W9-AYK-373

Photo © by Hulleah Tsinhnahjinnie

Winona LaDuke is an internationally known Native American activist. An Anishinaabe (Ojibwe/Chippewa), she lives on the White Earth Reservation in Minnesota. This is her first novel.

Praise for *Last Standing Woman*

"...LaDuke makes an impressive fiction debut....the novel skillfully intertwines social history, oral myth and character study in ways reminiscent of Leslie Marmon Silko and Louise Erdrich."

Publishers Weekly

"...a powerful first novel ...LaDuke's characters are as vital and fully realized as any in a Louise Erdrich novel....LaDuke finds ways for them to surmount their circumstances and offer support for one another. A fine work ..."

Library Journal

"...a lush, lyrical history of seven generations on a reservation."

U.S. News & World Report

"...LaDuke delivers an assured first novel....*Last Standing Woman* is a sweeping indictment of the racism and oppression directed at Native Americans....humor and compassion are ever present, and at its best, *Last Standing Woman* is a dignified and powerful retelling of one reservation's struggle for survival."

Booklist

"There are ... moments of wisdom and even lyrical poetry in the writing....There is an optimism at the core of the book that offers a certain comfort and reassurance that, despite all of the horrible things we human beings have done to each other, there may be hope for us yet."

The Tampa Tribune

"...a passionate and powerful telling of the story of White Earth.... This intriguing insider's [LaDuke's] view grabs the soul of the reader and breathes hope for regeneration."

NAPRA ReView

Last Standing Woman

by WINONA LA DUKE

Voyageur Press

First published in 1997 by Voyageur Press, an imprint of MBI Publishing Company LLC, Galtier Plaza, Suite 200, 380 Jackson Street, St. Paul, MN 55101 USA

Copyright © Winona LaDuke, 1997

All rights reserved. With the exception of quoting brief passages for the purposes of review, no part of this publication may be reproduced without prior written permission from the Publisher.

The information in this book is true and complete to the best of our knowledge. All recommendations are made without any guarantee on the part of the author or Publisher, who also disclaim any liability incurred in connection with the use of this data or specific details.

We recognize, further, that some words, model names, and designations mentioned herein are the property of the trademark holder. We use them for identification purposes only. This is not an official publication.

MBI Publishing Company titles are also available at discounts in bulk quantity for industrial or sales-promotional use. For details write to Special Sales Manager at MBI Publishing Company, Galtier Plaza, Suite 200, 380 Jackson Street, St. Paul, MN 55101 USA.

To find out more about our books, join us online at www.VoyageurPress.com.

Cover photos: Photograph of "We-no-na" circa 1858 by Whitney's Gallery of St. Paul, Minnesota; from the collection of the Minnesota Historical Society.
Color images: © Richard Hamilton Smith

Edited by Michael Dregni
Designed by Leslie Ross
Printed in China

Library of Congress Cataloging-in-Publication Data
LaDuke, Winona.
   Last Standing Woman / by Winona LaDuke.
    p. cm.
   ISBN 0-89658-278-7
   ISBN 0-89658-452-6 (pbk.)
   1. Indians of North America—Minnesota—History—Fiction.
  2. Ojibwa Indians—History—Fiction. 3. Ojibwa women—Fiction.
  I. Title.
  PS3562.A268L37 1997
  813'.54—dc21   97-1886
              CIP

ACKNOWLEDGMENTS

I owe a debt to many people for their help in creating this work:

My son Ajuawak and my daughter Waseyabin began this story and inspired its telling.

My parents Betty LaDuke Westigard, Peter Westigard, and Vincent "Sun Bear" LaDuke taught me to believe in myself and helped me to believe in myself.

Then there are some who loved me and encouraged me through some trying times: Paul Bogart, Faye Brown, Amy Ray, Lori Pourier, and the ladies of the Indigenous Women's Network. I also thank Teresa LaDuke, Ingrid Washinawatok, Audrey Thayer, Lisa Jackson, Eddie Benton Benai, Judy Fairbanks, Andrew Favorite, Florence Goodman, Emily Saliers, Reverend John Lee, and Reverend George Ross who lended their minds for help with language, nuance, ideas, and research.

Gracious friends and translators include David "Niib" Aubid (Ojibwe), Earl Nyholm (Ojibwe), and Brent Dershowitz (Dakota). Any mistakes of language, however, are mine.

The staff at White Earth Land Recovery Project, including Geraldine Bellanger, Donna Smith, Pamela Kay Ellis, Sandra Thompson, Theresa Stewart, Merrie Butcher, reviewed drafts and helped considerably with typing and transcribing my scribbles.

Thanks to Jeffrey Chapman and Juanita Espinosa who helped with artwork.

Finally, *chi-miigwech* to my editor, Michael Dregni at Voyageur Press, for his patience, compassion, and commitment.

DEDICATION

Dedicated to the memory of Fred Weaver, Dick LaGarde, George Aubid, Charlotte Jackson, and Elaine Kier, and those who struggle for justice and the people of White Earth.

*I want to die before all the Indians wear polyester
and all the gringos wear Indian clothes. . . .*
—Franz Blom

STATE OF MINNESOTA

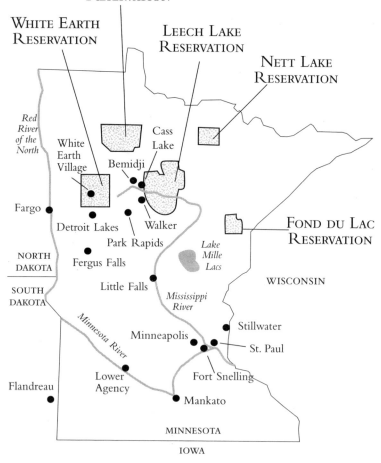

RED LAKE RESERVATION

WHITE EARTH RESERVATION

LEECH LAKE RESERVATION

NETT LAKE RESERVATION

Red River of the North

White Earth Village

Cass Lake

Bemidji

Fargo

Detroit Lakes

Walker

Park Rapids

NORTH DAKOTA

Fergus Falls

Lake Mille Lacs

FOND DU LAC RESERVATION

WISCONSIN

SOUTH DAKOTA

Little Falls

Mississippi River

Minnesota River

Stillwater

Minneapolis

St. Paul

Flandreau

Lower Agency

Fort Snelling

Mankato

MINNESOTA

IOWA

WHITE EARTH
RESERVATION

WHITE EARTH RESERVATION BORDER

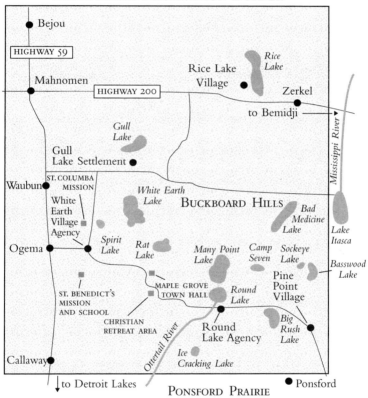

- Bejou
- HIGHWAY 59
- Mahnomen
- HIGHWAY 200
- Rice Lake Village
- Rice Lake
- Zerkel
- to Bemidji
- Mississippi River
- Gull Lake
- Gull Lake Settlement
- Waubun
- ST. COLUMBA MISSION
- White Earth Lake
- BUCKBOARD HILLS
- Bad Medicine Lake
- Lake Itasca
- White Earth Village Agency
- Spirit Lake
- Rat Lake
- Many Point Lake
- Camp Seven
- Sockeye Lake
- Basswood Lake
- Ogema
- ST. BENEDICT'S MISSION AND SCHOOL
- MAPLE GROVE TOWN HALL
- Round Lake
- Pine Point Village
- CHRISTIAN RETREAT AREA
- Ottertail River
- Round Lake Agency
- Big Rush Lake
- Callaway
- Ice Cracking Lake
- to Detroit Lakes
- PONSFORD PRAIRIE
- Ponsford

AUTHOR'S NOTE

This is a work of fiction although the circumstances, history, and traditional stories, as well as some of the characters, are true, retold to the best of my ability.

CAST OF CHARACTERS

George Agawaateshkan: grandson of a traditional war chief. *Midewiwin* leader.

George Ahnib, Sr.: husband of Janine Littlewolf, father of George Ahinb.

George Ahnib: son of Janine Littlewolf and George Ahnib, Sr.

Georgette Big Bear: wife of Selam Big Bear.

Selam Big Bear: grandson of Chi Makwa.

John Brown: Korean War veteran, church janitor, and caretaker of the drum.

Bugonaygeeshig (Hole in the Day the elder): war chief of the south-western *Anishinaabe*.

Bugonaygeeshig (Hole in the Day the younger): son of Bugonaygeeshig the elder, a leader of the White Earth *Anishinaabe*.

Cantetinza (Firm Fist): Dakota man, husband of Situpiwin, hung at Mankato.

Chi Makwa (Big Bear): grandfather of Selam Big Bear.

Claire St. Clair: second cousin to Jim Nordstrom, bingo player, and Minnesota lottery winner.

Lucy St. Clair: cousin to Jim Nordstrom. Versed in the art of love medicine and the cupid of White Earth. Given the name Ishkwegaabawiikwe (Last Standing Woman).

Philomene St. Clair: mother of Jim Nordstrom, grandmother of Alanis Nordstrom. Wolf Clan.

Maura Coningham: English teacher, wife of Jim Nordstrom, mother of Alanis Nordstrom.

D-Day: World War II veteran and buffalo hunter.

Kway Dole: gill net fisherwoman and deer hunter.

Equayzaince (Little Girl, aka Mary): wife of Mesabe.

Flatmouth (Eshkebugecoshe): *Anishinaabe* leader.

Boodoo Graves: father of Fred Graves, grandfather of Frances Graves.

Frances Graves: great-granddaughter of Boodoo Graves, daughter of Fred Graves.

Fred Graves: tribal councilman, son of Boodoo Graves, father of Frances Graves.

Moose Hanford: great-grandson of Namaybin Minnogeeshig and Ishkwegaabawiikwe, Vietnam veteran, best friend of Willie Schneider. Marten Clan.

Hawk Her Many Horses: Vietnam veteran, killed during the tribal offices occupation.

Ishkwegaabawiikwe (Last Standing Woman): wife of Namaybin Minnogeeshig, friend of Situpiwin. Great-grandmother of Moose Hanford.

Ishkwegaabawiikwe (Last Standing Woman): name given to Lucy St. Clair.

Ishkwegaabawiikwe (Last Standing Woman): the storyteller, daughter of Alanis Nordstrom and Willie Schneider. Loon Clan.

Maggie Jourdain: eternal caretaker and matriarch of White Earth village.

Little Crow (Tahoahtadoota): Santee Sioux leader in the 1862 war with the Minnesota settlers, known as Little Crow's War.

Janine Littlewolf: wife of George Ahnib, Sr., mother of George Ahnib.

Elaine Mandamin: great-great-ganddaughter of Mindemoyen, granddaughter of Mesabe, daughter of Geraldine Mandamin.

Geraldine Mandamin: daughter of Mesabe, mother of Elaine Mandamin.

Mayzhuckegeeshig: White Earth leader.

Mesabe: grandson of Mindemoyen, father of Geraldine Mandamin, grandfather of Elaine Mandamin, and revolutionary elder.

Mindemoyen: grandmother of Mesabe. Great-great-grandmother of Elaine Mandamin.

Namaybin Minnogeeshig: husband to Ishkwegaabawiikwe and Situpiwin. Great-grandfather of Moose Hanford.

Naytahwaush: grandson of Mindemoyen, brother of Mesabe.

Alanis Nordstrom: granddaughter of Philomene St. Clair, daughter of Jim Nordstrom and Maura Coningham, mother of Ishkwegaaba-wiikwe, the storyteller. Bear Clan.

Jim Nordstrom (Jim Good Fox): Hollywood movie extra, son of Philomene St. Clair, father of Alanis Nordstrom. Bear Clan.

Charlotte Oshkinnah: revolutionary elder.

Margaret Oshkinnah: sister of Charlotte Oshkinnah, died from the coughing sickness.

Izola Pemberton: sister of Philomene St. Clair and fellow church maid.

Willie Schneider: Vietnam veteran, best friend of Moose Hanford, father of Ishkwegaabawiikwe, the storyteller. Loon Clan.

Shingobay: the *Anishinaabe*'s senior war chief at the time of Little Crow's War.

Situpiwin (Tailfeathers Woman): Dakota woman, wife of Cantetinza, friend of Ishkwegaabawiikwe, wife of Namaybin Minogeeshig.

Browning Teaman: Comanche friend of Alanis Nordstrom and nationally famous powwow emcee.

Jim Vanoss: Roy Orbison lookalike.

Danielle Wabun: the rummage queen, daughter of Warren Wabun.

Warren Wabun: White Earth political leader, American Indian Movement leader. Crane Clan.

Wabunoquod: White Earth leader.

Lance Wagosh: White Earth tribal chairman.

Wazhaashkoons: brother of Ishkwegaabawiikwe.

Prologue

THE STORYTELLER

I was born exactly eight years to the day after George Ahnib took out the logging equipment. I was born two weeks after the old man, Mesabe, walked down the pathway of the souls to the next world.

As a child, I was bold. It is a trait I believe I inherited from my mother's clan, the *Makwa Doodem*, the Bear Clan of the Mississippi. My dad, however, was a Loon, and through him came my formal clan. Suited him funny, the Loon. He was a man who stumbled with words and was cheap with them when he did use them. But on occasion, he would fulfill his own destiny, and his voice would echo loud, long, and far.

The Bears are different. In times past, they were warriors, the *ogichidaa,* those who defended the people. Sometimes they still are. We are what we are intended to be when we have those three things that guide our direction—*our name, our clan, and our religion.*

The name I have was given to me by Lucy St. Clair. It is her name also, as well as the name of one of our ancestors. I am named Ishkwegaabawiikwe, Last Standing Woman.

There were two women once, a long time ago. One was a *Bwaanikwe,* a Dakota woman, called Situpiwin, Tailfeathers Woman. A woman from the west, she found refuge on White Earth. Another woman took her in. She was the one from White Earth, the *Anishinaabekwe,* the Ojibwe woman. The White Earth woman took in Situpiwin because they were both widows. One was a widow of the white man's war, another a widow of a man's war with himself, the war of a fool. Somehow they survived. They survived because of their own strength—and also because they had a friend that helped them, a friend who later was a husband to them, a husband to them both.

That was where the name came from. It was originally given to the *Anishinaabekwe*. She was a strong, proud woman. She had a generous heart, and she prevailed through hard times and kept that heart. I remember her in mine. She was not my actual relation by blood, but she was by name, and by spirit. They named her Ishkwegaabawiikwe, Last Standing Woman.

The story, though, was all of our story. Lucy St. Clair who named me was afraid we would forgot. But when the story flew into my ears, it made a picture in my mind I could never forget. A picture of how strong those old people were. And a picture of how we had these gifts we should keep.

There is a starkness in January. *Gichi Manidoo Giizis*, the Great Spirit Moon. The starkness of a searing cold, trees and limbs and all of the forest wrapped with thick ice and snow, piled higher and higher until it takes on the forms of the woods, bears, buffaloes, moose. But they are really asleep. When all the animals and spirits are asleep, we talk. We talk stories about them, when they are asleep.

There were stories all along. The same prophecies that directed the movement of the *Anishinaabeg* told of the coming of the light-skinned people and the hard times for the *Anishinaabeg*. Those same prophecies spoke of the *Oshki Anishinaabeg*, the new people, who came later. But that is not where this story begins.

PART I

The Refuge

WHITE EARTH

There were many migrations that brought the people here. *Omaa, omaa,* here. Here to the place where the food grows on the water. *Anishinaabeg Akiing,* the people's land, the land where the *manoomin,* the wild rice, grows. It had been perhaps a thousand years since the time the *Anishinaabeg* had left the big waters in the *Waaban aki,* the land of the east. And they now turned *Ningaabii'anong,* to the west.

Each day the migis shell appeared in the sky, and each day the people followed it. The shell was luminescent, gleaming in the sky. They traveled by foot on the land and by canoe on the rivers, traveling farther and farther to the west until they turned home. *Giiwedahn.* So it was that the families, the clans, and the head people of the *Anishinaabeg* came to the headwaters of the Mississippi. Here, *Gaawaawaabiganikaag,* White Earth, named after the clay, the white clay you find here. It's so beautiful, it is. Here the people would remain, in the good land that was theirs.

The *Anishinaabeg* world undulated between material and spiritual shadows, never clear which was more prominent at any time. It was as if the world rested in those periods rather than in the light of day. Dawn and dusk, *biidaaban, mooka'ang.* The gray of sky and earth was just the same, and the distinction between the worlds was barely discernible.

In the season round, the small camps, villages, and bands would plan their hunts by dream and memory, fill full their birchbark *makakoons* with wild rice, maple sugar, berries, dried corn, and squash. By snowshoe, canoe, or dog team, they moved through those woods, rivers, and lakes. It was not a life circumscribed by a clock, stamp, fence, or road.

But there was a law just the same, the Creator's law that still is. And with that law was the presence of ancestors, spirits, and magic. Always magic. Hunting magic, love magic, fighting magic, and the magic made between people. The spirits and the magic traveled with the Ojibwe to their hunting camps, traplines, maple sugarbushes, across lakes, and into the small lodges warm with fires and stories.

Forget the law, forget the magic, and you will be reminded. Hot fingers touched a face and burned a mark into the skin that stayed until you remembered why the mark came. Bony fingers reached through the ice to pull a greedy hunter down to *Mishinameginebig*, the Great Horned Sturgeon.

"*Gaawiin wan endam gin asemaa*," those old spirits whispered. "*Do not forget your* asemaa, *your tobacco.*"

The white man's law was different. The white man's law was all paper. A series of twenty or so treaties by the 1860s would leave the *Anishinaabeg* less land and more priests. One treaty took the copper and the big copper boulder. Another treaty took the iron ore. Yet another, the trees. The *Anishinaabeg* parlayed in good faith and to survive. The white man parlayed to get more than what he needed. Those old people—Martens, Cranes, Bears, Kingfishers, the clans—all went to see the white man and to talk with him. They received "assurances." But in the end, the assurances were just paper, just words. The old people, however, by some fortune, did secure White Earth. That reservation was to be the refuge for all those clans. It was a good land.

The *Anishinaabeg* were mystified and astounded by the appetite of the light-skinned men. And by their folly. Strange words, stranger ideas. The white man's government would have flicked the *Anishinaabeg* aside, flicked them all aside with the stroke of a pen on a sheet of paper. Except the paper, the *masiniaigin*, was not the land and it was not the people and it was not the magic. It was just the paper.

THE BORDER
1862

She was a woman drawn to the border. She was drawn to battle, into that cycle of war and revenge. She never professed to understand war or understand revenge, and as a woman, the fury puzzled her, but something inside of her pulled her there, and she could not explain why. It was burned into her heart, burning like a fire, unquenched by any snow, by any ice, by any cold. Perhaps the magnetism of the border and the battles of others came to her because she was a veteran of her own battle, her own war.

Ishkwegaabawiikwe traveled to the border of *Anishinaabe Akiing*, to where the land of the *Anishinaabeg* met the land of the Dakota, *Bwaan Akiing*. With her brother Wazhaashkoons, they paddled their canoe, fashioned from the skin of two birch trees, a canoe as beautiful and smooth as anything you could imagine. They canoed down the Ottertail River to the Pelican, and then crawled on their bellies up the side of a small hill and looked over at the Dakota camp. They could have killed them, those *Bwaanag*, but they did not. Instead, they watched.

The Dakota's camp of hide tipis and their herd of horses was a marvel to their *Anishinaabeg* eyes. Accustomed to bark lodges, dogsleds, and canoes, Ishkwegaabawiikwe was mesmerized at the first sight of the *mishtadim*, the horse, called the "big dog" by the *Anishinaabeg*. The animals caught her eye: They were fleet of foot, liquid in motion, and they pranced proud with their manes glinting in the sunshine.

Then Ishkwegaabawiikwe saw her, a Dakota woman as tall as any man, with long braids hanging far past her waist. A woman whose strides were quick and bold.

The Dakota woman glided into the herd of horses, walking between them as if she was their friend. Then she leaned forward and put her head near one of the horses. The horse's ears shifted, and then it lifted its head. The woman's leg flew across its back, and Ishkwegaabawiikwe saw her ride. She saw her ride and could not draw her eyes away. The woman rode simply for delight and seemed to float through the air just above the tall grass. Ishkwegaabawiikwe and her brother watched the Dakota woman's joy and saw a child run after her, a young boy of ten or so, running fast to catch his mother. She stopped the horse, leaned over, and plucked the boy up as he scrambled over the rear of the horse.

The sister and brother laid and watched for a long time, watching in *giimooj*, secrecy, as they knew how. And they enjoyed themselves. They would report back that the border was safe, that the *Anishinaabeg's* most honored enemies were at peace, and that they had beautiful horses and beautiful women.

Ishkwegaabawiikwe was a woman drawn to the border and to battle, and she attributed this to her husband. Her husband and his ways.

She had been married to a fool. Not unusual in the spectrum of time, but mournful nevertheless. He was a man constantly at war with himself, at war with the spirits, the Creator, and his wife. He was a man whose common sense was compromised by the fact that he had three testicles. Ishkwegaabawiikwe attributed his actions and features to his close relationship to his clan, *Ma'iingan*, or Wolf.

He had come from the north, met Ishkwegaabawiikwe on a trading party, and secured her as his wife. There had been a number of men in her own village who sought her companionship, but she did not show an interest. There was medicine for this. That was what her husband used, medicine. And that was how she fell for a fool. He had captured her with medicine, but he did not truly want her. He liked her by his fire and in his bed. But he did not care for her soul, did not truly care for her. She was just his possession, one of many.

It was not right to strike a woman. No one would have dared to do so then. No one but he. Foolish, he did not care, and he had no remorse.

She had delicate features once. Fine bones, angular cheekbones, and eyes that curved upward. She had those features until he beat her. Angry with whiskey, he tore her face with a sharp stick and a hatchet he got from the white man traders. He beat her and he cut her. Beat her until she could not see and could not feel.

She went inside herself, and in her pain, she laughed at her husband, belittled his person. She knew he was less because she knew he was the weak one then. At first she thought she should simply place his belongings outside her lodge, but she thought again. She remembered that every mark on her face had been earned and every mark had to be taken away.

In those times, a woman's relations would have avenged such an act. A husband would have been banished, sent to the deepest of the woods, or sent to the border with the *Bwaanag*. But Ishkwegaabawiikwe and her husband lived deep in the woods that winter, so it was long before her family saw her again.

Her relations did not see her until *ziigwan*, spring, when the snow and ice were less treacherous and daunting. Then everyone went into the sugarbush and would visit and share news. But by then her cuts had healed—she looked different, less delicate now. And with her silence, her relations did not comprehend what had befallen her. She had her pride, and she kept a silence. But her soul did not heal.

She told her husband, "You will never touch me again. You will freeze in your own glory." And she showed him her skinning knife.

She had got the skinning knife long ago at the trading post far away, paid for it with furs she had skinned. The knife was as sharp as the winter was cold, and she had a case for the blade quilled by her mother. Ishkwegaabawiikwe had taken all of this with her to her marriage. Her knife was her pride.

She held up the knife and let him look at the long blade as she told him, "You touch me again, and you will be a rabbit, a *waabooz*. *Aababishkaw*, I will turn you inside out."

Ishkwegaabawiikwe kept to herself then, throughout the seasons. He tried to win her back, but he had already done enough damage. He had stolen her with love medicine, taken that which he could not and should not have. And then not taken care of it.

And so she took herself back. She reclaimed first her hands, the soft touch. Moccasins she still made for him: it was the duty of a wife, the example for the family. But leggings and shirts he could fashion himself. And her beadwork designs changed ever so slightly, the flowers of her beadwork becoming bitter and sharp. He would not notice, but she knew. A woman would know.

Then slowly she took that back too, took back all else. Meat, hunting, fishing, syruping. She could set her own snares, and her snares were always full as she had hunting magic. She had plenty of dried meat, berries, and sugar cakes, and all of them were her own.

He had lost his place. She took it from him. And he would never reclaim it, no matter how brave he was, no matter how he begged.

He used to come to her at night, asking her to lie with him, and she just sneered at him. Flicked her eyes in the dark, smoldering in the firelight of the lodge. Once she awoke to his hands on her dress. She reached as quick as a snake, grabbed that knife, and held it against his neck. Slow, slow like a man who sees a bear and has no weapon, he backed out, backed away toward the fire.

He was a fool and he died like a fool. He was a brash and boastful hunter, one to flaunt his gifts. He always gave meat to the elders, the poorest people of the clan, and the widows. But he always took too much from the woods and kept too much for himself. And he spoke too loudly about the animals, at all times of the year. He boasted he could kill the cannibal, the *Wiindigoo* of Round Lake. He boasted he would kill him easy, easy with the medicine. That was an easy thing to say, and much harder to do. The *Wiindigoo* had power, and the *Wiindigoo* had an agreement with the lake and the *Mishinameginebig*, the Great Horned Sturgeon.

No one ever saw him again. He never got to the *Wiindigoo*, never even got close. Icy fingers reached from deep within the lake and pulled him down. Round Lake spoke to him, louder and louder, a roar into his ears. Until he saw *Mishinameginebig*. He saw him and knew him.

When he died, Ishkwegaabawiikwe did not cry. She had been a widow in her heart for almost two years already. She cut her hair short to mourn, and kept her secret. Then she burned his belongings, his moccasins and leggings, and she saved only a few of his best hunting tools. She saved them for herself. She had seared her pain with his and cleansed her soul.

That was where it came from, she was sure. Her fascination with the border, with the others, and her interest in the battles of others came from her own battle. Her brother, Wazhaashkoons, was kind and accommodating. He had sensed the discord of her marriage, but modesty had kept him from prying. And her own stubbornness kept it a secret and kept it well.

Her brother sensed her unrest, and offered that she should go scouting again with him. It was the second time, later that fall. He asked her if she would accompany him to scout the border with the Dakota. She joined him, and again they canoed down the Ottertail to the west, *Ningaabii'anong.*

The *Anishinaabeg* all knew of Little Crow's War. Who could not? The *Gichimookomaanag*, the white men, or the Big Knives as they were called, despised the *Bwaanag*, the Dakota. If the white men resented or disliked the *Anishinaabeg*, they hated the Dakota.

How many *biiboonag* after they had come she did not know, only that the white man called it the year 1862. By that year, the Santee bands of Dakota had learned much from fifty winters of treaty making with the white man's bosses, his headspeople. The *Anishinaabeg* watched them and learned as well, but some things no one would ever believe.

The Dakota had learned about the relationship between money and land. For one of the white man's nickels in trade for each of their "acres" of land, the Dakota had signed away over thirty million acres of Iowa, Minnesota, and the Dakota Territory. Suddenly, the Santee had the white man's nickels, but most of that money would go to traders, men who conveniently called in debts at treaty payment time. In the end, the Dakota received nothing except an understanding of the relationship between their poverty and the white man's wealth. They had retained only a "reservation" ten miles wide and one hundred and fifty miles long bordering the Minnesota River. And, like red coals below the ashes of a fire thought to be extinguished, they had retained a deep and smoldering resentment toward the white man's bosses, the traders, and the settlers.

Ishkwegaabawiikwe did not believe that one should ever wait for the white man, but people said that the Dakota did wait that year. People said they had put off the annual buffalo hunt past *AAbita Niibino Giizis*, the Mid-Summer Moon of July, while the people awaited the arrival and distribution of their treaty goods at the agency. The white man had begun to massacre the buffalo and so a shadow had set upon the prairies. Ishkwegaabawiikwe was not surprised to hear that the goods—the salt pork, flour, bolts of fabric, and sugar—were late in coming from the white man. Nor was she surprised to hear that the Dakota grew hungry. A local trader refused them credit on food, telling them to their faces, "Go and eat grass."

The *Anishinaabeg* knew the Dakota as a proud people. And the Dakota were not accustomed to being treated poorly in their own homes. Weary of intruders in their land and the hatred of the white traders, a group of young Dakota men went forth and broke down the door to a warehouse and began carrying out sacks of flour, sugar, and goods. The *Anishinaabeg* heard that the white man's soldiers fired on the Dakota and killed them. In retaliation, other Dakota killed five white settlers.

The Dakota called a council at the house of Little Crow, Tahoahtadoota, of the Santee. There was heated debate. While people wanted peace, they knew from experience that many Dakota would be punished for the actions of a few. The Dakota decided to attack first in hopes of discouraging the white man from waging a war.

The Dakota then sent messengers to their most honored enemies, now strategic allies, the *Anishinaabeg* of the north. The Dakota messengers came to the *Anishinaabeg*, crossing the border into the Ojibwe's lakes and woods. They brought the warpipe and asked for help. The messengers told of trouble at Fort Snelling, the big fort at the convergence of the Mississippi and Minnesota Rivers. The *Anishinaabeg* were not surprised. Forts were full of hatred.

The pipe was brought first to Bugonaygeeshig, Hole in the Day, asking him to join the Dakota against the white man. Bugonaygeeshig respectfully considered the appeal and smoked the pipe, agreeing to join. Other headsman followed Bugonaygeeshig, who was a respected veteran from the wars between the Dakota and *Anishinaabeg*. This time, however, the Dakota needed their help.

Bugonaygeeshig had no power to commit the *Anishinaabeg*. He was a lieutenant, not a general. Shingobay was the *Anishinaabeg*'s oldest war chief, and he possessed the authority to make war. His lodge was near Mille Lacs where several large wigwams adjoined each other, housing his large, extended family. As scouts returned to the village reporting that a peaceful party of Dakota was nearby, Shingobay moved to the Council House to await them. The Dakota tentatively approached the great war chief.

The four Dakota men placed the war pipe in front of the leader and earnestly made their plea. Solemnly, Shingobay heard the Dakota out, observing their demeanor, rank, and the gravity of the problem. He listened, noting with empathy their situation. It was then that he instructed them to take the pipe to Flatmouth, Eshkebugecoshe, and the other sub chiefs, while he considered the request. The Dakota were to return the next day.

Ishkwegaabawiikwe heard tell of how Shingobay summoned his *jiisakiiwinini*, the man who could see into the future. Two helpers came to the *jiisakiiwinini* and tied and bound him tightly in blankets and ropes, covering even his face. The helpers carried the old man inside the *jiisakiiwigamig*, a small triangular hide lodge known as the shaking tent. They laid the seer on the floor and left him there while Shingobay waited outside. The songs began. Singing, the *jiisakiiwinini* summoned his familiar spirits and clan relatives, seeking them to divine. Slowly the tent started to move. Now drums, voices, shrieks, growls, all came from the tent. Drums again, as Shingobay heard the *jiisakiiwinini* talking over the sounds. Singing again, then drums, and growls all emanating from the tent. It was two hours later when finally the shaking tent was quiet.

Shingobay watched the door expectantly. The *jiisakiiwinini* emerged, absent of ropes and blankets. All those present nodded in approval, and the chief walked with his advisor slowly back to the lodge, where deer meat, corn soup, and tea awaited the men. After refreshments, counsel was held in soft voices for several hours. Shingobay respectfully questioned the old man, and listened with his head bowed intently. Then he slept.

When the Dakota returned early the next morning, Shingobay

summoned them into the council lodge for their answer. Ishkwegaaba-wiikwe heard tell of the great chief's words:

"*I won't fight*," he said firmly. "*I have seen what will happen. If we fight, all the treaties we made with the white man will be void. And, if we lose the battle, they will get the land. They are too numerous, they are coming across the water, swimming onto our land. And, when they defeat us, for they surely will, with their numbers and guns, who will carry on? Who will carry on for future generations?*" He spoke solemnly and with great pain. Finally, he paused. "*I'm going to turn the pipe down.*"

He shook his head and passed the warpipe back to the Dakota. Shingobay would not smoke.

The Dakota left despondent. This was a bad omen. The *Anishinaabeg* were more numerous than the Dakota and would have improved the odds greatly. Shingobay's decision meant there would be no armed support for the struggle by the *Anishinaabeg*.

But for the *Anishinaabeg*, the future did not bode well either. In spite of *Anishinaabeg* neutrality, government informers reported that the Dakota brought the warpipe to the *Anishinaabeg* and surmised that the *Anishinaabeg* wanted war as evidenced by Bugonaygeeshig's smoking of the pipe and Shingobay's deliberations, whatever the outcome.

But chief Bugonaygeeshig had a son, named for his father and also called Bugonaygeeshig, Hole in the Day. This son of the chief was the flamboyant leader at White Earth, and he, like the Dakota, had grown weary of being treated as children by the great white men. One morning at dawn, he and a group of his *ogichidaaweg* took over the land office of White Earth and later, St. Columba Mission, the new Episcopal church enclave. They were tired of being ignored by Washington and wanted to show that they too could send the white men away. Bugonaygeeshig's raid coincided with those of the Dakota in Little Crow's War.

While the white man's government left White Earth alone for the time, within a year, the government would terminate the *Anishinaabeg* reservations of Gull Lake, Sandy Lake, Pokegama, Oak Point, and others. All those actions were perceived by the *Anishinaabeg* as punishment for having parlayed with the Dakota and for Bugonaygeeshig's raid. All of those actions also augured poorly for the future.

At dawn on August the eighteenth of the year 1862 by the white man's calendar, the Dakota attacked Lower Agency on the Minnesota River. Moving swiftly before full morning light, they began by killing the traders, including one named Andrew Myrick, the one the Dakota now remembered as Let Them Eat Grass. Myrick leapt out the window of his store and ran for the shelter of some nearby trees. But a bullet found him and pierced him. The Dakota pulled a handful of prairie grass from the ground and stuffed it into his dead mouth. And so it began, Little Crow's War. In the bloody time, more than five hundred settlers and many Dakota perished.

A month and a half later, Colonel Henry Hastings Sibley marched up the Minnesota River Valley with an army of more than a thousand soldiers to destroy the Dakota resistance. Within four weeks, Sibley decimated the Dakota villages. He sought to arrest any adult male even considered remotely capable of resistance, and in the end, collected more than two thousand Dakota prisoners.

Now Ishkwegaabawiikwe accompanied her brother to the border again. She wished to see the border. The *Anishinaabeg* knew that the white man would punish all Indians for the actions of a few. The white man chose not to tell the difference. The *Anishinaabeg* also knew that the Dakota would need help, that there would be refugees. They were the *Anishinaabeg*'s most honored enemies, and centuries of a border meant generations of war, retaliation, trade, hostages, love, and marriage. A sorrow for the Dakota would be a sorrow for the *Anishinaabeg*. And so Ishkwegaabawiikwe and Wazhaashkoons traveled to see and to understand.

The sister and brother moved carefully in this time of war. They moved by watching the stars, watching the fisher, the path of souls, watching them as they all traversed the night sky. The sister and brother moved in the daylight when they were able, traveling deep in the woods and along the rivers, hidden from the eyes of the white man. They promised their father that they would be safe, promised him they would not venture into the open. They were invisible in the woods, and they traveled to the edge of the *Anishinaabeg* world to the open plain that was the Dakota world.

The sister and brother climbed up the same hill on their bellies to look down in *giimooj*, in secrecy, on the same Dakota village. It was gone. There was nothing left of the gathering of hide tipis but charred remains spread throughout the small valley. There was not a sign of life: All of the people and all of the *mishtadimag*, the horses, were gone.

The sister and brother climbed back down the hill, stomachs sick with fear and pity for the Dakota. They looked and wondered at where they had all gone. Slowly and silently, they returned to their canoe and dipped their paddles into the water to make the journey home.

Ishkwegaabawiikwe was not surprised when she found her again, that *Bwaanikwe* that she had watched long ago. Sibley's troops had scoured the countryside by horseback, galloping up the routes they knew the Dakota traversed. When the soldiers found Dakota, they captured them to bring back to their town of Mankato, or they killed them.

When Ishkwegaabawiikwe found the *Bwaanikwe*, she thought the Dakota woman was dead. Huddled near the river under a tree, she had hidden herself poorly.

"I will take her," Ishkwegaabawiikwe said boldly before she even knew if the woman was alive.

Her brother looked at her in surprise.

"I will take her with us," Ishkwegaabawiikwe said again. "I will take her in."

Her brother moved close to the Dakota woman now and poked at her gently with his paddle. She shifted and moaned. His eyes wide now, he saw the blood covering her front.

"Help me," Ishkwegaabawiikwe said to Wazhaashkoons, as she wove her arm under the Dakota woman's and around her shoulders. Her brother lifted the woman from the hips, and they loaded her heavily into the canoe. Blood-drenched and exhausted, she murmured once, then slipped back into unconsciousness. Ishkwegaabawiikwe took her home, across the border, back to the woods, back to the lake, back to the refuge.

Ishkwegaabawiikwe was weary of the wars, the battles between the Dakota and the *Anishinaabeg*, the battles between the Indians and the white men, the war in her own lodge. Having seen one war ended by attrition, her husband's own folly, she was perhaps in need of ending another war with a small gesture. Ishkwegaabawiikwe took in the Dakota woman, her most honored enemy, her war trophy, her sister.

THE CAPTIVES
1862

She had a name then and a family once. The *Bwaanikwe's* name was Situpiwin, Tailfeathers Woman, and her family of four sons had perished at the hands of Sibley's troops. Her youngest son, the one who had once jumped astride her horse and ridden for joy, was dead now as well, shot through by a soldier's bullet. He died as she held him. Her husband, Cantetinza, or Firm Fist, had been taken prisoner by Sibley. Now she had nothing. She was a wife, soon to be a widow.

Situpiwin told her story. She was awkward in the *Anishinaabeg* language, but she persevered, speaking slowly, telling her story to Ishkwegaabawiikwe.

Her four handsome sons had been sleeping when the soldiers came. The soldiers descended upon the village with burning torches and guns. They arrested those they chose and killed many of the rest, leaving the dead and dying in their wake. Her last child had been killed before her eyes. She held him as he passed over, then she had to run. There was no time for proper burial. She crept out of the back of the tipi and ran for days. The soldiers chased the survivors ruthlessly, but she hid in the woods until they passed and then made her way to the river. She had hidden there until Ishkwegaabawiikwe found her.

All she knew now was that her husband Cantetinza was a prisoner of the government that took no prisoners. Word came of the court of justice. Sibley's court, it was said, was so efficient it could hold a trial in five minutes. The messengers said that the men were convicted for being Dakota. No one needed to prove their innocence or their crimes. No one cared. Cantetinza was one of those taken. Now he was to hang.

Situpiwin begged Ishkwegaabawiikwe to go. No longer her captive, Situpiwin was Ishkwegaabawiikwe's responsibility nevertheless. The Dakota woman begged her to go one last time to see her husband. Ishkwegaabawiikwe agreed.

Her brother Wazhaashkoons accompanied them again. Too cold for the canoe, they traveled by dog sled and snowshoe, then by wagon from Little Falls. It was still a dangerous time to travel, but Ishkwegaabawiikwe held by her treaty medals from the LaPointe Treaty of 1837. They had been her grandfather's, and the medals should guarantee them safe passage. She lent Situpiwin one of the medals and a dress. She disguised her as an *Anishinaabekwe*.

In Little Falls, they came to Bugonaygeeshig's camp and rested there for the day. Chief Hole in the Day sent two men to accompany them as they traveled south, a journey both difficult and grim. Finally they arrived at Mankato.

It was the day after the white man's holy day of Christmas. The thirty-eight condemned Dakota men were to be hanged at Mankato just weeks before the white man's boss, President Abraham Lincoln, signed the Emancipation Proclamation freeing the black-skinned people. Around a single scaffold built in the form of a hollow square, the crowd of spectators gathered.

It was not a place for the *Anishinaabeg*, not a place for Indians at all, but there they stood, Ishkwegaabawiikwe, Wazhaashkoons, and Situpiwin—the short woman of scarred face, the statesman, and the tall beautiful woman. They stood huddled in the far back of the large square. Other Indians were there too: some Dakota that had come to see their husbands and fathers; some Winnebago and other *Anishinaabeg*. All of them stood to the back of the square, fearful of what they were about to see and fearful of being seen. Situpiwin searched the crowd for a face, a relation.

Then the soldiers led out the Dakota men to the scaffold. The crowd jeered and threw rocks at the bound prisoners. Situpiwin squeezed Ishkwegaabawiikwe's hand, her nails digging into Ishkwegaabawiikwe's palm, her neck stretched to see the arriving men.

Situpiwin was tall and she could see far across the crowd. Her head jerked when she saw her husband, and she gave a deep sigh.

She began to push her way forward through the crowd of white spectators. Ishkwegaabawiikwe tried to hold her back. The crowd was angry and mean with hearts full of revenge. Ishkwegaabawiikwe pulled the Dakota woman's arm, grasping at her dress, trying to hold her back. But she moved forward undaunted. There was nothing else they could do to her.

Situpiwin pushed herself toward the scaffold, and Ishkwegaaba-wiikwe followed her closely, not daring to let go. A white man roughly shoved Situpiwin and she moved aside, trying to find a way to slither through to the front. Ishkwegaabawiikwe followed her every move, hands grasped.

Then Situpiwin cried out in Dakota as loud as she could, "Cante-tinza, Cantetinza. *Ded mawazin,* I am here."

Upon the scaffold, Cantetinza was dressed in nothing but rags, his hands manacled behind his back, his hair rough. He looked through the crowd hearing his wife's voice over the noise of the people.

But the crowd surrounding Situpiwin heard her calls as well. A white woman glared at them with an ugly mixture of fear and ven-geance. A big man with a grim smile across his face turned and yelled, "Quiet, you damn squaw." But another man, drunk with whiskey and with the prospect of a hanging, laughed aloud and grabbed hold of both Situpiwin and Ishkwegaabawiikwe by their arms and dragged them through the crowd.

"Make way, make way," he yelled in a whiskey-slurred voice. "These two squaws want to see the hanging."

Ishkwegaabawiikwe resisted, but the Dakota woman followed the man as the crowd parted miraculously before them, driven by curios-ity and the forcefulness of the drunk's demands.

"Make way," the man bellowed once again. Then he turned and leered drunkenly in their faces: "You need to see this hanging good so it will teach you."

Soon they were standing before the crowd and for the first time the short *Anishinaabekwe* could see the scaffold, the soldiers, and the condemned men. Her breath caught in her chest as the white man's flag flew proudly overhead.

Situpiwin was oblivious to the hatred of the crowd surrounding her, but Ishkwegaabawiikwe could feel it like the heat of a hot summer day soaking into her until she felt like running and leaping into the cool water of a river.

Again Situpiwin called out to Cantetinza, "*Ded mawazin, ded mawazin,* I am here, I am here."

Their eyes locked for a moment, his face puzzled by her appearance, she a shadow of sorrow and a small sign of comfort, but he was grateful for her presence.

"*Tehikecide,* I love you, you are dear to my heart," she called, oblivious of the crowd. "*Ake wanciyake kte,* I will see you again."

The crowd pushed them back now, straining to see as the soldiers lowered nooses over the heads of the thirty-eight condemned Dakota. Fighting against the tide of the crowd, Situpiwin stood stiff on her feet and would not move when Ishkwegaabawiikwe pulled at her. Her eyes were fixed on her husband as the noose of heavy rope was placed around his neck. He looked desperately for her again, and his eyes met hers. Then his head was covered.

"It's hanging time," the drunken man announced to the crowd.

The voices of the condemned Dakota rose into their death chants. *Hi yi hi yi hi yi hi yi, hi yi hi yi hi yi.* Ishkwegaabawiikwe watched as the Dakota grasped for each others hands as the final end came. The platforms dropped and there was silence, not a sound, nothing at all.

Then a roar went through the crowd as the onlookers celebrated their revenge, their conquest. Situpiwin's feet were still planted stiff, knees locked as her eyes watched her husband's feet move through the air like the ghost of a grass dance. The roar crescendoed now, as the Dakota men swung, their spirits rising into the sky. Situpiwin grew faint then, her knees finally buckling. Ishkwegaabawiikwe pulled at her and she followed. A hollow shell.

They made their way back to the wagon and Situpiwin laid down inside, her hands over her eyes, her pain so great at what she had seen. Wazhaashkoons steered them out of town.

Laying in the back of the wagon, Situpiwin finally spoke, calling to Ishkwegaabawiikwe in Dakota.

"*Bawakihankte.*" She motioned for her to cut her hair.

Ishkwegaabawiikwe obliged her, knowing that it was her way as well. She took hold of the soft braids, as soft as a mink's hide, as soft as any pelt, braids well past her waist. She cut the braids with her skinning knife, sharp and sleek.

The wagon moved north, away from the white man's Mankato, back to the border, *giiwedahn*, home.

Ishkwegaabawiikwe kept Situpiwin's hair. Her two long, thick braids, she kept them for her friend.

THE DRUM
1862

It was then that Ishkwegaabawiikwe dreamed the drum. The *Anishinaa-bekwe* got that dream, and she got that drum. Yellow and blue with thunderbirds on it. The old people said that it was a Thunderbird Drum. Songs were a part of it, and the drum songs were in the dream too.

She saw an old woman. Her face, too, yellow and blue with thunderbirds across it, and she had beads, shining silver metal cones, on her dress, on her yoke, and in her hair. Ishkwegaabawiikwe saw her, and then the old woman lifted up the drum—it was a hand drum, not another—and she showed it to the younger woman. Its face was naked at first, then, as she looked, the old woman's painted face was naked and the drum was painted. Just like that. It had a face.

She told Namaybin Minnogeeshig her dream. He had been her friend, and a true one at that. He wanted little except for simple companionship in return. He helped make that drum, and he talked to the others about it, the older ones who could *see*—Chi Makwa, her brother Wazhaashkoons, Mindemoyen, those who still remained in the woods, those who had not gone to town nor followed the white man or the white man's god. Those families that had drums, their numbers multiplied and their strength grew. They were determined to survive, to keep their ways, their songs, their medicines. To outwit the *wiindigoo*, the white man.

Ishkwegaabawiikwe and Situpiwin lived there, deep in the woods.

Namaybin Minnogeeshig was brave enough to court them both. They were a formidable challenge. Ishkwegaabawiikwe and Situpiwin laughed at Namaybin Minnogeeshig secretly at first, laughed at his ambition. But he won them over, that Namaybin Minnogeeshig, so persistent. He won them over with determination. And with beads and meat.

Trade goods, that was how it started. Someone once said that the love of fabric was the downfall of the Ojibwe women. Yard goods, black velvet, bolts of trader's wool all soothed the *Anishinaabekwewag* fingers. Smooth as a mink or beaver pelt, smooth as a brain-tanned hide, smooth as could be. Small glass beads mixed well with porcupine quill work and tufted moose hide. The most intricate designs, and the arrays of colors expanded their artistic universe immeasurably. Copper pots glittered to the dark crow eyes of the *Anishinaabekwewag* as much as the metal knives and guns spoke to the sense of the hunters.

Ishkwegaabawiikwe and Situpiwin admired those beads when he first presented them to the two women. Proud he was, proud as can be. He showed them the yellow, dark red, blue, and green. They saw them all there, the rosehips, the aster flowers, the wild rose, the greenest of leaves, and all the berries. They ran their fingers over the soft beads, shamelessly, and they saw all in those beads. They thanked him for the gift, knowing he wanted their affection in return. Ishkwegaabawiikwe and Situpiwin considered his proposition.

Then he brought meat.

Wiiyaas. Meat. Namaybin Minnogeeshig relied on the old standby, meat. The *Anishinaabeg* are a people whose culture revolves around meat. A hunting culture, a northern culture. Caribou, buffalo, moose, deer, rabbits, beaver, porcupine, goose, duck, turtle. If it can be eaten, the people eat it, the people eat it all. To bring meat to an Indian woman is to bring a much appreciated gift. Namaybin trapped well and he brought plenty. Namaybin reached into a beaver house on the Ottertail River and counted the beavers. Then he set his trap for the largest beaver. He set his trap and he waited.

Situpiwin would not have more children. She had nothing left in her. Ishkwegaabawiikwe was sympathetic to the idea of children and at times anxious. She observed her nieces and nephews, felt her breasts ache at the sound of a baby crying and her hands tremble as she rocked the *dikinaagan*, or cradle board, of her sister's baby. It had been two years since her husband had gone to the *Wiindigoo*, and now she was healing.

Namaybin Minnogeeshig struck her fancy. Modest as her dead husband was brash, gentle as he was coarse, she noticed him. It was hard not to, he had a magic as well, a magic of sweetness, and a strange backwards magic that appeared only sometimes. Sometimes he spoke contrary. Not only full of the actions, but the power, *Ayaagonwewaadizid*. On those occasions he would tell her that he despised her, and leave her a gift of putrid meat. Then Ishkwegaabawiikwe laughed. She did not love him those moons, she laughed at him. Sometimes full, sometimes softly, she laughed at the idiot. Then he would redeem himself, handily.

The final touch of the courtship was the large beaver. Namaybin had caught it in his trap and pulled it in, proudly bringing it to Ishkwegaabawiikwe. He must have known it would seal her affection, heal her scars.

Now her right hand clenched the handle of her skinning knife. Her left hand slowly pulled the beaver pelt, while her right hand carefully moved the knife back and forth to separate the skin from the fat and body. A huge beaver it was, snared on the Ottertail just south of Round Lake. The small pieces of fat spit into her hair and she smiled.

She focused her attention on the short legs, cutting the skin around the ankles in a sharp circle. She pulled the small black webbed feet through the hole. Just like undressing, turning inside out, *aababishkaw*.

Reaching deep into the body cavity with her hands, she carefully pulled the organs out, the lungs, the stomach, the intestines. Then she paused, looking into the palm of her hand.

"*Howaa . . . nisaaginishiwag.*" He had three testicles.

She reflected on this unusual organ, and was at ease. Then she slowly and deliberately finished cleaning the beaver, took him back inside her cabin and cooked him, cooked him long and slow, watching the fat drip out. She watched the three-testicled beaver from Round Lake cook.

She, Situpiwin, and Namaybin ate that beaver. He was good.

When the young chief Bugonaygeeshig was assassinated in the summer of 1868, it was if a shadow set across White Earth, a shadow that did not lift for almost one hundred years. Bugonaygeeshig was shot dead at Leech Lake, and Wazhaashkoons and the others reported that it was the work of lumber men and land stealers, men who had paid a handsome price for the chief's killing. Bugonaygeeshig had been the most feared, outspoken, and daunting of *Anishinaabe* chiefs—a strong orator, husband to four women, including a white woman, and a man with fine taste in clothing and horses. The *wiindigooweeg* had killed him in hopes of ending what the *Anishinaabeg* knew was theirs. Their ways, their land, and their drums. But the *wiindigooweeg* underestimated the *aanikoobijigan*, the old people, and they underestimated the drums. The old people drew further into the woods and brought the drum with them, the new one that Ishkwegaabawiikwe had dreamed, and they kept the drum to themselves. Those men of theirs kept the drum.

But the war of the God raged on the edge, and now moved into the village. The war of the God.

They kept a silence on the first priest they had seen. The new one, though, Father Gilfillian, had a coat of armor. He was like a turtle. Her brother Wazhaashkoons could not touch him.

Older now, her brother had decided that there was no use to waste his time fighting the priest. The priest would take the weak ones anyway. If they needed the white man's God, let them follow him. After all, if the white people had done so well, their God must have some power.

The others still kept their god and their ways, the *Midewiwin,* the shaking tent, the big drums, all of them. They had their own power.

Those men kept the drums. Namaybin Minnogeeshig had one, Chi Makwa another, and Wazhaashkoons a third. They kept those drums, fed them and cared for them. That kept the priests away. The priests could not touch those people. So they stayed, deep in the woods by Round Lake, by Many Point Lake. They stayed, never faltering from their path.

WEMITIGOOZHI
1800

The people watched the strange men come. They called them *wemitigoozhi*, the first ones they saw. The *wemitigoozhi* walked boldly into the village waving a crossed stick at the people. The *wemitigoozhi* did not surprise the people; no one could, especially not a pale-skinned man. His strides were strong and confident, his face hairy as a beast. He wore long, black, heavy clothes even in the heat of summer

The *wemitigoozhi* was covered with bites. The *zagimeg*, the mosquitoes, loved him. They sipped his blood with pleasure. The *zagimeg* were the *wiindigoo* in insect form.

The people laughed secretly at his misery. He flapped his arms at the mosquitoes and waved his stick, his crossed stick, walking into the village. And the people debated his demeanor. Either he was an amazing idiot for his brazen arrival in a camp gorged with warriors, or else he had a magic as strong as any.

Ishkwegaabawiikwe's dog pushed forward from behind her leg and rushed the feet of the *wemitigoozhi*. The dog did not bite, and the large hairy man in black stopped then, his face wide but without fear. He looked satisfied that he had the people's attention. It was not hard for him to get. He had made quite a spectacle of himself.

"I am a friend of your Great Spirit," he announced, with a tone of confidence. "I am a friend of your Great Spirit, and I have come to teach you."

The people listened to him, this talking boss, as he spoke on and on. He had learned the Ojibwe language from someone, although it sounded different to the people's ears; it was the Ojibwe language but from the north, a language from the Muskeg. But the people understood him. At least they chose to. That did not mean, however, that they believed him. He entertained them, that strange hairy man. He entertained them, and then they killed him. The people knew that was the best way.

The people knew of him and his others all along. The *wemitigoozhi* had long before come to the other bands. But they had never come to this village, never come this far into the woods, this deep into *Anishinaabeg* territory. Stories told of their magic and their solitariness, their brazen valor, and their strange ways.

Some villages prospered and others disappeared after the *wemitigoozhi* came. The people moved elsewhere, left their lodges, their drums, their otter hides, and moved with the strange hairy men. Other stories told of sicknesses that came with the *wemitigoozhi*, coughing and the pox. Sicknesses that killed the villages just the same.

The men with waving crosses, the *wemitigoozhi*, passed the people by. Later came the *makadewikonayewininiwag*, the other men dressed in black, speaking a different language but still waving their crossed sticks, and they too passed the people by. Passed them by until now. Perhaps the people's magic kept them at bay. Perhaps the people's reputation as ruthless sentries on the border with the *Bwaanag* discouraged them. Or maybe it was simply the people's inconvenient location. They were just too far in the woods, too far off the rivers, too far off the tracks of those who had come before.

The *wemitigoozhi*, however, eventually found the *Anishinaabeg*, found them and amused them for a while.

It was Ishkwegaabawiikwe's brother Wazhaashkoons who was the one to act decisively. He listened to the man with the crossed stick, he listened to him, and made up his mind. Her brother did not believe the *wemitigoozhi*. He shot him dead, an arrow piercing his chest.

"Not such a good friend of my Great Spirit," Wazhaashkoons said and scoffed. "He does not help you now."

The man looked puzzled, gasped words in a language the people did not understand, and then he died.

The people sent him down the Ottertail River in a canoe, one of their best birchbark canoes. They sent him away so that the *wemitigoozhi* would know not to come back.

FALLING OFF THE CROSS
1898

Onward, Christian Soldiers
Madjag enamiayeg,
Nundobuniyuk,
'Ga-widokag Jesus,
Ani-nigani.
Christ au kid ogimam
'Ga-migadamag,
Umbe mamaquiyok
Wabum enosed.

The Episcopal and Catholic priests were enraged. Fathers Gilfillian and Benoit were the two outposts of the great Christian faiths on White Earth. The churches had actively participated in the removals to White Earth and knew many of the families and bands. The Fathers believed they had done well with the Indians in terms of conversions. In spite of what seemed to be a constant battle, Gilfillian's flock had grown. He counted some two hundred and fifty souls among his converts, and Father Benoit could likely count three hundred souls having turned to the Catholic faith. Yet there were always those who needed to hear their word—hear it for the first time, or repeated many times over; it always seemed to the priests that there were many Indians who were hard of hearing. For that reason, any stones in the road to the Lord's Kingdom on Earth must be moved aside. It was God's word and intent.

Father Joseph Gilfillian fancied himself a patient person. Over the long term, he felt reassured that the Ojibwe would come to embrace fully the virtues of Christianity. Today, however, patience was required in endless supply. While on one hand they appeared grateful for everlasting security, on the other hand, the Indians were always unpredictable. It was clear that no seminary could prepare a man for such a life.

The Church had come to the *Anishinaabeg* in the early 1800s, bringing both the Bible and the smallpox. Jesuit Father Frederick Baraga came from Michigan, tirelessly carrying his teachings and his disease across the land. Opportunistically, he made his life's work the compiling of an Ojibwe dictionary and, not surprisingly, the translation of the Bible into Ojibwe. Hundreds were converted by his words, and hundreds died from his germs. Yet he had been among the most gentle of the men who looked like crows. The *Anishinaabeg* name for them was *Makadewikonayewinini*, the Men Who Dress in Black.

While the Catholics and Mormons took the southern and western tier of "Indian Country," the Jesuits and Episcopals divided up the northern half of the continent. The Men Who Dress in Black moved uninvited into communities, seeking and gaining converts. They followed the Indians as federal Indian policy dictated, assuaging the pain of the government's secular hand with a scapular and a cross.

Now, Gilfillian smoothed his cassock as he stood at his desk. He had completed his monthly report for the Indian Agency on Friday, and on Saturday he had undertaken a few more Ojibwe translations for his sermon. This was one of the great challenges of missionary work—the Ojibwe language was full of nuances and subtleties. For instance, with a slip of the tongue an unwitting translation could refer to a pipe or a penis. He had made that mistake while chastising the community for the use of their pipes. Disbelief and giggles were his response. He had lost some credibility, but pulled his black robe tighter and continued on.

As Gilfillian requested, two women were already preparing for the service. Philomene St. Clair was a wiry woman whose strength was hidden by her tiny stature and her eyes. She was of the Wolf Clan, and her face reflected her *doodem*, her clan—eyes set forward around a strong nose, eyes that saw and watched everything, then moved swiftly. She was good soul and an excellent housekeeper, and Gilfillian had never worried once about her since she was in his service. Philomene's sister, Izola Pemberton, had scoured the church on her hands and knees yesterday. Izola was a new member of the women's society at the church, and together they ensured that things were in order.

St. Columba Episcopal Church was constructed of rock, built stone by stone by the toil of the dedicated. This church was Gilfillian's pride, physical testimony to his success and the promise of the community. *He would be remembered.* His will would ensure his posterity.

Gilfillian went to greet his congregation as they came up the hill. He could see their buggies arriving. The female members of his flock wore calico dresses with high collars and bonnets; beadwork remained on some of the outfits. A few of the men had bandoleer bags, the large, intricately beaded bags worn for social and ceremonial events and dances. He would have to write a sermon on the need to abandon such trinkets and remnants of the past.

As the parishioners entered the church, Gilfillian shook their hands or nodded in approval. Some of the Indians had faces full of hope; others seemed to shuffle obediently to their pews. Gilfillian cared only that they were present. But for the most part, his congregation looked down so they did not meet his eyes, a sign of respect and a sign of fear.

As Gilfillian observed his flock's arrival, he could hear his choir begin now, voices raised in the beauty of a hymn he himself had translated into Ojibwe.

> *"Holy, Holy, Holy! Lord God Almighty!*
> *Pinzi, Pinzi, Pinzi! Enamiajig,*
> *Ki wawigenimigog waseyaziwining;*
> *Kakina ishpiming meshkawizijig,*
> *Kaginig ki wawijenimigog.*
> *Pinzi, Pinzi, Pinzi! Ano Kushkidibik,*
> *Agosin jiwabudaming kiwase yas-win,*
> *Kin su paniziyun; kin gaye go eta,*
> *Kin mayamawi, pinadiziyun.*
> *Pinzi, Pinzi, Pinzi! Kije-Manido!*
> *Kidun-kiwinun kidowijenimigonun:*
> *Pinzi, Pinzi, Pinzi! aadebeniged!*
> *Gaye dush au Panizid Ojichag."*

Only after his sermon began did Gilfillian notice the empty pews. He looked out to the place where Chief Mayzhuckegeeshig's family usually sat and found them missing, as was Wabunoquod, another chief. Then he noted that several of the Pembertons were gone, as well as the Chi Makwa, or Big Bear, family and others. It seemed that almost a third of the traditional and a fourth of the mixed-blood families were absent. He fought his own distraction and composed himself to continue his sermon. Mid-speech he found his anger overcoming his words. Now his mouth was pointed, accusing those who had fallen. He spoke of shame and the wrath that would descend. His face became more contorted, and his arms more animated. His finger pointed to the empty spaces and he called on those who were there to search out and vanquish the others as heathens. Grasping her scapular, Philomene began to move toward him, afraid he would choke on his own rage. He gasped, catching his breath. For the moment, he had regained his composure.

It was a far less composed Gilfillian who grasped Philomene's arm after the sermon.

"Where are our people?" he demanded.

He was met with a look of silence and dread.

"Is there a sickness in the village?" he asked again.

Again silence and dread. She winced.

"No, sir," Philomene volunteered reluctantly. "I don't believe there is any great sickness, although a number of children have flu."

"Is there a treaty payment?"

"No, sir," she said, never raising her eyes from the floor, "I don't believe there are payments now."

He continued, with any question he could find, and then began to dread the inevitable: "Are there Ojibwe ceremonies going on now?"

Philomene backed into a corner, cowering under the Reverend's questioning.

"Yes, Father, there are," Philomene responded, relieved that he had come to the right conclusion at last, but at the same time recognizing the consequences.

He was shaking now, and she was afraid to look at him. "What ceremonies are these?"

Philomene was in her late forties, a mother of four and grand-mother to nine children. But at this moment, she felt like a child herself, being spoken to by an adult. Father Gilfillian was a kind man. She knew that he would not strike her, but she was still afraid. She hated to be the one who disappointed him.

"*Ogichidaa dewe'igan* ceremonies," she finally said.

"What?" barked Gilfillian, frustrated again by the Ojibwe tongue.

"Big Drum ceremonies," Philomene repeated. A pause. "They last for four days. Since some of the people are working, they have taken to having these ceremonies on the weekends."

His face tightened as she spoke.

"Who brought these drums here?" he demanded. He had never heard of these rituals before and was furious that a new cult might have crept onto his reservation.

"It was a vision of the spirits." she said as if that explained all.

"There are no visions of the spirits except for our Savior's visions," he snapped. "This will not happen. The families will be punished. Who is involved?" The priest stepped closer, his breath hot against her face.

She spoke rapidly, trying to get all of her words out as quickly as possible so she could escape him. "A number of families from White Earth. There are now several drums in this village. There are church-going families involved as well as *Midewiwin* families. It makes no difference. One drum is with Chi Makwa and another drum with Minnogeeshig and another with Mindemoyen." She regretted her knowledge.

"That's enough," he said. Then he dismissed Philomene with a backwards wave of his hand and set his jaw.

Philomene was eternally grateful to be out of his sight.

After that the priest had no peace. It had been a great test to have a mission among these people, but this new distraction to Sunday worship frustrated him to no end. It was a step backward on the road to salvation. He looked over his monthly reports to headquarters in Washington and to his Church superiors. Before this he had been able to record progress—more Indians attending church and school, and other indications of forward behavior. This would not sit well with anyone.

"Let us hope this passes quickly," he whispered bitterly.

Joseph Gilfillian waited and watched. Many of the families came back the next Sunday and sat in church as if they had never missed a Sunday. But over time, families were missing again. He cornered Philomene St. Clair once again and discovered that a new drum had been given to the Littlewolf family in Naytahwaush, and other families had gone to welcome the drum into the community. According to custom, the drums were relatives, and as such, other drum families attended feasts and ceremonies with related drums. He could wait no longer. He went to investigate.

With an unhappy Philomene sitting beside him, he drove his buggy out toward Spirit Lake where the log house of Chief Wazhaashkoons could be found. The house rested next to an old lodge that had been abandoned when the family moved into the new cabin. But recently the old lodge had been resurrected. It was made of birch bark and willow and had fresh bark placed on the sides and brightly colored cloth tied at several locations. He had never seen this cloth before and it caused him to shudder.

He pulled his horse to a harsh halt and clambered out of the buggy, leaving Philomene to her own resources. He marched toward the doorway of the Chief's log house. When he was halfway across the yard, Wazhaashkoons suddenly came out of the cabin. He was a big man, dressed in a calico shirt and beaded apron, and he nodded to the *Makadewikonayewinini*. Father Gilfillian stood on the porch, looking directly into the deep brown eyes of Wazhaashkoons. But the chief looked past the priest, off into the woods. The priest moved his head quickly to each side, quite like a crow, trying to catch the Indian's eyes.

"Why were your people not at church this past Sunday?" the man in black asked the man in beadwork.

Wazhaashkoons paused. He spoke first in Ojibwe: "We had some doings." His eyes were level, still, turned away.

Father Gilfillian took a deep breath. *"It could be a funeral, a birth, many things,"* he thought to himself. Hopefully.

Then Wazhaashkoons spoke: "We have a new drum. I am caring for it."

Wazhaashkoons remembered the first priest, the *wemitigoozhi*. Perhaps he should have pierced this one as well when he first arrived. *"No,"* he thought to himself, *"this priest feeds some who need him, and he will never touch me. He can talk and wish all he wants, but his God will always be his own."*

Wazhaashkoons eyes still looked past the priest; it was disrespectful to look directly at an individual.

The priest froze. Why would Wazhaashkoons not look at him; was he being contentious or rebellious? Thoughts jumped through his head, then jumbled. He would ask no more.

"Good day," Gilfillian said, nodding, and he walked off the porch. Philomene watched the *Makadewikonayewinini* walk toward her. She had listened through it all and felt both jubilation and dread at the meeting of the two gods. Her priest was strong, but the chief was equally so. A small sense of pride eked into her at the sight of Wazhaashkoons.

As word came in from his faithful of other drums and other strays from the flock, the priest's temperament grew morose. *"They are whooping and dancing around the drum, very much as savages,"* he wrote in his report to the diocese. *"This is a veritable orgy which makes night and day hideous for weeks."*

Joseph Gilfillian was beyond patience. He deliberated carefully before making his move, then he made his way out of the Episcopal church and walked down the main street of White Earth village to the Catholic church, a large white clapboard building looming with vigilance and hope over the powwow grounds. He entered the church, and casting his eyes away from the high altar with its gaudy cross, luminescent savior, and velvet pomp, he strode in a straight line to meet his Catholic counterpart.

"Greetings Father Benoit," he nodded to the large man with a thick head of black hair.

"Greetings Father Gilfillian," returned the Catholic priest.

For two men in such fierce competition in spiritual headhunting, there was an underlying tension that was natural. Yet they had an understanding. Each had his families, and no raiding was allowed. The central priority for both should be conversion of those still lost and keeping the flocks together. Gilfillian believed that Father Benoit had a similar problem, and they should share in the solution.

Gilfillian spoke directly. "It has come to my attention that the presence of Satan is growing on this reservation. Heathen practices are broadening. They consist of dancing around a drum and other shameless behavior."

Father Benoit raised his eyebrows and acknowledged his dismay.

"Yes, I have heard of this savagery. A number of families have learned this practice from the Dakota." Unspoken, both Fathers shared disdain for the Dakotas, who they viewed as less civilized than the Ojibwe, and they believed that some of the ceremonies had been transferred between the two. Caught like a disease.

Gilfillian's curiosity now began to overcome his grace.

"Have you lost many parishioners?" he asked.

"Well, I must admit that there seem to be less attending church this month than last, although they do return, but only to disappear again," responded Benoit. "And your church, Father?"

"Yes, I too am missing some parishioners. I fear that something must be done before it gets any worse."

"Do you have a proposal, Father?"

Gilfillian had carefully considered this. He knew that this would require a major effort, but that it was essential to stop the frenzy before it spread throughout the community. The danger of losing converts was grave. He paused before he spoke. "We must outlaw the heathen rituals."

Father Benoit drew a deep breath and looked at his contemporary. This would not be easy, he feared, yet it might be the only solution.

Indian Agent Simon Michelet received the two Fathers with great interest. Only a mission of great import would have brought such a powerful ensemble to his office. Michelet was a practical man. He understood that both churches were an essential part of a successful Indian policy, and that any requests made by the Fathers should be given the highest consideration. He shook hands with each of them and then offered two chairs. His assistant brought a pot of tea.

Father Gilfillian told the story to the agent as the tea was poured. Michelet listened stoically, his features almost reptilian. His small eyes were set far apart in his big head, above a wide mouth and square jaw.

His thin lips parted finally at the end of Gilfillian's speech. "Oh," he said, simply.

Michelet had been in Washington a great deal lately, preparing for new Indian appropriations and presenting policy. He was vaguely aware of some new pagan dances on the reservation, but had not looked on them as a serious problem. But when Gilfillian explained that the dance came from the Dakotas, Michelet's ears were alert. "How did the Sioux come to our reservation?" Without question, he also retained a dislike for the Sioux.

"It was during the Sioux uprising," Gilfillian recounted. "A woman came from the Dakotas and took refuge on this reservation. It was around the time of her coming that the drum too came. She lives with the Minnogeeshig family now." Joseph Gilfillian knew how to capitalize on his assets, the assets of disdain: "There has been, it seems, quite a taking up of the dancing, and now many villages have one of these drums."

"Indeed, they are not content to attend only their own ceremonies," Benoit added, "but must attend the ceremonies of the other drums as well, calling them 'relatives.'"

Michelet finally understood the scope of the problem. "And this is having an effect on the churches, I gather."

The priests nodded in unison.

After a moment of reflection, Gilfillian presented his recommendation. "We would like to secure an agency policy that outlaws participation in any non-Christian ceremonies for an individual under fifty years of age."

Michelet understood.

"This would satisfy the older Indians who are prone to continue practice of the old ways, and thus, they would not be angry with us," the Father went on. "At the same time, this would stop the younger people. With hope, within twenty years there will be no living people who remember the ceremonies."

Father Benoit nodded his head vigorously as Gilfillian spoke.

"How clever," the Indian Agent applauded them. Small in stature in comparison to the imposing figures of the two priests, he had always been in awe of their power. "You would like me to pass an agency law," he said, reiterating his role in the action. They all understood the need for cooperation and diplomacy in such a situation. This was, of course, how things were best accomplished—each party doing its own part. The more the Indian Agent considered it, the more he liked the idea. "Yes, I can pass such a law. I am also sure that there will be support in Washington—the problem is on other reservations, as well. With the Sioux Agency, they have had bloody uprisings, largely a consequence, I believe, of these dances and drums."

"And enforcement?" Father Benoit asked anxiously. He had a particular interest in the role of discipline in the community.

"We have the rations," Michelet said.

The Fathers nodded knowingly.

"And we do have a police force," Michelet volunteered. "They will be authorized to arrest. This will likely deter most of the Indians."

"Yes, that should be sufficient," Father Gilfillian concurred, pleased to have once again secured the cooperation of the agency. "We will see which families return to church, and whom is missing, and report this to your office."

"Very good. I am sure that we can lay this matter to rest in short order," the man with the reptilian face smiled again. Now he rose from his chair to shake hands with the priests.

"Thank you, Mr. Michelet," said Father Benoit, rising from his seat.

Father Gilfillian added appreciatively, "We will keep you informed."

The two Fathers left the agency office, pleased with their work of the morning. Outside the office, they shook hands and parted. In a garden nearby, two large crows landed and seized on a shiny tin piece that had been discarded. After a short exchange, they tore the piece in two and flew their separate ways.

THE DESCENT
1898

The retaliation was swift and relentless. Simon Michelet undertook the new challenge with remarkable zeal and enthusiasm. He deputized ten new agency policemen and dispatched patrols to the villages. He posted the new decree and notified the Indian newspaper of White Earth, *The Progress*. There was no excuse for continued practice—all must know the order. Interpreters were sent to the families who spoke no English, and they too were informed. He expected, and would get, complete compliance.

He enjoyed this task and the status associated with any success. In the circles of federal Indian policy, tolerance for native religious practices was scorned at best. Indeed, it had been scarcely ten years since the cavalry had silenced the Ghost Dance ceremonies at Wounded Knee—*"Unfortunate,"* Michelet thought, *"that all those women and children had to be killed as well, but perhaps it would squelch those uncivilized activities once and for all."*

His new counterpart in the Dakota Agency had devised a brilliant strategy, a strategy for which he was envious. The new agent had built a mental institution in Pierre to house the so-called "medicine men" from all of the Plains tribes. The agency's simple—and admittedly brilliant—philosophy was that it was easier to confine those who had alleged "visions" then to have to police the whole community. Michelet had read with great interest the reports from the Dakota Agency, and thought he should send some perpetrators there—

Chi Makwa would be the most likely candidate. Any shaking tent men—*jiisakiiwinini*—could easily be deemed *insane*. And maybe that Ishkwegaabawiikwe: She seemed to have a strange power as well, she and her consort, that Dakota woman. He had been unable to pry them apart and force the Dakota woman back to her own reservation. And now he was paying for it with this trouble.

But on second consideration, it would be better yet if he could handle his agency's problems himself. His superiors in Washington had given him a great deal of latitude, especially since he had met with so much success in instituting the land allotment policy on White Earth, dividing up and making worthwhile use of much of the reservation for logging. For now, he would try his own methods, but the institution in South Dakota, or alternately the Minnesota state mental institution in Fergus Falls, just on the edge of the White Earth Reservation, could come in handy.

Food would be the key to controlling the Indians. Michelet knew that a number of families now depended on the government rations for food, particularly some of the older families who had lost children to illness or to removal. At each distribution center, he explained the new laws and emphasized that any family found to be in violation of the law would not receive rations. In turn, families who reported violators would receive additional rations.

Then he waited and watched. He could set a trap as well.

Winter turned colder, and the price of furs dropped as the northern trade routes expanded. With little to trade, the families faced dire hardships and came to be more dependent on the goods the agency provided. Then Michelet urged the trading posts to call in their credit. It did not take long for some Indians to turn against others and report the drums. As spring ceremonies set in, so did the police. Unrepentant and steadfast Indians were swiftly punished. A hundred or more people were arrested. Other families simply hid their small children, and then, in secret, brought them to the ceremonies. The law did not stop the drum, it only forced people to retreat into the woods.

The old man Chi Makwa was singing the second song in the sequence. His strong, low voice lead the other singers as the drumbeat punctuated the melody. Now members of the Minnogeeshig family began to dance, slowly shuffling their feet in a small circle near the drum, while others danced in place. The undulating lights of the kerosene lanterns flickered off the beadwork on the drum and onto the *Anishinaabeg* moving in a circle to the sound of the drum.

Hidden by the woods, Philomene St. Clair stood, clenching her rosary beads, knuckles whitening from the immense pressure coursing through her veins. Only the cloud of her breath in the cold air gave away her hiding place in the snow. She listened as the drum songs began again, and then turned, walking quickly toward town.

It was an hour later when the two agency policemen arrived. They were smartly dressed in navy-colored uniforms, black hats, and stars. They came by buggy, reining in their horses to an abrupt halt outside the log lodge used for the drum ceremonies. Quickly climbing down from the buggy, they walked through the remains of the winter snow and approached the door. They hesitated, then opened the door.

Inside, Chi Makwa's voice resonated as he led the song, other voices joining in again until a child shrieked at the sight of the policemen, scurried behind her mother, and enveloped herself in her mother's long wool skirt.

The *dakoniwewinini*, literally the Men Who Hold Someone, charged inside the log lodge now, as children rushed to hide. Only Chi Makwa continued to sing, looking up at the two *dakoniwewinini* with fierce contempt in his eyes, then looking through them, as if they were not there. The old man continued to sing, while the two *dakoniwewinini* stood just inside the doorway, confused by the elder, causing them to halt their charge.

When the song finished, the policemen quickly moved toward the old man, grabbing him roughly. Wazhaashkoons and Namaybin Minnogeeshig jumped forward to hide the drum away and pull the policemen away from Chi Makwa. A policeman swung at Namaybin Minnogeeshig with his club stick and Namaybin winced, then turned back and twisted the club away from the policeman, and threw it to the ground. Ishkwegaabawiikwe meanwhile grabbed the drumstick and fled with Situpiwin and the other women and children outside to disappear into the woods.

The policemen could only take two hostages, as those over fifty years of age, the elders, were exempted from the law. Chi Makwa's son and an Oshkinnah boy of nineteen or so twisted and writhed to escape the policemen. But the agency men held the boys tight even while swinging their batons wildly to fend off the others. A baton struck Wazhaashkoons, who fell onto a table, upsetting a kerosene lantern. As the shattered lamp burst into flames, the men rushed to squelch the fire. The policeman took advantage of the confusion and retreated to their buggy, dragging the two young men in tow.

Chi Makwa stood in the doorway and shook his drumstick at the policeman. His voice was hoarse as he screamed after them. "You should be ashamed of yourselves. Where is your Indian heart? Where are your grandchildren to be? In the villages of white men?"

One of the *dakoniwewininiwag* glared at him, half scared, half proud in his power over the elder.

"Old man, be quiet," he howled, almost hysterical. "Old man, you stay in the woods with your blankets and beads. Old man, times are changing. New times. This is the new law."

In a panic, the policemen turned their buggy toward the road, pulling tightly on their horses' reins in their hurry to escape the old man's wrath, the horses bucking in their harnesses. Wazhaashkoons and Namaybin fought to put the fire out in the lodge.

In spite of his age, Chi Makwa ran after the policemen now as fast as his old legs could carry him. His voice boomed in their ears.

"Your time is short here. Ours is forever. You can't stop us. You can't hold us back. You can't hold us long."

The buggy picked up speed, the horses galloping down the road, and Chi Makwa's voice was lost to it. From out of the woods, the men, women, and children of the drum society slowly reappeared. The old man shook with anger, tears welling up in his eyes. Namaybin Minnogeeshig put his hand on the old man's shoulder and brought him back inside to his chair. The fire quelled, the men brought the drum back from the woods. The women sobbed for the two abducted children, but knew the drum ceremony must be completed before they could act.

Ishkwegaabawiikwe gave the drumstick back to Chi Makwa, and

he began singing. Slowly, solemnly, the people reassembled, wading through broken chairs and the smell of burned wood. There were two more songs before the ceremony would be done, and their voices rose in unison.

PIMAS, AFRICANS, AND MONKEYS
1915

Dispensed by the powers that be in the white man's land, the distinguished Doctor Ales Hrdlicka arrived one fine summer day at White Earth. A small man, graying at the temples, with a shock of black hair that framed his angular face and piercing eyes, Hrdlicka was singularly possessed by the pursuit for pure physical specimens of humanity and the determination of their positive origins.

In a world resounding with the collisions between cultures and peoples, he had found his manna. Through Hrdlicka's practical physical anthropology, he could chart, utilizing a series of clever instruments of his own devising, both the "full bloods" and the "others" who were a mixture of the three great stocks of humankind: the whites, the yellow-browns, and the blacks or *negritos*. It was a passion that had taken him from the University of Paris to the tombs of most museums and major military hospitals. From there he had traveled by pack mule, by steamboat up the Amazon, by train, by foot, by dogsled, traveling through the villages of Mexico, Peru, the Arctic, and much of Indian country.

He was a man of immense resourcefulness. He had studied most stocks of the world, making tables, charts, averages, evaluations, and groupings of his millions of measurements. The work that was perhaps the most dear to his heart was his comparative studies of Pimas,

Africans, and various species of monkeys. This analysis of cranial capacity and supraorbital ridges he believed held the key to understanding the clear evidence of evolution. Until recently, his favorite research location remained the great Smithsonian Institution in Washington, with which he retained a special relationship as he sifted through the thousands of bodies, corpses, and skeletal remains unearthed from around the world by archaeologists or donated as booty of war. From the dead, he could collect much in terms of raw data, but it was from the living, whom he yearned to observe, that he could truly study cranial capacity, breadth of septum, character and retention of hair, and the personal histories of individuals and allegations as to their lineage.

White Earth was prime for the plucking. Under the 1887 Nelson Act, the reservation had been divided into individual eighty-acre allotments in a policy intended to civilize the White Earth *Anishinaabeg* through the learning of American concepts of land tenure and private property. The allotments also inexplicably followed the boundaries noted carefully by logging companies who now flourished in the northwoods. Having allocated all the lands on White Earth, save four entire townships of prime white pine that were conveniently transferred to state jurisdiction, new laws authorized the sale not only of trees, but of land itself—but only of land owned by those determined to be "mixed blood" Indians. Mixed bloods, it seems, were deemed "competent" by Indian Agent Simon Michelet and his superiors at the agency to handle their own affairs. Full bloods, of course, were known to be unable to do so. The task ahead for those with a vested interest was now to enumerate the number of mixed bloods.

Hrdlicka theorized that Pima Indians from Arizona represented "the most Indian of all Indians," and utilized them to construct a "full blood" physical standard against which the *Anishinaabeg* might be judged. *Large* and *important* tribes, he expounded, are already so mixed that it is a task for the anthropologist to find a sufficient number of full bloods for his studies. Under these circumstances, the need grew more urgent to determine the physical type of the most important tribes. He had looked forward to his time with the Chippewa, whom he found to be "quite typical, ordinary Indians, without any special attributes." The expression on their faces he found to be "kindly, their behavior cheerful and friendly, but not too forward."

It was *ziigwan*, the springtime, prior to the good doctor's visit, when Mindemoyen began to have her dream. It was always the same, and no one could offer an explanation. *She wore her dark blue town dress, one sleeve rolled up. She had cut her arm with her own knife. And now the blood flowed quickly. She held her arm over a wooden bowl, one her father had made. She watched the blood drip into the bowl until it was half full. Then she wrapped her arm in cloth to stop the bleeding. She sat down, bowl in hand, next to her friend* Ishkwegaabawiikwe*, who had a bowl filled with blood as well. Now they walked together toward a small white tent. Looking to either side, they saw their relatives and friends all walking toward the tent with bowls of blood in hand, arms wrapped in white gauze.*

In the summer, Hrdlicka and his colleague, anthropologist Doctor Albert E. Jenks of the University of Minnesota, came to the village. They traveled by buggy to the villages where they set up shop in a small white tent. Their office consisted of a few chairs, a table, and an assortment of equipment that Hrdlicka himself had crafted in aid of his science—several varieties of andropometer, spreading calipers for adapted and advanced work on the skull, and a special device for measuring cranial capacity.

The Indian Agency issued a special decree that extra rations of salt pork would be given to those who would contribute to the fine medical research of the doctors. By now most families could use extra meat on the table. Agent Michelet also made it clear that the agency would be less than forthcoming with monthly rations to families if they did not cooperate.

Lined up like ear-tagged cattle at auction, the Pine Point people anxiously awaited the pronouncements of "the doctor who knows what Indians are." Mindemoyen had the dream the night before Hrdlicka came to town; now she too waited in line. She watched as the Essens brothers emerged from the tent, puzzled looks on their faces.

"What happened?" she whispered. Everyone craned their necks to hear.

"They are crazy men," the younger brother said.

The two brothers slowly opened their shirts as a small group of *Anishinaabeg* gathered round. Each brother had a scratch on his chest. Eyes widened in astonishment.

"Are they *wiindigoos*?" asked one of the older women in the village fearfully.

Some crossed themselves.

"No, they are not *wiindigoos*," the older brother said, then shrugged. "They are just strange white people."

Then the other brother spoke: "The doctor man says I am a full blood and my brother is a mixed blood."

The crowd was silent, stunned.

The older brother spoke again: "The doctor also wanted to know the blood of my father and his father before him. I said, 'He is dead long ago. I don't know exactly what he was. You can go dig him out of his grave, and then you can find out.'"

The Doctor summoned Mindemoyen from the dwindling line of those presumed to be full bloods. She held tightly to the hand of Ishkwegaabawiikwe and now fearfully looked straight ahead. The Doctor repeated her name again, then came out of his small tent looking for her.

"Mrs. Mindemoyen," he said quietly. "This will not take long and will not be painful."

She thought back to the Essens brothers' scratch marks and looked fearfully at the tent. Remembering the promised food and her hungry family, she stood up and strode toward the tent, following the doctor.

Her eyes grew wide when she saw the strange things of the doctor. First he bade her take off her bonnet and sit in the chair. He took down her name and began to make notations in his book.

Age: 45, estimated

Eyes: Fairly slanted

Hair: Straight, thick, black

Nose: Foot stout, bridge concave, less evolved

Mindemoyen sat straight and quiet, looking toward a space on the tent wall on which she imagined a birch bark pattern that made her feel more comfortable. The doctor circled her now, clucking with some reassuring tones. "This will require just a minute, just a minute, ma'am, not to worry." The doctor put his face directly in front of her now, looking at her eyes, then closer, with his notebook still in his hand. She did not look at him, just through him, toward that birch bark pattern again.

She was determined not to show her fear to the doctor, who smiled at her now, apologizing ever so slightly for any discomfort. She tried not to look and closed her eyes when she saw him pick up a set of circular forceps that looked like the jaws of a giant metal bear to her, closing in on her head.

"Do not worry," he explained. "This is nothing but a spreading caliper." He placed the metal tongs on her forehead and she felt the coldness of the steel like a knife blade against her skin. He made some notations, then moved the instrument to her nose and cheeks. He continued examining and measuring her forehead, chin, and skull from several different angles. He wrote again in his book, adding lists of numbers, figures, measurements, and observations.

Cheek bones: Pronounced
Supraorbital brow ridges: Strong, primatal
Forehead: Low in appearance, large protrusions
Occipital bone: Large, protohuman
Incisors: Shovel-shaped, sharp

Finally, he stood back and calmly asked her to stand and open her dress so he might look. With some hesitation, she complied, continuing to look at the wall. He pulled his thumb and forefinger across her chest in a deep scratch, which caused her to jump back quickly, gasping, and grasping her dress back close around her.

But he had already turned his back on her and was writing yet again in his book. He spoke to her over his shoulder. "You may close your dress now, Mrs. Mindemoyen." He turned to look at her, announcing his prognosis like a benediction: "You will be happy to know that you are of mixed blood descent."

At long last, Mindemoyen reappeared from the white tent, her head ducking out of the flap. She hurried to Ishkwegaabawiikwe's side, still shaking, still tasting the salt of her tears on her lips.

"*Chimookomaan geweenadis,*" she gasped. "The white man is crazy."

Ishkwegaabawiikwe looked at her cousin as her own name was called out from the tent.

"*Anish kah a way buck?* What happened?"

"*Ikido chimookomaanikwe, Indaaw*" Mindemoyen said in a whisper so no one else would hear: "He says I'm a white woman."

WIINDIGOO
1915

The old man Namaybin Minnogeeshig, his wives Situpiwin and Ishkwegaabawiikwe, and their children lived deep in the woods now, preferring their traditional life to that of town or agency Indians. And frankly, they were shunned by some of the same, who in their newly christianized enthusiasm, rankled against traditional religious and marital practices of the *Anishinaabeg*. Namaybin had more than one heated argument on the makeup of his family during a rare visit to the agency store and wondered aloud if they would rather he cast one of his wives out to fend for herself or find her way to town and the alleged charity of the white churches and good citizens of the border towns. And so the family chose to rely only on themselves, remaining steadfast and content in their stretch of woods and a life of their own determination.

The Minnogeeshig family watched as the logging teams encroached closer and closer to their trapline. The animals behaved differently now, moving nearer to the Minnogeeshig family camp, the logging companies close on their tracks. The logging companies had moved onto the reservation with the blessing of the Indian Agency and now began a feeding frenzy that would last for thirty years. Lumber camps were set up near the lakes as teams of men and horses moved the great pines from their homes in the woods to the lakes and then down the rivers to the mills of Little Falls further south and far from the reservation. It was a mystery to most, save perhaps the Indian Agent and a few timber cruisers, how the Pillsburys, Weyerhaeusers, Steenersons, and Walsh families had the papers to cut the trees, but somehow they did, and they kept on cutting.

When old man Namaybin Minnogeeshig would go to town with his horses, he would see the lumbermen cutting, or in the least, see their work. Shaking his head, he would say *"So much greed, so much greed,"* wondering where it would end and what would be next.

Namaybin was a huge bear of a man, stocky through the chest, with arms as strong as a horse. He had coal black hair with a shock of white at the temples. His deepset eyes could show the greatest sparkle of kindness to his children and wives, or the deepest hatred, a look rarely used by *Anishinaabeg*, who preferred generally to look through or ignore completely those with whom they disagreed. He had used the glare of hatred only on a few occasions and to ward off the boarding school superintendent.

He could hear now the sounds of men and Swede saws, the sounds of workhorses straining as they pulled the big logs, and smell the timber just recently cut, wafting on the wind toward his front porch. The dirt road that came to the Minnogeeshig cabin meandered through the woods, circumscribing beaver dams and ponds, and carefully passing between the large white pines that were the grandfathers to the *Anishinaabeg*.

Namaybin looked now toward the road, and he saw the logging foreman coming down his trail in a small buggy pulled by a bay horse. Namaybin's stomach ached now. The buggy lurched to a stop, and the small man in town clothes climbed down from the buggy, followed by a tall, lanky Indian also dressed in town clothes.

Namaybin poked a stick into his fire and sat on the stump in his small yard. A teapot was warming within the flames, surrounded by hides stretched on sapling hoops or wooden frames that embraced the smoke of the old man's fire as they prepared for their new life as a medicine pouch or garment.

Namaybin looked at the lumberman and did not stand. With some hesitation the foreman came forward, his eyes taking in the Indian's life and filing it in his mind. Namaybin regarded the lumberman and his Indian. He remembered that there had once been a *wiindigoo*, or cannibal, at Round Lake, many winters past. It had been long since the cannibal had been there but Namaybin remembered him just the same.

The wiindigoo's *small lodge had stood on the north side of Round Lake, a lake rich with beaver, fish, and wild rice. But the foods did not please the old man now. The* wiindigoo *had starved once, long before, starved during a cold winter of too much snow and not enough rabbits. Starved nearly to death. Until he found a family, also weak from the winter. He culled those animals, culled them right from the herd. He culled them out of hunger and out of anger too. His own wife and family were long gone from the small pox. His bitterness at those who brought it had not subsided. He was alone, his family gone. His face and hair were unkempt, his moccasins hard with use. He ate his visitors now. Never again to be a victim of invisible death. He ate those who strayed, were weak, or were just plain unfortunate. He ate the bold and the foolish, and he ate the young. He relished in his evil, and he forged a magic, a strong magic with the* Mishinameginebig, *the Great Horned Sturgeon, saying "Ninitim, ginitim. Ninitim, ginitim. My turn, your turn."*

Namaybin looked again at the lumberman. *"The cannibal is here again,"* Namaybin observed.

The lumberman looked down at Namaybin and now the old man spoke.

"There is no use to make small talk with a cannibal," he said in Ojibwe and paused, looking to the interpreter. The interpreter had been gazing down somewhat dismissively at the old man, but he now drew a quick breath and drew back, surprised by the sharpness of Namaybin's words. The interpreter hesitated, then dutifully translated Namaybin's words, and the man in town clothes shifted uncomfortably. The interpreter looked somewhat apologetically now at Namaybin.

"An Indian can sit and talk to a cannibal, making all kinds of jokes, telling stories, and drinking tea," Namaybin continued in Ojibwe, his eyes locked on the lumberman, "but both the Indian and the cannibal know exactly what the cannibal is thinking."

Namaybin stopped now and turned his back on the lumberman, moving toward a beaver hide he was working on. Carefully scraping off the flesh with the blunt of his knife, he listened with one ear. The interpreter spoke softly to the lumberman. The town Indian's face had been guarded before, but now it held the beginnings of a small, secret *giimooj*, an Indian smile. The lumberman did not notice the smile.

The lumberman spoke now. "Mr. Minnogeeshig," he said abruptly in his harsh, awkward white man's language, irked by the silliness of the Indian's veiled words and secrets. "I have papers that say I can take the trees off your land. I have the papers."

The interpreter translated for Namaybin. "White man says he can take the trees. White man wants the trees. White man has paper."

Namaybin looked at the two men and held his hand out, beckoning the paper toward him. The white man passed the paper to the old Indian.

The Indian looked at the papers, puzzling over the strange writing of the white men, unable to read, yet understanding clearly what the lumberman wanted.

The lumberman shrugged. "I am only coming here out of courtesy, Mr. Minnogeeshig," he said. "The Indian Agent gave permission to cut the timber off your land."

The interpreter translated now, looking somewhat detached, and Namaybin glared at the men. The interpreter pointed to the signature on the paper, as Namaybin grasped the paper, looking closer at the marks he could not understand. He understood the intent of the paper. He understood the cannibal.

Namaybin tore the paper now and threw it into his fire as the cannibal gasped, lurching forward to retrieve his precious document from the flames, the fire scorching his fingers as small, burnt cinders of the paper were lifted away by the breeze. It was an unsuccessful rescue. The Indian looked back at his beaver hide and walked toward it, knife in hand. The cannibal sputtered, shaking his head, and now his finger, at Namaybin.

"Your trees are mine. And your trees are coming down," the lumberman said coldly. He turned on his heel and returned to his buggy, leaving the embarrassed interpreter to translate words that needed no translation.

Rousing Namaybin's anger was a mistake, much like waking a hibernating bear prematurely from its slumber. There is no getting around that the bear is predator.

Namaybin watched the cannibal and his associate as they retreated hastily down the road toward the logging camp. The cannibal gone from his presence, he stood up, stayed his fire, and moved to his horse.

In the afternoon he paid a visit to Mindemoyen's family, Chi Makwa, the Wabizi family, and others near Round Lake and Many Point. He asked them all the same questions. Who had sold their trees, and who had not. All nodded in agreement. None had sold. The Indian Agent had sold their trees for them.

By night, Namaybin, Ishkwegaabawiikwe, Situpiwin, and others moved into the logging camps and took as the booty of their lumber war the tools of the trade—saws, axes, chains, harnesses, skids, and adding insult to injury, the best team of workhorses, a pair of beautiful gray Percherons. Stashing their cache in the woods, they moved to fix their post. From deep in the forests, moving stealthily by canoe, the Indians crossed the lake toward the outlet into the Ottertail River, and by dawn they had positioned themselves below the logs, at the conflux of the two bodies of water.

The next morning the cannibal returned. Anticipating the glory of a new clear cut, he was stunned to find his camp dismantled. Groaning, he slammed his fist on the side of his buggy. "Damn Indians," he yelled into the woods.

A foreman arrived amid a flurry of horse hoofs. Breathless, he bounded from his horse and ran to the lumberman.

"Them Indians have taken over the lake. They've got the lake, they've got the lake," he repeated over and over, stuttering with disbelief.

The lumberman looked at him, incredulous.

"How can they?" he asked.

"Look for yourself. They've blocked the logs, all of them, with their canoes and rafts."

The lumberman hit the buggy again. "Damn Indians," he roared, and mustered his horse for the ride to the other side of the lake.

His anger festered as he rode. Maneuvering through a crowd of frustrated loggers, he came to the front of the throng to better assess the situation. He scanned the faces in the canoes—maybe fifty Indian men and women armed with Winchester rifles, sturdy in their canoes on the river and holding the shores. His eyes met those of Namaybin. He winced. The Indian glared.

Now, in perfect English, the Indian spoke, his voice carried swiftly across the water. "It is no use to make small talk to a cannibal," he said, and he cocked his gun.

AGWAJIING
THE SANITARIUM
1920

"Ingiikaj, Nimisenh," Margaret Oshkinnah whispered to Charlotte in the next bed. "I am so cold, Sister."

It was night now, *Gichi Manidoo Giizis,* the Moon of the Great Spirit, the white man's January. From her bed, Charlotte Oshkinnah looked out of the open window at the moon and stars. She felt the chill of the north wind blow over her. All of the windows of the sanitarium were open to the night to allow the fresh wind to carry away the sickness. The white light of the moon reflected off the hard-crusted snow and illuminated the vast garden, dark trees, and grounds at *Agwajiing,* meaning literally "Outside," the *Anishinaabe* name for the Minnesota state sanitarium at Walker. Charlotte too was cold, but she feared that her sister's coldness was of a different kind.

The girls huddled in beds within the scant, foreign buildings that were nothing more than stone walls with their open windows, wooden plank floors resting on the earth, and a low plank roof above. *Agwajiing* was a resting or languishing place for many Indians. The large, stone main building presently housed more than three hundred souls with an entire wing dedicated to the people of White Earth, Red Lake, and Leech Lake Reservations.

Charlotte and Margaret Oshkinnah slept in the small dormitories outside the main building. When first nine-year-old Margaret, and then eleven-year-old Charlotte, began to cough, people had feared the worst, the white man's coughing sickness. Their parents had both passed over from the diseases that spread like fire through the villages. Their father was an Oshkinnah, a Little Boy; their mother, a Littlewolf. When the Indian Agent Michelet overheard the girls' cough one day in the White Earth agency store, he quickly covered his own mouth with a handkerchief and ordered them sent to *Agwajiing*. The white doctors had prescribed this cure; they felt it was best for their charges. Charlotte and Margaret were on strict bed rest and not allowed to walk at all, not allowed to leave their beds.

Charlotte heard her small sister whisper again, softly insistent, pleading. *"Ingiikaj, Nimisenh."*

The white nurse was resting in the next room. The nurse would scold her for getting out of bed, but again Margaret called. The floor was so frigid that Charlotte feared setting her bare feet on it. Finally, she braved the cold: She climbed out of her bed, felt the icy floor instantly chill her whole body, and ran in quick, small steps to climb into her sister's bed. She was thoroughly cold in the brief bolt from her bed, but even so she felt that her sister was colder. Charlotte held the nine-year-old close and tried to warm her. Margaret was slight for her age, a condition augmented by her illness. The nurse had not yet noticed Margaret's severe state; the little girl had sought to hide it from her, lest she be moved away from her sister and put elsewhere in a ward where she knew no one. Patients were divided by severity of illness, not relations.

Margaret turned away now, head to the pillow, and coughed again and again, shivering in her older sister's arms. Charlotte gathered her sibling closer now, rocking, rocking, kissing her head.

Finally the little girl's shivering eased, and she spoke in a whisper. "What would mother say? Remind me."

"She would tell us stories. Now is the storytelling time." Charlotte responded, whispering directly into her sister's ear.

Charlotte held her sister close, smelling her hair and feeling her small hand in her own. She pointed through the open window toward *jiibayag niimi'idiwag*, the northern lights. Looking out the open window, past the expanse of white snow, a slip of white pines, and on to the edge of the horizon, they could see lights like arrows shooting up from the edge of the world into the night. They undulated and transformed themselves in a slow dance with the sky.

"Kegosha iwedi jiibayag niimi'idiwag," Charlotte spoke into her sister's ear. "Look there, that is *jiibayag niimi'idiwag,* the northern lights. Those are the ancestors and those who have passed on. They are dancing to the drum."

"Dibaajimowin," the younger child pleaded again, firmly. "Tell a story."

A pause. Then Charlotte began.

"It was long, long ago," she said softly. *"A brave man named* Kinaeu, *or War Eagle, journeyed to the Land of the Souls. He was determined to go there. And it was far. He walked for long. And finally, he came to a path, which he followed. Looking ahead, far ahead, he could see a dark gray column of shadows and shapes. They were ahead of him on the path. They were Spirits. They were dressed in their finest clothes, as if they were going to have a great dance and feast. Yet they were all gray as dusk. He followed them, hoping to get close enough for company on his long trip. Finally, he caught up to them, approaching them with respect. They hissed and drew back, waving him away. 'You do not belong with us,' a young woman Spirit said. 'Go away.' He was scared. He followed slowly, at a distance, seeking to come close several more times, but he was chased away each time by the Spirits. Finally, he found his own path."*

Now Charlotte shifted her sister's head carefully and felt the warmth coming back to her. She continued: *"Long he walked down this path. On either side of the trail was a beautiful forest. In the distance, he could hear a river. Ahead of him, just above the tree line, was a row of lights, close to the horizon. That, he knew, was his destination,* jiibayag niimi'idiwag, *the northern lights. He continued to walk toward them, but they seemed to be many days away.*

"He was challenged many times by the Spirits and tempted many times to stop in the Land of Spirits. But he was strong and he kept walking. He defended himself against monsters, against the temptation of beautiful women who pleaded with him to stop and lay with them, and many other obstacles that would delay him. He kept walking. And, at long last, he saw ahead of him a village, a small town beneath those northern lights. This was the destination of the Souls, he knew it now.

"He drew close to the edge of the village. He watched from the shadows.

There, they danced and feasted. All of the Spirits, the Souls, danced in their fine outfits. With joy, and peace, and happiness. There were no wounds, deformities, or sickness. All was gone, only joy in the dance."

A pause now. Charlotte could see that Margaret was nearly asleep, peaceful now.

"That is the northern lights. That is where our mother is. You will see her. You will see her dancing to the drum. You will see her looking down on us."

"Can she see us?" A sleepy response.

"Yes, she can see us. She watches us." A pause, then reassuring, "She is always with us."

Content, Margaret snuggled closer to her sister, her head on her sister's chest, arms wrapped close around her neck. Charlotte kissed her warm head and listened to the girl's uneven breaths, raspy, yet restful. She softly stroked her hair.

In the early morning, Charlotte stirred, awakened now and suddenly aware of how cold she was. The bed was cold. The bed was wet. Margaret's arm lay across her chest. No sound, no sound at all. Her breathing had stopped.

"Goshkozin, goshkozin," Charlotte gently shook her sister. "Wake up, wake up."

There was no breath, no warmth.

Charlotte gasped and gave a muffled cry. Then she held Margaret's body and spoke to her softly. She rocked her back and forth, singing to her now, softly, *"Way hey hey, way hey hey, way hey hey,"* over and over and over.

It was some time before the stout nurse approached. Clucking with dismay, she softly caressed Charlotte's head, the little girl still in her arms.

"It's alright, it's alright," the nurse said gently, offering hope in a situation with no hope. Charlotte continued to rock her sister, now singing softly, a hymn learned at *Agwajiing's* religious instruction.

". . . Kaginig minocumini
minwa bigoninig
me eta go ni nibowin
Kebish kage makug

Kichji Misawinagut su Oiwedi agaming
Oma ondas nakakegam
Onza bundjigeshig. . . ."

The nurse slowly turned and walked out. Other patients quietly watched the proceedings on the bed until Charlotte Oshkinnah extricated herself from the pile of blankets and her sister's body. She walked over the cold floor and out the door, holding only herself. The nurse returned and clucked again over Margaret.

"She's gone," the nurse said to the small children still watching with wide eyes. "I didn't think she would go, she was a strong one."

Charlotte held back in the doorway and watched the stout nurse. Charlotte was bundled heavily now in a coat, hat, and mittens. The nurse wrapped Margaret's body in a blanket and then carried her out the door and toward the main building some yards away. Charlotte followed behind, accompanying her sister with a small wrapped bundle.

As best as she could, Charlotte attended to preparing her sister for the journey to the Land of Spirits. From a trunk, she had retrieved a paisley dress with a beaded yoke and moccasins of smoked deerhide and black velvet with small beads sewn on the top, a pair of moccasins her mother had made before she had passed on. Now they were to be Margaret's traveling shoes to the next world.

Charlotte then went to find an elder. The responsibility of dressing the dead was reserved for women who would bear no more children. Charlotte was now an orphan. She had no direct family, yet in the sanitarium, somewhere, was at least one member of every family from home, from White Earth.

She slipped by the nurses now, moving into another ward. Health regulations prohibited the patients from mingling, but she paid the rules no mind. She needed an elder—that was all she knew. Slowly she walked between the beds in the dormitory, peering at faces, looking for a glint in the eyes, a smile, a familiar glance. Her eyes came to rest on an old woman who looked somehow familiar. She hesitated and then quietly walked to the bedside. The old woman looked up. Charlotte remembered her now from the Drum Ceremonies.

"Boozhoo Nidanis."
"Boozhoo Nookomis."
"Nindizinikaaz Waywayeumigokie Nidanis."

Charlotte remembered her well. Her name was Waywayeumigokie. A stout, strong woman who danced, smiling across the drum from her family. She always had maple sugar sweets for the children. Now, however, she was a shell of her former self, here in the white man's hospital. Her skin hung on her bones like burlap bags, but her eyes were clear and her voice strong.

Charlotte moved closer to Waywayeumigokie.

"*Aseyma, Nookomis, Aseyma,*" The girl said softly. "*Nishim neeboowin.* My younger sister is dead. Can you help me?"

"What do you need, *Nidanis?*"

"I need to dress her and send her off."

"*Ahem.*"

The old woman climbed out of her bed with much effort, and then together they dressed Margaret, braided her hair, and placed her small feet in her traveling shoes. Then Waywayeumigokie placed the medicine pouch in the girl's hand, closing the tiny fingers over the beaded pouch. Wrapped in a blanket, she was lowered into a shallow grave at *Agwajiing,* one of those who would not return home.

For four days, Charlotte attended as best she could, singing those songs she remembered and returning to the grave with a plate of food for her sister's journey. Then her sister was gone.

Late at night, Charlotte Oshkinnah wrapped her blankets tight about her to ward off the cold and looked past the flap through her open window, across the expanse that was the yard, gardens, and trees of *Agwajiing,* and toward the sky. If she looked hard, she could see her sister and mother dancing in the lights.

ONDENDI
TO GO AWAY
1930

The priest arrived in the buggy with three other boys already on board. Boodoo Graves peered out the window of his family's log lodge, watching Father Benoit, the man dressed like a crow in black, as he looked over the lodge, his eyes widening with recognition as he spotted the boy watching him out the window. Boodoo dashed away from the window and ran back to hide with his smaller brother under a bed. The priest waited, then slowly unloaded himself from the buggy, one eye to the boys already in hand.

"You stay," he said to them in his firmest tone. The boys remained frozen on their seats, following the priest with their eyes as he walked toward the log house.

"*Bimibatoon, bimibatoon,*" the boys whispered in their minds, urging Boodoo to freedom. "Run, run."

From under the bed, Boodoo heard the heavy boots on the porch. He lived with an aunt as his parents and two sisters had passed away from tuberculosis last year, leaving him and a younger brother to find their way in the world. His older cousins—his aunt's sons—had already been taken by the priests to Flandreau, a government boarding school that was several days journey by buggy. Now all that remained in her house was himself and his four-year-old brother. For this year, his brother would be safe from the watching eyes of the priest and

Indian agents, but Boodoo's time had come.

His aunt sat at the table watching the priest out the window. Now she rose and took to her broom, sweeping the floor as she already had four or more times that morning. She had hidden her own children and Boodoo twice successfully, yet the priest always returned. His aunt whispered the words to Boodoo and watched her nephew out of the corner of her eye: "*Bimibatoon, bimibatoon.* Run, run." As the priest neared the front door, Boodoo crawled out the side door, racing for the woods. His aunt continued sweeping. Now the knock came, and she opened the door.

"*Mino geeshiguck,*" Father Benoit greeted her.

"*Mino geeshiguck,* Father Benoit," Mrs. Hand said.

"I have come to take the boy to school now." He paused as his eyes looked beyond her, searching through the darkened room.

Mrs. Hand made no response.

"It's the time to go. The other boys are waiting in the buggy," the priest continued.

A brow furled now as he looked at her face. She gazed past him, in typical style, not wishing to meet his eyes.

A branch broke at Boodoo's feet and the priest spun around and saw the boy running into the woods.

Both frozen for a second, predator viewed prey, and Boodoo gasped at the fury in Father Benoit's look.

That second of locked eyes was too long. The priest, now fast as lightning, bolted from the porch and ran for the boy. Boodoo ran through hazel brush, basswoods, popple, and birch that smelled like his land, his home. Then he stumbled, and the priest grabbed his leg. The boy wriggled and fought against the priest, but he was no match for the larger man.

"*Wenshkaan,*" Benoit said to the boy. "Get up."

Holding him by the arm, the priest walked the boy back to the buggy, then lifted him up and into a seat next to the others.

"Stay," he commanded the boy as he would a dog. Boodoo's head hung down to his chest, and he felt shame and fear as tears filled his eyes. The priest retrieved his black hat from the yard and placed it on his head, tipping it then to Mrs. Hand who stood inside her doorway, broom in hand. She paused, then went deeper inside the house, returning with a small bundle that she carried out and placed in Boodoo's hands. She stood on her tiptoes to kiss the boy on the cheek, tasting his tears on her lips, whispering softly into his ear. Kissed again, he looked fearfully at her, hardly seeing her through his tear-filled eyes, then looking down again, at the bundle. She walked away then as the priest nodded once more to her. When Boodoo turned his head one last time to view his aunt, she stood in the doorway, broom in hand, watching the buggy disappear down the road to the Flandreau Boarding School in South Dakota.

It was two weeks later that all the boys arrived at the boarding school. Unloaded from carts, buggies, and train cars, they all stopped talking as they were herded into the dark corridors and gray rooms of the school.

"Line up, line up," a priest ordered them. Priests in their black cloaks moved around them like carrion, briskly placing the boys in a long line by order of size.

The boys stood, weary from travel, terrified, trying to be brave. They were the hopes of their nations—*Anishinaabeg*, Dakota, Lakota, Shawnee, Winnebago, Mandan, Hidatsa, Potawatami. Braids and scalplocks carefully wrapped. Beadwork vests of woodlands and plains styles. Moccasins, leggings. Clutching medicine pouches, memories, and prayers of their mothers.

The priests looked them over, taking down a few notations in black ledgers. Then a man with a strange black box came to stand in front of the boys. He danced around the box like a seer. The boys stared back into the box's single, large eye, stunned with a fear they struggled against. Priests came to stand on either end of the line of boys. They smiled. The man with the box got under a dark blanket, then there was a flash of blinding light from the *mazinaakizigan*, the camera.

The priests stopped smiling and herded the boys down a hallway to another large room. "Undress," ordered a priest. Other priests loaded their arms full of the beadwork vests, leggings, and moccasins, and then disappeared. In their nakedness, the boys pulled close together.

Then came a shiver of cold metal on their necks. The boys clutched at their hair as huge scissors cut it away, leaving them groping for their lost braids. Cold metal blades snapped at their heads, shearing their scalps to the skin. The boys were left standing like shorn sheep surrounded by piles of glossy black hair.

They were led into another room. From out of the walls above them came scalding water. Priests smothered them in pungent soap, scratching at them with rough brushes. The smaller boys cried out and the older ones searched for an escape with frightened eyes. The water stopped and the priests dried them off with towels like sandpaper. Other priests appeared, dumping boxes of white antiseptic powder on the boys from head to foot, turning them into white ghosts of their former selves. New white underclothes were passed out along with somber navy blue two-piece suits and stiff black leather shoes.

The metamorphosis complete, the boys were pointed back to the first room. They were lined up in their new clothes and new faces. Smiling priests took their places at each end of the row. The man with the blanket and the dark box returned, and the *mazinaakizigan* flashed its blinding lightning once again.

Then food came, strange to them, hot and tasteless. It was served at long tables with metal utensils. Then to bed in long rows of cots. The boys whispered to each other until priests come to their side, and the boys were quiet. From far down the line of beds came a solitary muffled crying, and then sleep at last.

Only a month passed before the nightmare began for Boodoo. It was a nightmare brought on by one of the priests, Brother Thomas, who took a special interest in what he called the "great spiritual potential of the boy." That was during the day, but this was the night.

Boodoo stood in a closet. Deep inside, he screamed. He bit his lip as he felt the hands pull at his underpants. Brother Thomas's breath was hot against the back of his head, but his searching hands were cold claws as they tore at his pajamas. More than once, Brother Thomas had summoned him from his bed near the east door. Each night the boy lay frozen in fear, hoping the priest would not come for him. Tonight, Brother Thomas had called him.

At first he fought the Priest, but the man was much stronger, and the subsequent beating he received was severe. The priest had his way in any case, and made the boy stay locked in a separate room crying for three days so as to teach him to mind. On the second night, the Priest had come to the boy anyway.

The humiliation was almost too much to bear. He had thought to kill himself. The Priest was ready for this and watched the boy in his every move. There was no escape. After three or more lockups, the boy's resistance waned. His only hope was that the Priest would focus his attention elsewhere. The boy closed his eyes and placed his clenched fists against the wall as he felt the weight of the Priest. Inside, he screamed again.

Boodoo Graves thought only about those woods, far away, the smell of birch and popple, the smell of leaves, the sound of a paddle on a clear lake. He forced his mind to concentrate, to think only of that life, his home, his land, in the days when no priests were allowed there, none at all.

MESABE

He was born in *Ode'imini Giizis*, the moon of the strawberries, the white man's month of June. It was a week before the annual celebration of the signing of the peace treaty that reserved for the people the land that was White Earth. His parents were Ottertail Pillagers who had moved to Pine Point in the 1880s. There he lived, on the north side of Many Point Lake, on land allotted to his grandmother, Mindemoyen.

Each season brought a new wealth to the family. The *Anishinaabeg*, in turn, provided their prayers of thanksgiving for their food. And so, in their simple way, they followed their own instructions.

Their life followed the circle of the seasons. In the deep of winter in *Namebini Giizis*, the Sucker Moon of February, Mesabe's father taught him to walk on top of the snow by wearing the giant feet they called *aagim*, snowshoes. He followed his father into the woods on his snowshoes where they set their traplines to snare beaver, rabbits, and porcupine. He learned how to skin the animals for their pelts, clean them for their meat, and never to take more than he needed.

With the coming of *Waabigwanii Giizis*, the Flower Moon of May, the forests bloomed with plants and flowers. Into the woods Mesabe followed his grandmother, who wore her straw hat and carried a large basket. Mindemoyen showed him which plants were good medicine to heal and help. She taught him how to identify the leaves, blossoms, and roots and how to make teas, poultices, salves, and washes, what to add to soup and what to chew slowly.

In the warmth of *AAbita Niibino Giizis*, the Middle of the Summer Moon of July, he learned how to throw a gill net into the waters of Many Point Lake and then haul it back in with a catch of silver fish from the lake's depths.

With the coming of *Manoominike Giizis*, the Ricing Moon of September, he helped his family patch the birchbark canoe with pitch so it was ready to harvest the *manoomin*, the wild rice, the food that grows on the water. His grandfather taught him how to select a length of soft, light cedar and carve his own *bawa'iganaak oog*, a ricing stick used to coax the rice from its stalks. His mother showed him and his brother, Naytahwaush, how to sew *makakoons*, the birchbark baskets used to winnow the rice. Then the whole family, along with all of the Ottertail Pillagers, took to the lakes and the sound of the ricing sticks filled the air along with songs and talk between the families in their canoes.

As *Gashkadino Giizis*, the Freezing Moon of November, came once again, Mesabe built the fire high in the family's lodge, and the snow covered the forest. It was then that his family told the stories.

Mesabe grew up in the world of his ancestors, but he learned as well from the world of the *Gichimookomaanag*, the white men that were settling into villages and farms on White Earth. He learned in the town to speak the white man's language, and still he kept his own. He learned to read and write, and at the same time he learned from Mindemoyen how to collect the sap of the maple trees and boil it down to make syrup in *Iskigamizige Giizis*, the Sugar Making Moon of April. He learned of the white man's god, and he also learned the songs and ceremonies of the drums, the pulse of the people, their way to make an expression of thanks to the Creator.

Born into a time of chaos and change, Mesabe witnessed the families scattered asunder by the white man's laws and shook his head at the folly of *wiindigoo* plunder. In a world that was fraying and unraveling before his eyes, he rankled against the white man's god and government. He held onto and followed the strands of his ancestors' lives and rebraided them into a rope that would lead him through the twisted steel and shorn fields of America.

KNIGHTS OF THE FOREST
1916

"A secret order called the Knights of the Forest was formed by two men from Mankato and one from Garden City, for the express purpose of the removal of the Winnebago and all Indians from the state of Minnesota. The Knights grew to considerable size to include many of the most prominent and influential men of . . . both political parties. One noteworthy act of the Mankato lodge . . . was the employment of a certain number of men whose duty it was to lie in ambush on the outskirts of the Winnebago reservation and shoot any Indian who might be observed outside the lines. . . ."
—*Blue Earth County Historical Society Review*, April 27, 1886

The Knights of the Forest were born from the ashes of the Minnesota Territory farmhouses ravaged in Little Crow's War forty years past. Bankers, politicians, businessmen, farmers, tradesmen, and good family men by day, they were sworn in the secrecy of their meetings to drive the scourge of the red man from Minnesota.

Their sworn oath spelled out their purpose as they recited it, hands on their hearts: *"We have learned at the cost of many lives, that the white man and the Indian man cannot dwell together in peace and harmony. The chief objective of this order is to prevent the permanent location of any tribe of Indians in this state. . . . The objects for which we are assembled are worthy of our cause. It is no less than the preservation of our lives, our families and our homes. Let us be ever watchful and keep constantly in mind the sacred obligation which binds us together as brothers in one common interest . . . the determination to banish forever from our beautiful state every Indian who now desecrates its soil."*

Over the years, the Knights tactfully charted their course with the precision of military maneuvers and the luxury of many powerful allies. The Knights moved in the color of the law, or outside the law, depending from which vantage point of justice one observed. Enforcing dubiously mandated evictions with a torch thrown through the window or a ring of fire was expedient and rarely punishable. Especially since few witnesses could or would be found, and those that did come forward could rarely testify in English. Their work continued.

On alternate occasions, the *Detroit Lakes Tribune* called the fires that erupted at Indian homes "unfortunate" and "mysterious." "Unfortunate" was an apt, understated description for the obviously tragic backdrop of the times in which the Indians inexplicably found themselves. Yet the white man's newspaper often regarded the findings of federal investigations with bewilderment, reporting on national commission findings that described conditions some twenty miles from the place of publication with absolute astonishment.

The federally empowered Moorhead Investigation of 1916 uncovered diseases and dismal living conditions: "Fully sixty percent of the Indians were afflicted with tuberculosis, thirty percent with trachoma and twenty percent with syphilis, and all diseases on the rise." Ten Indians were discovered living in a tarpaper shack, and blinded old women with trachoma were found to be signing away their land.

These stories of the dismal conditions into which the Ojibwe had been forced would crop up at various times in the pages of the *Detroit Lakes Tribune* almost as if they had dropped inadvertently off the national wire services. Then the stories would disappear entirely for months on end, the paper resuming coverage of sumptuous weddings, the price of pork, interesting fashion and style topics, and the rise of opulence and the standard of living in a flourishing town that bordered the reservation. There was never seen to be a correlation between the growing destitution of the reservation community and the swelling of the coffers of the businesses in Detroit Lakes.

It was not altogether surprising that the tarpaper houses caught fire. Various illnesses, dangerous wood stoves, and overcrowding were often found in combination, and fire was a potential result. It was the frequency, however, that could not be deemed a coincidence. Nor the nocturnal moving of white men on horseback.

It was in one of these fires that Mesabe's parents would perish. He and his brother Naytahwaush ironically were saved by their abduction to boarding school thirty miles away. When his grandmother Minde-moyen arrived with the news three days later, the two boys stumbled after her, speechless, never again allowed by Mindemoyen to step back in the white man's schools.

The coming of the land stealers and the great sicknesses drove the families further into the woods. They trapped, hunted, fished, and harvested, emerging to barter at the trading post in the settlement or occasionally make the journey to town every three months or so. Each time Mesabe would leave, he would return with the news of removals and deaths. Family after family was stricken with the diseases, and many perished with no survivors to carry on their songs or stories.

Each season, fewer attended the ceremonies. At first it was four of the Ahnib family. Next the Minnogeeshig family. Mesabe remembered the day that the old woman Ishkweniibawiikwe died. She died not on the day that her spirit left her body to walk the path of souls; she had died much earlier, watching first three of her four children succumb to the coughing sickness and then the death of her great friend, the Dakota woman, Situpiwin, ancient as well. Mesabe remembered Situpiwin wracked by the coughing, strangled by the convulsions that were taking away her breath. It was said that one night she coughed for hours without pausing for breath until finally she could breathe no more.

After that, after the death of her three children and her Dakota sister, Ishkweniibawiikwe seemed dead to the world although she still tread the earth among the living. Mesabe remembered her working around their lodge when he came to visit, remembered her in the ceremonies, a living ghost emptied of all that was alive. When she too finally died with the coughing sickness torturing her body, it was only a physical death. Her spirit seemed to have left her body long before.

That year many were to go. Soon there were no longer enough officers for the drum or those to carry on the ceremonies. The drums were left on their own. Old man Minnogeeshig had left his drum in a special cache near his trapline, carefully wrapped in cedar, to ward off the varmints and bad spirits.

It was strange how old man Minnogeeshig knew he would leave this world and began preparations several weeks before. He gave various treasures to his last, surviving child and to his favored nieces and nephews, delivering the best of town dresses of his recently deceased wives. He slowly distributed all of his items to those whom remained, those not yet dead from the white man's diseases, whether tuberculosis or alcoholism. Minnogeeshig had not yet passed on his *Midewiwin* drum when he died, his heart sick from the sadness he could not escape. Like a great tree, he fell all at once with a crash, a heart attack, and tumbled to the ground. Yet on his face was peace and a smile. He had given his life back to the animals whom had sustained him for sixty years.

After three ceremonies, the empty spaces of the lodge stared back at those who remained. Prayers for those who had passed on, and to cleanse the grief of those still living, consumed much of the time.

Mesabe and his family returned to his grandmother Mindemoyen's allotment after the ceremony. The land went broke that winter. The beaver and rabbits were scarce, almost as if the quietness at the ceremonial lodge called fewer animals forward. Mesabe continued his prayers, yet each time he checked the snares, fewer animals had given themselves. It was then that he decided to look for work in Park Rapids at the logging company.

Mesabe and his wife, Equayzaince, or Little Girl, also known as Mary, moved into the logging camp north of Park Rapids in midwinter. Mesabe was forced to cut down the trees he loved, peeling pulp for the white man, and Equayzaince was able to hire out for washing the clothes of the lumberjacks. They made a living, they had food and were able to save enough each month to bring home to the others at Many Point Lake.

It was on one of the visits back to Mindemoyen's allotment that his grandmother told Mesabe that she had borrowed money from Lucky Waller in Detroit Lakes to pay her grocery bill at the store. Mindemoyen promised to pay back the loan with the fall's treaty money. Mesabe had heard of Waller, and what he had heard was not good. Waller was more than a loan man, he was a land stealer, and he knew many ways to steal land from Indians. Mesabe took his grandmother to town to pay back the loan, less than a month after the money had been borrowed.

The offices were in a big brick building downtown. Waller's office consumed much of the ground floor and was prominently placed on the main street. He himself was a stout man in fine town clothes: a smart bowtie topped a new wool suit, commensurate with his formal status as banker and land speculator, and enhancing his shadow status as a leader of the Knights of the Forest. His face bulged over his tight collar, teeth yellow and gold with bad habits and soft food. The white man's eyes were a cold gray, and colder now as he flicked the Indians aside with one look.

"You keep that money," Waller puffed. "It's all taken care of."

Mesabe insisted on paying back the money. He pushed the pile of fifty single dollar bills across the desk to Waller, but the speculator would not touch the money from the Indians.

"No thank you," Waller said, as if he was politely refusing an offer. "I bought that land, and I don't intend to sell it back," he said, impatiently stating his version of the obvious.

Mindemoyen whispered to her grandson and pointed to the thumb mark on the paper for money. Mesabe translated her words into English.

"She has not sold the land. She only borrowed money from you. Now we're here to pay it back."

The stout man stood now, laboriously pushing himself from the chair. He shuffled toward a door and his backroom. "You wait," he commanded.

Waller returned from his backroom with the paper. Pointing to the paper, the loan shark said, "This is a deed. Your grandmother sold her land to me."

Mesabe looked at the paper and stumbled over the legal terms—releases, clauses, parties of the first and second, and descriptions of land he knew on the ground but not by section designations, numbers, or a map. Between the "whereas, heretofore, and other valuable considerations," the words were a tangled muddle. He could see the thumbprint at the bottom.

"Is that your thumbprint?" he asked his grandmother.

"Eh heh," replied the old woman, signifying her agreement, "but I did not sell the land, I only borrowed the money."

Mesabe repeated her story to the land agent, but Waller had no more interest in their presence. He called for his assistant to remove them from the room. Mesabe rose to strike Waller for lying to his grandmother. His grandmother held his arm.

"That will only cause them to take you away, with my land," she warned him. "He cannot keep it forever, it is not his."

True to his promise, Waller now had a thumbprinted deed in his possession and by that fall, Mindemoyen's land on the shore of Many Point Lake had been sold to a land speculator from Chicago. Mindemoyen was never to pass another winter on the lake, and two winters later, was to die in Pine Point village, falling like others to the diseases and to the despair. Mesabe took her back to Many Point Lake, and after a four-day *Maajaa'ind*, or sending off ceremony, he buried Mindemoyen on her land. The man from Chicago had never seen the land, nor them.

OGICHIDAA
1925

The Knights of the Forest faded into the psyches of the people who made their homes in the small border towns. Sometimes in the boldness of day, but more often in the safety of their evening bars, emboldened by a whiskey or beer, they would glare to the north, east, or south, speaking in muted tones about how *the Indians had it coming*.

Except for a few. They mourned the plainness of English words, cotton and steel that spread now from the towns of white clapboard houses. Like a fog, it enveloped the woods that diminished tree by tree, supplanted by orderly rows of corn, beans, sugar beets, and fields of alfalfa. Cropped close by steel blades, penetrated, torn, and supplanted again, the land endured an unnatural succession that even Darwin could never have concocted.

It was the dawn of a new war, a cold war.

War was not a continuous practice of the *Anishinaabeg*, only a tactic used when necessary, and only in the most disciplined manner. *Ogichidaa*, those who defend the people, was a word borrowed from the most honored of enemies, the Dakota. Yet all the same, the *Anishinaabeg* had become the subjects of war, a cold war more maddening than any battle fought with the Dakota. A cold war waged from Washington that was to last a hundred years, if Washington would even retreat then.

Starvation, loss of traplines and hunting areas, and the anger and frustration of battling an invisible enemy were enough to drive most men mad. Not to mention loss of honor.

And so they ventured forth from the deep woods, into the white man's world. First singularly, tentatively, then in pairs, and finally flocks, much like the geese on which they had relied for generations. They carried with them, hidden, a medicine pouch, a lock of a mother's hair, several sprigs of cedar wrapped tightly in a smoked deerskin piece, and a pungent memory. Mesabe and his brother Naytahwaush too were forced from their home; they joined the United States armed forces.

There was honor in the status of *ogichidaa*, far more honor than would ever be afforded an Indian man who found himself in a white town.

On the front lines during the Great War, Mesabe would dream about home, the aroma of sage and balsam, and the sounds of the drum, distant but constant, like a heartbeat would come to him, sometimes when awake, and often when asleep. But Naytahwaush could not. Naytahwaush would only dream of war. It had invaded his soul, and Mesabe knew then that his brother had to return home if he were to live at all.

After two long years, Mesabe and his brother returned to the reservation. The smell of death was all around them, and they spent many days in the sweat lodge to send back the spirits that had followed them home. After the ceremonies, Mesabe had only the memories of the war, and his soul was cleansed. Naytahwaush, however, could only find part of his mind. The demons and ghosts were to torment him to his grave. He was forever pointing to the horizon and screaming that the German line was moving closer.

Naytahwaush never did come home. Preferring instead a small canvas tent with plank sides and a stove, he delved deep into the woods, and from his enclave he trapped, hunted, and only rarely socialized with his family, while plotting his battle strategy.

Naytahwaush remained a warrior to his last breath. The *ogichidaa* retained the practice of ambush much to the disdain of the Indian agent and those policemen who had the duty of delivering salt pork commodities to the outlying areas.

Counting coup. It was an exercise, that was all. From a hill he would watch for the truck to slowly come around the corner, heading down the dirt road toward the small government building. As the truck approached the stop sign, he would vault toward the driver's window, forcing his hunting rifle inside.

"Give me your food, money, and tobacco," he would demand of the bewildered driver, shaking at the sight of the fatigue-clad Indian.

"Slow down, slow down," the driver would yell, arms raised, shaking, fumbling his way out of the truck under the maniacal scrutiny of the warrior of Round Lake.

"*Ambay, Ambay, weeweeb,*" Naytahwaush would say, "Hurry, hurry, let's go."

Furtive glances toward the road, a nudge from the rifle, and the agency man would carefully place a hefty supply of commodities in the ditch by the road

"Tarp, too, I need a new one," Naytahwaush would say gruffly. "Now back in the truck and away, if you value your life."

It was a simple proposition, and the driver was soon gone, gasping for air.

The strange Indian soldier would ferry his booty to a hiding place in the woods, then carefully and deliberately carry what he needed to his camp until his stores were replenished. The counting coup ritual occurred on several occasions unbeknownst to the agency superintendent, from whom many losses, illicit sales, and various doings were concealed. It might have continued indefinitely, as graft had existed in the Indian agency since its birth, but the strange Indian soldier of Round Lake was eventually ferreted out by the Indian police who judged that one day the gun might just go off.

There are some diseases of the white man for which the Indians have no cure. The *giiwanaadizi* disease settled on Naytahwaush and would not relent. The Indian agent finally placed him in the state mental institution at Fergus Falls, sixty miles to the south.

Log cabin, smell of wood stove, balsam boughs in a hunting camp boiling sap, Indian tea, smoked moccasins, hues of brown, red, and green. He could remember, sometimes. *Bright and white, smell of antiseptics, medicines, lights that burned eyes, pulsating and glaring.*

The mental institution was too bright, as radiant as bed sheets left outside to bleach in a February snow. Naytahwaush would try and close his eyes to it all, shut his nose to the smells, and fold his arms close so as to avoid the harsh cold of steel and frigid tile. Then there were the stares, observations of various unnamed physicians, nurses, and orderlies who encroached on all that was his own, his body, mind, eyes, teeth, and soul, thrusting themselves into his presence as they pierced his shield of armor.

If you cannot choose your life, there is some redemption in choosing your death. A warrior would know that. Surrounded by the whiteness of the institution and of a society that slowly choked him, Naytahwaush hung himself one morning at dawn. The orderly said he heard an eerie song just before light, *a death chant*, and then nothing. The warrior had gone home to the woods.

THE RESURRECTION
1930

It was long after Wazhaashkoons, Wabunoquod, Chi Makwa, and the others had passed over. Carefully fitted into their finest beadwork and traveling moccasins, their souls had journeyed to the land of the spirits. Their bodies remained. They rested high on a hill overlooking Spirit Lake, resting and watching from beneath aging cedar *jiibegamig*, or gravehouses, and granite headstones embellished with the scrolling and detail worthy of their esteemed stature.

They were long gone. He, however, had outlived them all. He had outlived them through his cunning, his immunities, and, of course, his path with the Savior. But most of all, his will.

Now he wondered at his folly.

Father Gilfillian could not sleep. Tormented nights and pursued during the days, the spirits of missionaries before him and the ghosts of his superiors in the church, *bless their souls*, called out to him. Scolding, scolding. His tasks were incomplete, his life's work a sham.

Joseph Gilfillian no longer ministered. His senses were dimmed by his advanced age, his mind a scramble of English, Latin, Ojibwe, and a smattering of the cursed Dakota. He was largely incomprehensible, except that is, to his fine team of Percherons.

Coal black with fur as thick as a bear's in the winter, the Percherons stood seventeen hands tall and weighed sixteen hundred pounds apiece. The horses remained his constant friends and understood his garbled oratory, particularly when his commands of *Gii*, *Haa*, and *Whoa* were interspersed with a sharp flick of the lines on a flank—or a treat, of which they received many: carrots and apples in season, grain and sugar cubes in the cold times. They were his children. His only true disciples.

He had a solution. Rising slowly from his chair, he willed his tired bones, muscles, and joints forward. He was bitter at Philomene St. Clair for dying before him, especially now that he needed her, needed strong arms and a strong back to help him in his daily tasks, attending to the mundane details of this life on Earth. Today, however, this task was his alone.

His light coat and hat near the doorway, he ambled toward them. Black, always black. Stretch and crane, his coat and hat on now, Joseph Gilfillian slowly walked to his barn, *the way to peace and salvation ahead*. His ancient frame was steadied only by sheer determination as this morning in *Waabigwanii Giizis*, the Flower Moon of the month of May, surrounded him.

He walked into the small barn behind the St. Columba Episcopal Church and grasped the lead rope that hooked the halter of his mare, paused and rubbed her cheek, greeting her gently. Her immense head and mane shook with freedom as he slowly walked her outside, tying her to the post near the barn. This process he repeated again with the filly, her daughter, marveling at her muscles, her head, her beauty. A perfect beauty.

He gasped now as he placed the heavy leather hames and harness sets over their backs, pausing to catch his breath amid the task. The horses observed him with patience and curiosity as to the pending adventure. Arthritic hands struggled with buckles, clips, and loops as Joseph Gilfillian persevered on the road to his salvation.

Finally readied, the lines in hand, he called, "*Azhetaan, azhetaan.* Back, back," as the two immense coal-black rear ends moved closer to him. Then, "Haaa, haaa," and with a constant pull on his line, the two horses turned and slowly walked toward the wagon. There they stopped, and again he paused to capture what remained of his breath.

Then "*Azhetaag, azhetaag.* Back, back," again to them, until they were set on either side of the pole, which he now placed with heavy breaths through the loop on their yoke, hooking their harnesses to the front of the wagon. Clutching the lines, he walked slowly to the side, and with the help of a small wooden footstool, heaved himself clumsily onto his wagon.

A set of clucking sounds and the two horses rumbled forward down the long winding road from the back reaches of St. Columba toward civilization, a civilization he had made. Forged with his iron will and the hand of God. He allowed himself the small pleasure of recounting his successes again, remembering their names and histories.

Now, he collected two of his successes: Philomene St. Clair's grandsons, a pair of boys with strong backs and obedient natures who lived just on the edge of White Earth village.

"You boys will be in good standing with the Lord," he reassured them as they climbed onto the wagon, firmly instructed by their mother.

The young men were nervous in the presence of the old man. His stern reputation had stood the test of time, reinforced by the stories recounted by their grandmother, which still echoed in their ears. All of these stories, however, were no match for the fear. The fear of falling out of favor with God.

The boys had helped the old priest on a number of peculiar missions before this one of today. Missions the priest had called "Setting things right." His impeccable sense of order included stashing Indian religious items in the storage room of his church as well as rectifying the records of his baptisms, births, marriages, funerals, and other events. *"All must be in order,"* he would mumble. *"All must be in order in the eyes of God."*

Clucking sounds to the horses continued as now he passed the reins to the oldest boy and observed him as the wagon moved north of White Earth. At the curve in the road, he beckoned to the boy to take a sharp right and drive the team up a dirt trail to Spirit Lake.

"We're here," Gilfillian finally pronounced. The wagon abruptly lurched to a stop, throwing the priest forward. Righting himself with some difficulty, he motioned the boys out gruffly.

The hill looked out over Spirit Lake and was full of cedar *jiibegamig,* gravehouses. Traditional granite headstones marked the graves of Chi Makwa, Wazhaashkoons, Wabunoquod, and the others who had walked the pathway of the souls. Not the pathway of the Episcopals.

The boys stared at the headstones, then at the aged priest. While their family had followed the church, they were careful about entering into such traditional cemeteries.

"They are over there," Gilfillian pointed to the boys. "The ones I want, *iwedi, iwedi. . . .*"

His eyes gleamed now with renewed determination. The boys looked at him as he motioned them to the back of the wagon.

"*Mangaanibiiwag, iwedi. Naadin.* The shovels are in the back, go get them." His commands were short and direct. He was used to giving orders.

The boys glanced at the headstones, then looked again at the priest with some trepidation. Bright, young eyes met a steady, stern look from small, dim eyes. The boys turned again to the headstones and pierced the sandy soil with their shovels, moving the earth away from the granite headstones. The priest listened to the sound of shoveling with satisfaction as the boys continued digging until the bases of two of the old stones were exposed.

The old man motioned for the boys to move aside now and directed them to unhook the horses from the wagon.

"Unhook them, unhook them," he rasped impatiently, as they scrambled to remove the yoke from the center pole. The horses stood, somewhat more restless now, immense hooves shifting as they observed the young men.

"*Aaniindi biiminakwan?* Where's the rope?" Gilfillian asked. Then, swinging his arm wildly, he motioned again for the boys to move aside.

He pulled on the reins to motion the Percherons backward, but the two horses stood as still as mules, jittery from the conflicting commands and the spacing of stones and holes in the earth. Gilfillian pulled back again and resumed the clucking sounds to the horses, "Easy, easy." Finally the twittering horses took an awkward step backward, and he maneuvered the team until they were positioned exactly in front of the headstone of Chi Makwa.

"*Biiminakwan, biiminakwan.*" He motioned now for the rope as one of the boys took the lines. The Father walked slowly now to the headstone. With gnarled hands he looped the rope over the stone, wound it around, and, breathing heavily now, he dropped to his knees as his bony fingers painfully worked the ropes into a fierce and angry knot. Then the priest put his hand on the headstone, tracing his fingers over the name.

Chi Makwa.

Gilfillian grinned as his mind wandered, and he contemplated the sermon for this momentous occasion. His voice rose and crescendoed as he spoke to his sleeping congregation:

"And Moses took the bones of Joseph with him, for he had placed the children of Israel under solemn oath, saying, 'God will surely visit you, and you shall carry up my bones from here with you. . . .'

"The bones of Joseph which the children of Israel had brought up out of Egypt, they buried at Shechem, in the plot of ground which Jacob had bought from the sons of Hamor and the father of Sechem. . . .

"And Joshua declared to the people, 'Behold this stone shall be a witness to us, for it has heard all the words of the Lord which He spoke to us. It shall therefore be a witness to you, lest you deny your God. . . .'"

Content, he smiled with satisfaction, slowly leaned against the stone, and painfully arose.

"*Miizhishin reins.* I'll do this one myself."

The boy passed the reins to the old priest now and moved aside as the old man straightened his back and placed the reins over his shoulder.

"*Maajaadaa, maajaadaa,*" he urged the horses forward.

The diligent Percherons pulled the rope taut, then leaned against the weight, hindquarters flexed. They paused, their muscles protruding through the thick fur again as the horses leaned forward. The boys watched in wonder as with one more jerk, the stone tumbled forward, the powerful horses easily dragging it five feet now from the gaping hole.

After a short rest, the old man and his two black horses pulled the stone aside the wagon. Then he vigorously motioned for the boys.

"*Omaa atoong.* Put it in here."

With straining backs and legs, the two boys lifted the granite headstone into the wagon bed. Breathing heavily, they leaned against the wagon now, as the old man drove the horses back to the cemetery site. His eyes surveyed the remaining sixteen headstones of the plot and spied the next most contentious stone.

He paused now as he contemplated moving his body again and looked over his shoulder at the two boys who had recovered from their task. They walked over now to the old priest and observed as he set his jaw and urged the horses into the cemetery again in front of a headstone.

Wazhaashkoons.

He passed the lines again to the boy. He personally attended to this stone as well, repeating the painful wrapping and knotting as he murmured a hymn to the old chief, his cracking voice rising into the quiet of the spring morning to the tune of *Onward, Christian Soldiers*:

"Madjag enamiayeg,
Nundobuniyuk,
'Ga-widokag Jesus,
Ani-nigani.
Christ au kid ogimam
'Ga-migadamag,
Umbe mamaquiyok
Wabum enosed."

With a sigh of relief, his task was completed. He stood, took the reins, and watched, full of pleasure as the stone was slowly unearthed, tumbling toward the wagon.

Under the watchful eyes of the old priest, the boys again lifted the stone into the back of the wagon. His tormented soul somewhat comforted, Gilfillian laboriously pulled himself into the wagon and sat now, supervising the relocation of four of the less significant headstones.

Now the old wagon lurched and creaked as the Percherons leaned against the weight, and pulled the priest and his headstones back home. The horses led the wagon up the winding road to the St. Columba cemetery where gaping holes awaited the stones in their new home. The boys reluctantly climbed down from the wagon and paused, awaiting the priest's directions as to the precise location for replanting the headstones in the Episcopal cemetery.

The priest had carefully plotted the new converts' final resting places, arranging each family in respectful order and placing strays or widowers on a special knoll. He impatiently walked between the headstones, knocking his cane against them as he counted the stones and re-ordered them in his mind. He paused at a fresh hole, made a small smile to himself, and pointed with his cane to the hole.

"Chi Makwa. His other people are coming too. We will place him here and leave room for the rest."

This strange process continued over the next few days until the headstones of all sixteen of this flock of unconverted had been recovered and reconciled. Only then did the priest sleep long and hard.

GAAJIGEWIN
TO HIDE AWAY
1930

That year, many were to go. Soon there were no longer enough to attend to the ceremonies. The drums were left on their own.

It was a white hunter from Detroit Lakes who "discovered" a small water drum, carefully cached away by Chi Makwa at his trapping camp. The white hunter was exercising the privileges of his society on some newly tax-forfeited Indian land on the reservation, now held by Becker County, when he stumbled on Chi Makwa's winter trapping cabin. It was an unusual find, he thought, as he carefully packed it up and brought it into the museum in Detroit Lakes. And there it would sit, in the display case filled with similarly procured items, all gathering dust and absorbing the ogles of hundreds of tourists for years and years to come.

Ishkwegaabawiikwe's drum fared somewhat better. It was a women's dance drum. Mesabe held the job as the janitor at the Episcopal church in White Earth village. Besides the Indian Agency, the church was the only employer in town. Mesabe took home meager wages, but the small check supplemented that which he still got from the land—deer, fish, beaver, wild rice, and his garden. It was land on which the white man would say he was a trespasser, the only land he knew.

There was no one left living who had been on that drum, no one but him. Each day, he would feed the drum with tobacco, and a few times a month bring it out to see the sun and feel the life around it, the life of the people. That was what had begun to worry Mesabe. Despair had seeped into their hearts, cold and paralyzing. Tighter and tighter the ropes of the government seemed to be enclosing the village and the people of Pine Point, wrapping them within the confines of laws, policies, commodity foods, and that life the government had picked for the Indians. If you could call it a life at all.

So Mesabe cached the drum away, put it in the only hiding place he was sure would outlast the times. The rafters of the Episcopal church. The ribcage of the beast.

PART II

The
Re-Awakening

THE PASSING
1960

"*Gii-aynadog ninimoshenh wenjibonynan goshaa niin*
Niinimoshenh goshaa wiin gaa-takoozid
Gii-minwendam goshaa wiin gii-kanoonag
Niinimoshenh goshaa wiin gaa-takoozid"

"My sweetheart must be back where I come from
My short sweetie
She was happy when I called her
My short sweetie"

He held his infant daughter in his large, work-hardened hands and rocked her, humming an old love song as a lullaby. An olive-skinned man with deepset eyes and jet black hair, Jim Nordstrom rocked Alanis back and forth and kissed her head now. He cooed to her, *shhh, shhh, shhh.*

For a moment, he remembered his grandmother Philomene St. Clair's songs. He remembered the hymns she sang to comfort him in her small house near White Earth village. *Packed dirt floor, swept twice a day, chinked logs you could see through when the moss dried too loosely. Later additions had clapboard walls, dark rooms, oil lamps, a sparse china collection brought out for Sunday dinner. The ironing board was always busy with linens. A wood stove waited, warm to the touch, on which fluffy biscuits, bannock, and cakes were cooked.*

Now he sat in a small, cluttered apartment in East Los Angeles. The air smelled like the exhaust of cars. A eucalyptus tree knocked on the window. The air conditioner rattled.

Alanis had been born in East L.A. to Jim and his wife, Maura. Maura Coningham was an English teacher in training, Irish by birth. A writer by gift, a storyteller by love. It was the story that drew her to Jim. The images, songs, and mysteries of the northern woods pulled her in until she was a character in the story of his life. At one time she felt flat and undefined. Now she struggled to find her role and make her own way. After Alanis's birth, she worked her way through college, trying to finish her teaching degree while she student-taught at a local grade school.

While his wife was at night school, Jim Nordstrom conducted his affairs in a way that passed for baby-sitting his little girl. With Alanis in tow, Jim Nordstrom attended powwows, went hunting, butchered meat, or panned for gold in the hills around Santa Barbara. Alanis also accompanied him on visits to various women he referred to as his "cousins," but whom by and large were far too buxom and Nordic to pass for a close relation.

Jim Nordstrom was an extra in the westerns. There were few places an Indian man could get respect in the big world in those days—working on the railroad, shilling carnivals or wild west shows, marching in the army, and as an extra in Hollywood.

Jim Nordstrom was a star among the Indian extras as he now and then had speaking parts in the films. Nothing fancy—only a line here or there—but it earned him extra respect and an extra twenty-five cents an hour on his wages. A casting agent considered his Ojibwe way of speaking perfect for an Indian, and he was prolific in roles as Comanche chiefs, Apache warriors, Sioux braves, and even one part as an Eskimo hunting polar bears. He sang a few wailing songs that were scripted for him and were presumed to originate from sacred rituals; they were an essential part of most westerns. He spoke several singularly memorable lines: *"My people here, yours there." "I go now." "White man speaks with forked tongue."* The scripted lines succinctly summarized the emotions of the Indians.

By and large, Indians were mostly action figures, evil characters, and backdrops to the drama of the white man. They were occupied with riding horses back and forth on the horizon, burning wagons or farmhouses, and making the all-important smoke signals. Resourceful and a survivor, Jim Nordstrom taught himself how to do all of these things and more. Caught up in the fever of the period, he, the Ojibwe hunter from northern Minnesota, began to live out a fantasy world of the Plains Indians. He became an expert at falling off galloping horses, counting coup, buffalo hunts, and placing a knife at a white woman's throat. There was always plenty of action for a villain.

Yet it was inevitable that the scene always ended tragically with the Indian's head down, riding off into the sunset, or dead on an expanse of prairie with a musical score crescendoing, images of happy pioneers or singing cowboys on the distant horizon. And interestingly enough, in spite of a plot line that traversed thousands of miles and told the epic story of the West, the film crew rarely left Monument Valley.

Talented as he was, Jim Nordstrom would never become more than an Indian extra. Tony Curtis, Rex Barker, and Tom Ward all played Indians better than Indians did. These white actors got all of the best lines. They babbled away in *Indian talk*, memorable oratory punctuated with phrases like, "So long as the grass is green and rivers flow, so long as the sun shall rise and set," and other lines that reaffirmed the eternal status of Indians in America's psyche. Still, Jim Nordstrom wished he had said those words—and received the extra few bucks for the speaking part.

Later, when Alanis had grown up, she kept in her head an image of her father: She remembered him in full headdress on a white horse. He was stunning. His black wig of braids was long, thick, and sleek. His skin was shiny from a coffee-colored paint that made the actors' skin color even-toned and more *authentic* for the film. Then there was the fringed buckskin outfit and the full Hollywood headdress made of turkey feathers. For a finishing touch *all Indians* required face painting: bright, bold lines, zigzag lightning bolts, and colorful streaks. It was war paint that a make-up artist had determined was accurate for all tribes—Comanche, Navajo, Cherokee, Sioux, and anyone else who ever used a bow and arrow. Her father was an image made in Hollywood, an image forever set in her mind.

While his daytime was filled with action and adventure, by night Jim Nordstrom was just another Indian. He was one of the thousands who now lived on the West Coast, having followed the railroads, movie scouts, or simply the highways until they ended in Los Angeles, Riverside, Oakland, Portland, or Seattle. He, like thousands of others, had to adapt to survive. That he did well.

As Hollywood's fascination with westerns waned, Jim Nordstrom's identity changed and he became a modern Indian. He offered Indian wisdom for a small price, sage thoughts for the needy. Words from a wise Indian filled a hole in the spiritual world of the adventuresome hippies, deadheads, or dabblers in eastern religions who had landed once again reluctantly in the western hemisphere. Jim Nordstrom came to be known as Jim Good Fox, and he relished in the role. It was acting more genuine than his roles in the westerns. He could develop himself. In the process, he recovered himself, recovered what he was amidst all he was seen to be. He found his pipe, found his vision, and found a new life. It fulfilled him and let him be a full man in a world where Indians were one dimensional, or in a museum display. Fortuitously, he soon found that gifts in the form of knowledge, sacred items, and blondes seemed drawn to him. The more he did, the more his attraction grew until the phones, mail, speaking, and ceremonial requests filled his days and nights.

Maura Coningham had had enough. One bold summer morning as the scent from the eucalyptus wafted through the muggy air of East L.A., clogging into exhaust, and the sound of motors, horns, and Spanish, Maura Coningham packed her daughter and a meager collection of books and clothes into a Nash Rambler and headed north. The story had changed and the characters were in different chapters. The women found a home in Mill Valley, and Maura became an English teacher in a local public high school.

Then Alanis only remembered pieces of her father. A camera side shot of him during a rerun western on TV, a quick scribbled birthday note with a bracelet, poster, or necklace that he sent along. Rarely a face. And each time on the phone, a different woman would answer in her best Ojibwe accent and call to her father, *"Niinimoshenh, Niinimoshenh."*

Alanis's last image for many years was a news clip that showed her father driving a van of food into Wounded Knee in 1973 to support the armed occupation of the church and cemetery by the Lakota people.

So it was that under her mother's care, and later a second marriage to a Norwegian mathematics teacher, that Alanis was removed from the fringe world of Indian Hollywood. She found herself in a quiet story of cookouts, school work, slumber parties, and college. There was always a feeling that something was missing, but she couldn't put a name to it. A sound, a face, a smell would knock a fragment of her memory loose, and she could sense the smell of Great-Grandma Philomene's bannock cooking on the stove. The visceral smell of horse sweat and manure reminded her of a distant, Indian world, or the sounds of geese moving in their eternal circle from north to south and south to north made her recall seasons. Occasionally a wind blowing through the trees would recall the sound of rice sticks and wild rice knocking and falling into the canoe. In the smell of spring, the clean scent of maple sap wafted through her nostrils.

Jim "Good Fox" Nordstrom finally ran out of women. Five brides later, he was wifeless in Denver when he was diagnosed with cancer. When news came of the illness of her father, Alanis moved to Denver. Fending off an entourage of New Age followers and the family of wife number five, Alanis tried to reconstruct a relationship with a dying man. It was too late. Cancer finally killed him. The Ojibwe called the disease *asabikenhshii*, or the Spider.

Jim Nordstrom passed over in his own house, Alanis at his side. Only when her father was gone could she remember what she wanted to say to him.

Collected by the county hospital, which officially designated him as "deceased," Alanis had the time of her life getting her father back. Alanis enlisted an old college friend and the director of the Denver Indian Center, Browning Teaman, to help her. In the end, it took Browning, Alanis, and two huge barrel-chested Ojibwe men to rescue her father's body from the hospital.

"You know he's dead," an exhausted Alanis explained to a hospital attendant. "Just let him go."

"We can't, Miss. Hospital policy, you know," the attendant's monotone voice stated matter of factly. "We need to release his remains to the funeral home."

"He is not going to a funeral home," Browning interjected firmly. "He's going home."

"Not without an official release," the hospital attendant began stubbornly, her eyes flicked, wincing slightly as the two large Ojibwe men moved, ever so slightly behind Browning.

"Just watch," Browning said, his eyes twinkling. He moved his head to the side, puckered his lips toward the other men, a silent signal, and together they carried the stiffened body from the basement of the hospital. If anything, he was experienced in retrieving Indians from the county, Alanis smiled to herself.

"Move fast, before they send a posse and steal him back," Browning whispered to his crew. The hospital workers looked on aghast, afraid to confront the war party. The hospital attendant quickly dialed security, fumbling the numbers and dialing again and again until she got it right.

They loaded Jim's blanket-wrapped body into the back door of the station wagon. Alanis sat between the two men in the front seat, with the other following in a second car behind. They sped from the parking lot.

"Miigwech," Alanis whispered to Browning.

"Don't thank me," Browning said, "thank the Great Spirit for helping us out." He touched the eagle feather on his rearview mirror, then shot her a smile. One of the other men sprinkled some tobacco out the window.

Browning's sophistication was astonishing to Alanis. They stopped a couple miles from the hospital and clambered out of the two cars. Browning and his two Ojibwe friends transferred their possessions and prayers into a van, the stiffened body laying diagonally across the floor, wrapped in a wool blanket.

"Just in case the hospital sends the cops out after us," he explained to a puzzled Alanis.

Then, chips, pop, and smokes in stash, the entourage struck north for the Wyoming border.

"Twenty hours 'til Minnesota," Browning announced, looking to Alanis. "I'll need help with the driving."

It was three days later at a traditional cemetery in the woods north of Pine Point that a small group of Ojibwe gathered. Wrapped in a star quilt and placed in a simple pine coffin, Jim Nordstrom was finally home from a long journey.

EZHE'OSED
HE WHO WALKS
BACKWARDS
1970

George Ahnib laboriously pulled on his sweatshirt and pants, nervously looking for anything that might have climbed onto his clothes—a mouse or spider that he imagined could crawl onto his skin. He hated buttons and snaps as well. Buttons involved touching too much of the fabric. The sound of snaps made him cringe, as if a gun had been fired outside his door. As a consequence, he was destined to a wardrobe of simple items. And, due to his meager collection, he was forever indebted to his extended family for their wringer washer.

As his thick hair fell onto his face, he furiously pushed it back, running his fingers through its length to his shoulders. As much as he detested anything else touching him, his hair could fall to his knees and crawl all over his back and he would relish it all the more. "Real *ogichidaa* have long hair," George would say, one of his few phrases. This he repeated at the most unusual times. He would flick his long locks back and laugh raucously, his dark eyes set deep beneath a chiseled and scarred face, smoldering while he took on a fierce *ogichidaa,* or warrior, stance. Then, a few moments later, the everyday George would return with the eyes and mind of an eleven-year-old child.

George could remember little or nothing about most things. Day to day, he had enough wits to get dressed, but regular meals were beyond his basic comprehension. If not, cooking more than the most simple meals certainly was. His relatives collected him from his house twice a day to make sure he was fed, and his cousin dispatched her brother to ensure he was washed and had brushed his hair.

George existed in another world. He had existed in this world for the eight years since he had done in his brain by sniffing too much gas. At eleven years of age, George and his friends "huffed" at every chance they got, siphoning gasoline from cars, and inhaling whatever they could find. It was a cheap high that made him giddy and let him see a different world.

George saw things when he was high. He saw a wolf in that world, a large gray-black male that watched him from the distance. At first, George had been scared and ran away, far into the woods north of the village. In his mind's eye, the wolf followed him, at the edge of his peripheral vision. Finally, George stopped to rest. The wolf watched from a distance then slowly came closer, carefully moving several steps each time the boy closed his eyes. Then George heard the wolf talk. And like the secret entrance to an immense cave revealed before him, the world opened up. *"Bindigiin, bindigiin."* The wolf spoke Ojibwe. *"Come in, come in."* Slowly and deliberately, the wolf ran next to him, not close, but near enough for George to hear him. George heard the wolf, then the trees and the drum. The world came alive for him and was his own.

The drum had a soothing sound that surrounded him and made him feel more at ease. The drum made him dance. Slowly, he shuffled his feet to the drumbeat and then stomped his right foot twice to the beat only he heard. He was an old-time men's traditional dancer, slightly off rhythm. Swaying slowly with his drumbeat, he danced in a circle clockwise again and again in his own dance. People whispered and wondered what George was hallucinating, but George would just say that he had gone away.

George Ahnib's Pine Point village was a tormented town. The ghosts of Ottertail Pillagers past wandered the streets of the newly built HUD housing project looking for their traps, sugaring pails, and sacred items.

Some ranged like banshees on the Ponsford Prairie, while others appeared as silent lights in the forest, emanating from the dark of the pine trees left standing by the white cannibal seventy years before. From where they hung above the fireplace mantle in the homes of collectors or as curios on the log walls of the local resorts, medicine pouches, quivers, pipebags, and bandoleers watched and waited for their people to return. Plied from their owners by drink and desperation, the continuity between prayers and conduits was disrupted.

Some said that the Ottertail Pillagers of Pine Point were being punished extra for resisting the white people. They had been reticent to visit the strange Doctor Hrdlicka, not cooperating like the other villages. And then there was the Round Lake Uprising and the strange raiding wars that ensued. The Indian Agency had been furious with the Indians from Pine Point for almost a decade after that setback in the growth of lumber revenues and the debacle of Indian policy. By the time that the epidemics of tuberculosis and trachoma had wreaked their havoc in Pine Point, few were left to carry on the songs, dances, and stories. Most had moved to the cities, seeking a refuge from the cannibal.

Those who remained, chiseled out a life from a government policy of stone, cold as cement. George's family lived in a small simple house and worked jobs in nearby border towns as loggers, pulp peelers, and cooks. The Pine Point people prevailed, drawing from the deepest wells of their souls to outlive president after president, one Indian agent after another, and four decades of stingy, malevolent, and sometimes just plain bizarre Indian policy. Except for a few. Unreclaimed by the long path, there were those who succumbed to the deepest of poverty—material and, later, spiritual.

It was truly remarkable that anyone survived intact. By the 1960s, a new program of the white people came to the reservation. The War on Poverty knocked over trees and family boundaries, moving people from their small modest homes and placing them side by side in an architecturally perfect housing project. The pastel collection of ramblers stood on a treeless field, divided by boulevards on newly paved streets. The people of the forest winced at the bright colors and desertlike panorama into which the government hoped they would move. Then, lured by running water and electricity, George's family slowly brought their old, browned family photographs, veterans' flags, homemade quilts, and sparse collection of mismatched furniture into the housing projects. If before the solitude of the woods could heal their heartaches and sorrows, the housing project offered no shelter from the storm.

In the poverty of no opportunities and a set of options controlled by men in the granite buildings of Washington, despair set in for many. For George's aunt, the despair was dulled by the strict adherence to Christianity and the hope given by the Episcopal and Catholic missions. For George's mother, that despair and the pain of loss was dulled by a bottle of liquor, generously supplied by a local bootlegger.

To his mother, Janine Littlewolf, the loss of control over her life and the accumulation of intergenerational grief was drowned in Colt 45. She liked the way the malt liquor tasted like ordinary beer but had a kick like a horse, or like a pistol held to her head. She had no parents: The nuns of nine years of boarding school were her memories of intimacy. And her children were gone, all except George.

Welfare had barged into her home one day after her infant son and toddler daughter. Clucking about poverty and squalor, the social worker had conducted a terse and one-sided interview with the bewildered woman, and within twenty minutes, walked out the door with a bag of clothes and her two children, leaving George's mother empty and confused. Many years later, she heard that the children had been moved from foster home to foster home across the state of Minnesota, until they were finally adopted into separate white households. Having signed over her parental rights, she never could locate them, and they could never know of her, their blood family, or even of each other.

George had been with his father that day. They had driven up the Camp 7 Road to shine deer. George Sr. and George Jr. had shot a buck, returned home, and then his father had driven back out with a twelve-pack. An accident claimed George Sr.'s life.

As time passed, Janine Littlewolf's commitment to life waned. She strewed beer cans and cigarette butts throughout the house that the government in Washington had so generously supplied her. She would stare blankly at the television blaring reruns of old westerns, watching for the movie star from White Earth, Jim Nordstrom, resplendent in his white headdress.

At six years of age, George would cook simple meals for himself and his mother: macaroni and cheese from a box, hard-fried eggs, and Lucky Charms cereal were his specialties. He attended to himself as best as he could and attended to his mother as minimally as he could. George became a master of concoctions, building monuments such as towers of beer cans to entertain himself and then demolishing them in a calculated fury. Ducking from falling beer cans, and later from social workers, he would stealthily creep out of the back door and move quickly between the backyard junk car collection and off into the woods. Here he found peace.

Running with the other Pine Point boys, he discovered sniffing gas. It began with inhaling exhaust from idling cars, then they siphoned gasoline from a neighbor's car and took it to their fort in the woods back of the Project. Passing the can back and forth, they breathed deep and laughed until they passed out. Later it was house paint. The boys would buy it at the hardware store in Pine Point, until finally the store owners got wise to the paint marks on the boys' faces and stopped selling it to them. The more George sniffed, the more he escaped, and by the time he was seventeen, the gasoline took him to a place from which he was unable to return.

At almost the same time, George's mother passed from this world to the next. To the Indian Health Service, she became another statistic: One of those Indian women over forty-five who is sixty times more likely than a white woman to die from cirrhosis of the liver. The truth was that she died from a broken heart. In any case, she had so pickled her wasted body that they barely needed to preserve her with formaldehyde when they laid her to rest in the Episcopal Cemetery in Pine Point. George inherited a small social security check and a HUD home from his mother.

George aged but he never truly grew older. In 1988, George was twenty-three years old, but his mind remained that of an eleven-year-old. Through it all though, the wolf stayed with George. Walking beside him, calling to him across the ball diamond, and dancing beside him in his strange dance, George had a protector in his own world.

In the material world, his relatives cared for the man-boy. They protected him from Becker County Social Services. Arriving in unmarked station wagons, the polyester-clad women armed with clipboards and accompanied by police officers, conducted monthly raids into the HUD project, searching for welfare fraud perpetrators, fathers of AFDC children, child support fugitives, and any "misfits" who might garner more money for the impoverished county services. They kept track of Pine Point people like jam in a pie cupboard, but miraculously George escaped their net. When Social Services came to town, George was gone, and this is how he was able to survive.

The reservation was his home. Not only was he related by blood to many families, he was related by the tragedy and joy of the village's collective history. Everyone had a place and a role, and George had his, if only to laugh and enjoy the drum and remind people of simple things. George's place was in his mind, and White Earth was his refuge.

THE THAW
1980

The winter was unforgiving. It came in a seemingly endless cycle of freeze and thaw, searing winds, and the deepest colds. Gloved hands gripped steering wheels like claws. Lips murmured prayers to unseen spirits on icy roads. Jaws were set to steady fear.

The ever deepening snow put all to sleep. Even the spirits. The soft blankets were made glossy by the blinding sun of *Namebini Giizis*, the Sucker Moon, the white man's February. The earth became a hard, frozen surface after a month of freeze and thaw. Animals ventured from their sanctuaries, and snowshoe-clad Indians ventured into the woods to find food or onto ice-covered streams and lakes, cut open with augers, to find fish. There was no choice but to survive.

Through it all came the spring. Willow buds were the most brave, emerging from frozen limbs and then covered at once in their innocence with a blanket of new spring snow. A persistent spring wind blew through the dedicated warmth of early suns. The ice created honeycombs on the lakes, and a determined wind brought the ice crashing to the shore in sheets.

Finally the geese came. A few geese, solitary and bold, began the journey north. They called out, *It is spring, it is warm, and we are alive.* Then slowly more and more geese until the flocks moved against the skies overcast with the promise of the first spring thunderstorms.

Each spring, like a religious rite, Mesabe drove the backroads to the

Indian Agency in Cass Lake to ask the Great White Father when he would help the Indians with their land. Along the way, Mesabe shook his head in wonderment and sadness at the world around him. Log skidders crushed *jiibegamig*, gravehouses, as the lumberjacks rid White Earth of the forests. Chainsaws severed the *ininaatig*, the maple sugar trees, the lifeblood of the *Anishinaabeg*. Logging trucks careened down the narrow dirt roads, their trailers precariously filled with White Earth's trees. Tractors and cattle trampled medicine plants into the ground. White hunters arrive en masse to obliterate anything that moved in their line of sight. Like clockwork, the dayglow orange invasion transformed the woods into a war zone, bodies gutted and strapped to car racks, or strewn in truckbeds, legs stretched, eyes rolled back. The deer began their final journey to freezers in suburban homes. On the lakes, like an *asabikenhshii*, a cancer, the summer cabins spread along the shoreline until there was little or none left for the Indians. Elbow to elbow, the city people migrated north, chasing swimming or canoeing Indian kids off *their* beaches and penetrating the lake with docks, motor boats, pontoons, and the accoutrements of their vacations.

At the Indian Agency, Mesabe's spring rite played itself out just as it had all of the many years before. The Indian agent's assistant would shrug his shoulders, a religious rite of his own. He made various hand gestures illustrating his helplessness. "In those situations . . ." the assistant would say and leave off, the future dangling with his unfinished sentence.

Mesabe had his monologue memorized by now. "We had eight eighty-acre allotments in my family," he would say. "Those lumbermen, those Indian agents took them all. Basswood, Many Point, Round, and Sockeye Lakes. They were all there. We could make a good living from those lands, and we wouldn't have to be as poor as church mice. We took good care of the land."

The Indian agent nodded noncommittally, like he heard but could not listen.

Mesabe wondered if government people went to a special school to learn to nod like that.

"Your agency, you people are supposed to protect us Indians. And our land. You all get paid for it." Mesabe raised his voice now and leaned forward into the airspace of the Indian agent. The agent leaned back and nervously pushed his glasses back up on his sweating nose. His hairy arms were pasty from inside work.

"What are you going to do? You've got to stop them from cutting . . ."

The Indian agent nodded again, knowing and superior in his position.

"We're looking into it, Mr. Mesabe. We're investigating all of these issues. Washington is apprised of the situation."

It was always the same set of answers. Only the staff personnel would change, like a seasonal rotation, every two years their tour of duty would move them back from the outposts of Indian country to the security of their stone buildings in Washington.

It was during the spring thaw that Mesabe began having the dreams again.

He was a grandfather now. He had survived his wife, Equayzaince, and two of his five children. The rest were scattered like maple leaves from Minneapolis to Winnipeg. There were no jobs, houses, or land for the Indians of White Earth. Only a promise of justice, and a memory of what was once. And, of course, the land itself remained, through it all, battered, scarred, and shorn. The wind still whispered to the oak leaves, fluttering in the dead of winter, and sang to the rice beds full of loons, ducks, and the ghost voices of Indians laughing when they harvested.

Elaine Mandamin was his granddaughter, the only child of his daughter, Geraldine, who had died in a car accident. Elaine's father was not discussed, although everyone knew he was a lumberjack from Nett Lake. A man who hit it hard. The drinks, the work, the women. Then moved on. Geraldine and Elaine had lived with Mesabe when the girl was young, living in a small log-and-tarpaper shack that pre-dated the government housing projects but post-dated the great plague and the Knights of the Forest. There, the three of them lived— Elaine, her mother, and her grandfather.

Geraldine Mandamin was hitchhiking to Park Rapids one day when she was hit by a Holsum bread delivery truck. The driver claimed she had stepped in front of the truck, and no one could say any different, although the driver had a reputation for dooring—swinging open a car or truck door to hit a walking Indian. So she was gone. No court, a small Episcopal funeral, and Elaine was alone.

She spent much of her teenage and adult life missing the softness of a mother. There were other aunties and relatives in the Minneapolis Indian community who cared for the girl. By the 1960s, at least one generation of White Earth people had been born in the city and learned to navigate between the growing emigrant populations who fed the skyline. By the 1970s and Elaine's arrival, three-fourths of the White Earth people were away from home, most of them in Minneapolis and St. Paul. Her aunt was a nursing assistant; her uncle, a carpenter. Between the garage sales, baking, and hard work, they made enough to support the extended family. A trip home to Ponsford for ricing or deer hunting made all the difference to Elaine. The food tasted clean in her mouth, the rice tasted like Basswood Lake, and Elaine never once forgot the smell of maple sap boiling in her grandfather's kettle in the woods.

The Indian community became more organized and vocal as Elaine grew up. She remembered being dragged to a protest of police brutality against Indians, she recalled how her aunt and uncle changed their hair styles and finally grew it long by the time Elaine was ten years old. The American Indian Movement had started to grow in the cities. Men and women patrolled the streets, keeping police "in check." And then she remembered Wounded Knee and the caravan of Ojibwe who went to support their most honored enemies in their time of need.

Elaine drenched her skin in the smoke of sage, sounds of pow-wow drums, and the voices of her aunt and uncle discussing "Red Power" and the *Oshki Anishinaabeg*, the new people. She let the words and images caress her skin and comfort her. It was like a warm fire far away in the distance she could feel. One she longed for but could not touch, one she walked toward, yet, it seemed, remained still distant. She sensed that her mother was somewhere there in all those voices, but she could never get close enough to touch her. So she just kept walking.

After a few years at college in Minneapolis, she returned home to Mesabe, two children in tow, to live with her grandfather and work for the tribe's biology department. And now, Mesabe's hopes rested with the girl. She was the only one of his descendants who had come home. He encouraged her, teased her, and watched her and her children through frustration, tears, and joy. They shared it, and he shared his hopes with her.

He had told Elaine now about his dreams, the ones which recurred for weeks on end, and of which he took particular note.

"Those old ladies are coming to me. Talking to me, but I can't hear them," he said to Elaine as she came from the kitchen to sit in the living room with him. The room was sparse, a collection of blanket-covered thrift-store couches and aging pictures on the wall: his ancestors and descendants, John F. Kennedy, and the Pope. In one corner a television blared showing Vanna White in another new dress, turning letters and pirouetting herself. Elaine's two small children sat and watched, playing with blonde Barbie dolls.

"Are they from now, or from a long time ago?" his granddaughter asked.

"They are old ladies from a long time ago, and some young girls, too. They are wearing long dresses and straw hats, just like they used to at the feasts and dances or just to go to town."

The old man wore a flannel shirt, his thermal underwear peeking out at the neck. His work pants were worn smooth from the woods and from the family's wringer washing machine. His face had few wrinkles, considering his age, and his jaw was still set strong. His eyes were bright and his mind lucid.

The old man looked at Vanna's dress, cut low in back and covered in sequins. She was spinning around, moving smoothly from one side of the screen to another, her dress shimmering as she moved. He could not understand the immodesty of white people. It hurt his eyes.

"They talk to me, and then sometimes, they motion me to come and look at something. Last night they came again. They took me to walk down an old road by my grandmother Mindemoyen's allotment. That was out by Many Point Lake." He continued as Vanna turned more letters. "The trees were grown up high and big just like the old days before they cut them down."

"Maybe it was back then," Elaine said to her grandfather.

"No. It was now. Or in the future. It was about something to happen, like it would be that way again."

"That's good, isn't it?" Elaine asked hopefully.

"That's real good," the old man said.

The two little girls undressed the Barbie dolls from their own sequined dresses. Someone had made dresses of calico, ribbon, and leather for the dolls, and now, arms distended and twisted, they were stuffed into the new Indian clothes. The old man watched. Elaine looked on as well but kept her mind on the dream. Dreams were important to the *Anishinaabe*, especially the dreams of old people. Elaine had learned this long ago. Many religious traditions, hunting secrets, or medicines came from dream instructions.

"What do you think it means?" she finally asked.

"Sometimes it could mean that I'm going to pass on. But not this time. I'm not going to die yet. I think something is going on with them lands."

"Which lands are you talking about?"

"We should have eight allotments, from all my old people. But it seems they stole them all—those men that knew how to do business. Those lands are up by those lakes, and some are in the woods. The county and the boy scouts and some resorts got them now. They stole them from us Indians."

"Maybe we should find out what's going on. Should we go to Cass Lake again and look at the BIA?"

Mesabe scoffed.

"Hell, I've written letters to the Bureau for fifty years now about them lands and how they were stolen. They never help."

They both sat in silence, lost in their thoughts, the girls playing with their Indian Barbies, the Wheel of Fortune spinning.

"Yes," Mesabe finally said. "Something is going on with them lands. Something bad and something good both."

INDIAN HATING
1980

There is a peculiar kind of hatred in the northwoods, a hatred born of the guilt of privilege, a hatred born of living with three generations of complicity in the theft of lives and land. What is worse is that each day, those who hold this position of privilege must come face to face with those whom they have dispossessed. To others who rightfully should share in the complicity and the guilt, Indians are far away and long ago. But in reservation border towns, Indians are ever-present.

The poverty of dispossession is almost overwhelming. So is the poverty of complicity and guilt. In America, poverty is relative, but it still causes shame. That shame, combined with guilt and a feeling of powerlessness, creates an atmosphere in which hatred buds, blossoms, and flourishes. The hatred passes from father to son and from mother to daughter. Each generation feels the hatred and it penetrates deeper to justify a myth.

Norman Grist suffered from the Indian Hating Disease. He had it bad, knotted tightly and pungently in his gut, and he handed it down to his son Robert like an heirloom. Norman had a farm near Mahnomen on the reservation. Norman's family had bought that reservation land, fair and square, like all the others. They purchased it in 1932 from a land salesman named Lucky Waller, an agent who offered good terms and plenty of God's land to the immigrant German, Norwegian, and Czech farmers who moved into the reservation territory. His grandfather started out with three hundred and twenty acres, a team of horses, and a lot of determination. Four old Indian allotments, Waller told him: The Indians did not use them, so there was no reason the white men could not.

With the sweat of horses, men, and women, the Grists built that farm, acre by acre, pulling out rocks, breaking the sod, plowing the soil under, clearing trees, and filling the sloughs. Acre by acre they built their farm and family until there were plenty of Grists on the prairie, Grists who had earned their way into God's—and the bank's—favor. And in a small clearing behind the house was the family graveyard from the early days where small granite headstones marked the spot where Norman's grandfather and grandmother slept under the soil they had farmed.

By the 1970s, Norman Grist's family had 1,280 acres on which they broke their backs to make a living. For years, the soybeans and cattle had done well for them—if they worked through the twelve hours of available light each day, seven days a week. The truth was, when the farm was at three hundred and twenty acres and the equipment less expensive or even borrowed, it was possible to do the work and take a day of rest. That was then, and this was now. *Today it seemed like the farming business had more to do with what machinery they had on the farm: a 270-horsepower Versatile four-wheel-drive articulated tractor, an International Harvester row-crop tractor, chisel plow, moldboard plow, Wil-Rich thirty-foot-wide harrow, John Deere drill and attachments, an Owatonna swather, John Deere fully enclosed combine, haybines, choppers, disks, silage blowers, boom sprayer, and a couple of Dodge pickup trucks.* All of this came with a thirty-thousand-dollar annual operating loan and two hundred thousand dollars borrowed against machinery and the land.

It was true, the farmers and the Indians had traded for many years. "Heck a couple of Indians even came to work for me as hired men," Norman would muse and editorialize with the other farmers in a midday reprieve over a cup of coffee and piece of pie down at the Red Apple Café. "That was back in the fifties and sixties. Mike Littlewolf worked on the farm for two years and Jim Kettle did the same. When they were working for me, they did well enough and put in an honest day. They were reliable men, that they were, sure."

Something had happened, though, Norman figured: "One day, they just never came back. Just like that, they disappeared. I used to see the Littlewolfs in town every once and a while after that, but not much besides that. Those Indians are almost spooky the way they disappear, sure are."

To Norman, those were "good Indians." As time passed, he saw less of Indians and had little opportunity to speak with them. He became more withdrawn into the white farming community on the reservation. To that community, there were "good Indians" and there were "bad Indians." Good Indians worked for the businesses in town or for the farmers. Bad Indians did not want anything to do with white people, had hoards of children, stole from farmers, and collected welfare checks. Over time, Norman used to say, "There are just too many bad Indians and not enough good ones."

As he repeated his refrain, his audience at the Red Apple would nod their heads slowly in a chorus of agreement, sipping their bottomless cups of coffee.

Robert Grist, or Bob, as he got to be called, saw few Indians as adults. In the Mahnomen school system, about half the kids were at least part Indian. That was when he started, though. By the time he was in high school, the number had dwindled, and by the time of graduation only six Indians remained. Most Indians didn't make it through school, Bob knew, but he could not understand why. It didn't seem that the Indian kids were dumb. Just that they were quiet; and each year, they became more withdrawn.

Except for a few. He attended school with Lucy St. Clair and Selam Big Bear, both tough Indian kids. Hell, you no more had to glance at Lucy wrong and she would belt you across the face for looking stupid. She was pretty too, and that bothered Bob. It bothered him because she was a bad Indian, bad Indian stock through and through.

One time when they were all juniors, Bob, Miles Spaaker, and Kenny Jiworsky were out by the lakes drinking beer in someone's Ford Falcon when they decided they needed to "train" Lucy. Someone laughed, then they started to goad each other until the idea set in. Everyone knew that Lucy was no virgin, but Bob wanted to see for himself. You couldn't blame him or any other farm boys for wanting to try. They threw out their empties, started the car, and went cruising. They found her walking on the south side of Mahnomen.

They pulled the sedan up right next to her, slowed down to her walking speed, and Bob and Kenny Jiworsky rolled down their windows. Miles looked straight ahead, his jaw set with nervousness, his eyes looking wildly to see who might observe them.

"Lucy, Lucy," Bob crooned to her, "Jeez, you're one pretty girl."

Without even looking his way, Lucy flipped him off. The other guys laughed but Bob's face turned red, half hurt, half angry. The car kept steady with her, and she turned the corner down a residential street. She stopped, crossed her arms in front, and looked at the three farm boys.

"You're all ugly. Real ugly white boys. Shut up and leave me alone."

She spun on her heel and walked away.

"You don't have to be so mean, Lucy," Kenny Jiworsky said, mocking hurt feelings. "We ain't so ugly, not compared to some of those drunks in your family."

"Fuck off," she screamed, spinning back around and in one smooth motion she slammed her arm toward Kenny's face. But just as smoothly, he grabbed it. Quick as a cat, Miles Spaaker in the backseat opened the door and wrapped his arm around her waist, yanking her inside the car. Kenny got in the other side of the Falcon now and squeezed her between the two of them, pinning her arms behind her.

They drove just a little farther out and pulled onto a section road near Noeske's farm, south of town. Lucy hollered the whole way, and Miles Spaaker was trying to keep her in the car and quiet enough to head out of town. Kenny tried to get her out of the car. She fought him, but he did manage to get her out. Then he no more than started to pull her shorts off when she let out a kick that got him square in the balls. As Kenny doubled over, Bob went after her, and Miles Spaaker tried to pin her hands behind her. Just as Bob was coming for her, she freed herself, and pulled out a buck knife, the kind you gut a deer with. Then her expression changed. What had started with disgust moved to fear and now turned to rage. But not an uncontrolled rage. That was not Lucy at all, she knew control. She had a conscious rage and maneuvered her knife with slashes aimed at piercing skin, not organs. Her eyes were stone cold with hatred and her arm fast and strong.

She slashed Bob across the chest, slicing his skin like she would skin a deer. Then she shredded it, a mistake with a deer but not with a white boy. She kept right on slashing and tore up his shirt, all through his arms and his chest until he was bleeding real bad. Miles tried to stop her, but she turned around on him fast, too. Miles never had been that swift, so she only took one lunge at him, and he backed off.

Lucy hiked up her shorts and took off running back toward town. Kenny was still rolled up sick like and Bob was bleeding all over from the slashing. All they could do was pile back into the car and turn around. Lucy had taken off over a couple of fields. There was no way they could get her, and their ambition had been lost.

Bob was going to have a hell of a time explaining the cuts to his father. He stumbled through the kitchen door, immensely relieved not to find his mother home. Dripping blood, he careened to the bathroom and hung his body over the sink as he found some dark-colored washcloths. He wet a cloth and pulled it over his wounds, wincing and crying like a baby. The cuts looked bad but were not deep, just painful, really painful.

Now as he washed his wounds, he worked up an explanation for his misfortune. *"Lucy had been drinking and attacked me with a knife."* That sounded good. He winced again as he salved the cuts. Deep enough to cause incredible pain but not deep enough to need stitches. He had been really lucky. He bandaged himself up with all the gauze in the cupboard, then wadded his shredded and bloody shirt and set it aside. He ran a washrag over the floor, mopping up the drops of blood, and threw that rag into the wash. Then, out behind the silo he burned the shirt on a manure pile. He came back inside just in time to see his mother arrive in the station wagon, and he quickly set to work on his chores.

After that, Bob steered clear of Lucy. His curiosity and that of the other farm boys was less important than his own survival.

As Bob grew older, the fine line between bad Indians and good Indians began to fuzz. Fewer Indians came to the farm, and he only saw most from a distance. They were quiet, so he never knew what they were saying or thinking. And most of them seemed dirt poor. "Hell, they could make a living if they wanted to," his dad used to say. "They don't need to be poor if they don't want to be."

In the late 1970s, things began to change on the farm. The price of soybeans dropped, as did the price of milk. The Production Credit Association, federal government, local banks, and insurance companies had lent to farmers on the promise of tomorrow's prosperity. Suddenly, future prosperity did not seem so certain. Land prices jumped from three hundred dollars per acre to anywhere from five hundred dollars and up to a thousand dollars. That positive climate of credit shifted, and interest rates went up. Wheat markets plummeted, reflecting international trade policies, and soon loan payments were almost equal to income.

Bob had gone off to college in North Dakota about that time to take up business management, anything that wasn't farming. He was not around when his dad almost had a nervous breakdown from the bills. His ma pretty much kept things together and had taken night job plucking birds at the turkey farm in Detroit Lakes to bring in a little extra cash. Things were tough then, and his dad began to look at selling off some of the farm to reduce the debt.

Bob returned from North Dakota with a wife named Jane and two kids. From the family banker they secured a mortgage on a small resort on White Earth Lake and christened it the Happy Woodsman. Forty acres, three hundred feet of beach front, eight cute cabins, and a one-hundred-thousand-dollar mortgage.

The day had turned sunny with westerly winds blowing the cloud cover toward the big lakes. Jane Grist merrily peeled potatoes in the kitchen of the Happy Woodsman. The phone rang, breaking the silence. Jane picked up the receiver to hear Norman Grist's voice booming over the line, saying something about a certified letter he had received from the government. Jane motioned to Bob to get on the other phone.

"Wait, Dad. Bob's getting on the line."

"We got a certified letter from Washington," Norman began again. Bob's voice tensed. "What's it say?"

Norman started slowly to read the letter. He stumbled over some of the words as his fourth grade education encountered federal language.

"Dear Mr. Norman Grist. This letter serves to inform you that title dis, dis, creep, in . . ."

Bob puzzled, then interrupted his father: "Discrepancies."

"*Discrepancies* have been found with your properties located in SW1/4 19 14640, W1/2, NW1/4, 19 14640, SW1/4 17 14640, N1/2 NE1/4 Sec. 8 145-41, according to the federal invest, investors . . ."

"Investigation."

"*Investigation* mandated by USC Sec 25, 2415 of the U.S. Congress. Sec. SW1/4 19 14640 was tran, transact, transacted by a forced fee patent, involving Napoleon Brisbois, an in, incom . . ."

"Spell it, Dad."

"I-N-C-O-M-P-E-T-E-N-T."

"Incompetent."

"*Incompetent*, and Lucky Land Co. Sec. W1/2 NW 1/4 19 14640 was transacted by a full-blood sale between *Equay*—Hell, I can't say that Indian name—someone and the Weyerhaeuser Land Co. Sec. SW 1/4 17 14640 was transacted by an illegal tax forfeiture of 20 acres of this parcel. Subsequent discrepancies with Lucky Land Company . . ."

The old man's voice trailed off as he stumbled over the last of the letter. Reading made him uncomfortable, and even the mention of Washington made him angry.

Bob and Jane were sure that the trouble had its roots in the mid-seventies with the so-called Civil Rights Movement. The Grists watched it on the evening television news, blacks and whites fighting it out over bus seats and drinking fountains far away down south. It did not make much sense to Bob and Jane; it was something you watched without understanding, waiting for the football highlights and weather report.

Then the Indians got some kind of wind of it and started to act up, first in Minneapolis. Occasionally Bob would hear word of an Indian demonstration here or there, but not much more than chatter over coffee. "I can't see what they've got to complain about," he would say to Jane as she poured him a cup of coffee. His elbows rested on the Formica tabletop as he looked into his wife's deep gray eyes. "I can't understand why those Indians aren't just thankful for what they have in this life." Jane sat down and tidied up a small stack of bills in the napkin holder.

"You bet," she said, affirming his observations. The simple life of country people seemed good enough to her. "What else would they want?" she asked her husband. "We all get the same things here," she said as she motioned with her arm to her modest collection of avocado-theme appliances in her rambler's kitchen. "We had to work hard for all this, and they want it all and to get it for nothing."

Bob nodded his head, agreeing with her.

"Those Indians get everything free of charge from the feds, all paid for by you and me: their education, housing, health care—they even get their teeth fixed and their funeral as handouts."

She shook her head at the shame of it all. "Some of us are equal, and some are more equal than others."

Neither Bob nor Jane could see what good change could possibly bring to the reservation. For the time being, however, they didn't need to worry. The problem was in the cities.

It was when the trouble came to the Minnesota reservations that things changed, Bob remembered. In the early eighties, trouble came to the Red Lake Reservation in northern Minnesota, not far from White Earth. The Indians occupied the tribal and BIA headquarters, and all the white people were thrown out. There seemed to be some kind of corruption in the tribal government, at least that is what the protesters said, but no one knew for sure. All anyone knew is that most things federal were in flames and most white people were no longer on the reservation. A couple of weeks went by, the siege ended, and no one was sure what had come of it except a bunch of arrests and a lot of burnt-out buildings and pickup trucks.

If there are two groups of people in America who feel a bewilderment and resentment concerning the scale of the federal government's power and intervention into their lives, it is farmers and Indians. National policies made thousands of miles away in Washington, D.C., seep into the cornfields and woods, into the udders of the dairy cows or the minds of tribal children.

The fire over the land disputes was rekindled in 1977 by a descendant of Bugonaygeeshig, the war chief of the southwestern *Anishinaabeg*. Now an old man named George Agawaateshkan refused to sign papers issued to him by a county agent, by which he would relinquish his rights to a parcel of land. Instead, Agawaateshkan went to court and won in a case subsequently upheld by the Minnesota Supreme Court. The decision stated that the county and state had illegally taken the *Anishinaabeg* land almost sixty years before.

When the war chief's grandson slapped his beaded mitt down on the table with that lawsuit, the rusty wheels in Washington began to move again. Like Rumplestiltskin awakening from a deep slumber, the Departments of Justice and Interior launched an investigation into land titles on White Earth, rubbed the *miiniingwaan*, or eye boogers, from their eyes, and began to dig out of the archives the yellowing affidavits and paper signed by the likes of Lucky Waller, Mindemoyen, Chi Makwa, and Minnogeeshig. As the dust particles were blown off the papers and deeds in the archival vaults, the dust blew into the air of the northwoods and cornfields, the lakes and prairies, and all that was old and resting remembered their words, thumbprints, and blood samples taken by land agents and anthropologists. They stirred from their long restless sleep, listening for the sound of their language, their beadwork and jingle dresses, and their drums.

The federal investigators opened file after file, awkwardly repeating name after name, until a third of the ancestors were awake, clamoring for their bones, beadwork, and land. The more files opened, the worse the situation appeared. There was no straightforward answer, the government investigators said, as to how the land had ended up in others' hands. Some land had been taken for taxes, which under federal law was illegal. Much had been taken with the stroke of a pen and the print of a thumb from a full blood, none of which was legal. Others had simply been cheated out of their land with a threat plied by a torch and a mysterious fire.

It was the law and it was news. The same *Detroit Lakes Tribune* that had carried perplexed reports seventy years before concerning the strange land transactions now reported again with similar astonishment on the findings. The newspaper published four full pages of legal notices issued to farmers and townspeople alike. The article said the federal government and the agency had placed all their land titles in question and that the federal agency said much of the land on the reservation had been procured illegally. The list of legal notices had originated in the Federal Register and was required to be publicly posted so as to inform all parties of the legal status of their land. As Bob Grist looked down the list he saw the names of everyone who had received certified letters: his neighbors, relatives, and classmates.

He found it difficult to believe how much it hurt simply to see his family's name printed in the newspaper.

It was several days later that Norman Grist sat across the desk from his banker who had supplied him with operating loans for the past twenty years. Norman laid his balance sheets on the big oak desk and told the banker he needed thirty-five thousand dollars for seed, fertilizer, fuel, and a little bit for his hired hand.

The banker's eyes met his, and Norman felt the anxiety bite into his stomach again, just as when he had received the certified letter.

"I can't do it, Norm," was all the banker said.

Norman was silent. Finally, the banker broke the quiet.

"I'll be straight with you, Norm," he said, nervously twirling his golden pen around his manicured fingers. "Ever since this title question, your land ain't worth nothing."

"What you mean, it ain't worth nothing?" Norman fired back.

"It ain't worth nothing 'cause your title ain't clear."

Norman was silent again. And again the banker broke the silence.

"That's the way that it is," he said, "and I am very, very sorry about it."

Norman felt the fear turning his stomach. Suddenly an image from his childhood jumped into his head: he and his father working side by side clearing stones from their fields, and then sitting in the shade of a tree eating a glorious picnic lunch brought out to them by his mother. A feeling of intense hatred toward the banker filled his soul, focusing all of his fear and anger on this one man. Then, just as quickly as the hatred had come, it went away, and he felt like the young boy that had worked the fields so long ago. Wearily, he spoke to the banker, talking not like businessmen, but like a friend asking for help:

"What am I supposed to do, Chuck?" he said. "I got all kinds of loans and they all expect to be paid."

The banker shook his head.

"I don't know, Norm. I just don't know."

When Norman Grist told the story to Bob at the kitchen table, Bob looked into his father's face and thought he had aged ten years within a handful of days. He was suddenly an old man, small and fragile. For the first time in his life, Bob Grist took charge.

With a copy of the newspaper list in hand, Bob and Jane looked up the people's phone numbers and made fifty phone calls inviting them all to a potluck at the resort to discuss the problem.

On a crisp fall evening, Jane looked out the window at the pickup trucks and sedans filling the resort parking lot. Men with tanned faces and seed caps emerged from the driver's seats as women with pantsuits or flowered dresses under big sweaters came from the passenger's side. The women carried hot dishes, Jell-O salads, and homemade cookies. Bob greeted the Jiworskys, the Spaakers, and other big farmers from Mahnomen and some of the smaller farmers from the Ponsford Prairie.

The resort dining room was soon packed with grim-faced men and women. Everyone dined on the hot dishes, talking quietly among themselves. When the cookies and coffee were served, Bob passed out some government papers he had picked up at the library on the title situation. Whatever enjoyment people seemed to have had from the food waned with the papers. Bob broke the ice.

"Glad you all finally made it out to our resort, although I wish it was under better circumstances." He felt uncharacteristically confident, a sense of leadership emerging. "We've got some problems with these Indian claims, and we thought we should try to come up with a plan to fix the problem. My dad, here," he motioned to his father, "we've been told we have bad title on eighty acres. And I know most of you are in the same boat."

"Hell, you've got eighty but we've got one hundred and sixty with bad title," a farmer named Henderson from the prairie interrupted. "Most of it is sowed up in corn already. The bank is saying they're gonna pull our operating loan, and you can be sure as hell the FHA is going to pull the whole works if we fall behind at all. The pissin' thing is I've been good to the Indian all these years, so I can't see why they'd take it out on me."

A couple of farmers voiced their support, and then another stood. "What I can't understand is how we could have bought this land in the first place if it didn't have good title. After all, my Dad paid good money to the Indians for the land, so how could that be illegal?"

From the back, Miles Spaaker called out, "We shouldn't have to pay them twice for it."

"It's not the Indians' fault," John Makela said loudly from the midst of the murmurs and nods. He was a tall, lanky man in a plaid shirt with rolled-up sleeves. The room went silent as all eyes turned to him. Forks rested now on plates. "This has to do with the federal government screwing us all up, and they only just figured it out."

"How do you figure?" Bob asked finally. This kind of talk made him uncomfortable and made the situation more difficult. Things suddenly were not so black and white. He was wondering at the thought.

"Well, according to what I've been reading, all of this here land was originally the White Earth Reservation, and it was supposed to belong to the Indians," Makela continued. The tension mounted, and sighs and more murmurs surrounded him.

"Hell, the whole country was supposed to belong to the Indians, but that was a hell of a long time ago," Kenny Jiworsky blurted out. There were a few laughs, and some of the tension eased.

"This here, though," Makela rebutted, undaunted, "was a place the Indians thought they would keep, only it didn't work that way. Somehow, the land got taken from them here too. There was a lot of crazy things that went on."

"Yeah, but that was then and this is now," Bob Grist said authoritatively, with a sense of being on the prevailing side. "What the hell are we supposed to do about something that happened a long time ago. Everyone knows that a lot of things happened way back then, but we can't be responsible for 'em now."

"That's right," Makela agreed. "But we've got to figure out a way to fix it up."

"I think we should get legal counsel," Jane Grist volunteered. "There must be some attorneys that know how to deal with these Indians."

"Hell, lawyers are high priced and usually only get you more confused," said Warren Danielson, a resort owner from the south side of Many Point Lake. He was skeptical, a weathered man of the northwoods who had lived through many seasons of bounty and scarcity. "I think we should kick some ass."

"Getting a lawyer is a good idea," Henderson said. "And we should do some research besides. My sister-in-law works for the BIA in Cass Lake, and she might give us some information on what exactly these claims mean and what to do about them."

"Good, good," said Bob, relieved to finally hear some ideas. "So who wants to do what and how are we going to pay for it?"

"Well, I'll put up a hundred bucks for a lawyer if the rest of you reach into your deep pockets too," Henderson volunteered. Soon Jane was passing an International Harvester baseball cap around to collect checks and cash. Judy Makela counted the money when it came in and found $1,362 in the hat.

"That's a good start," Bob said, very much feeling to be a leader now.

There were some sounds of approval and a few questions. Warren Danielson interrupted, unconvinced by the plans. "So what are we supposed to do about our title in the meantime? And how do we know that this will stop these Indians for the long run? I'm sick of them all. The only good ones are those Indians I find in graves in the back of my place."

As people started to get excited, the meeting disintegrated into a number of small conversations. Others rose to leave, packing up cold casserole dishes, and shaking Bob's and Jane's hands at the door.

Bob stopped Warren Danielson as he was leaving. "What you were saying back there reminds me," Bob said. "I heard you got some kind of contract to let a university archaeologist dig up your back forty acres?"

"Shhh," said Warren, holding up his finger to his lips and emitting a mock laugh. "Don't tell my secret, or everyone will do it. Sure, I got a good deal with the university. They let their students dig up my old field there and pay me a little something for the privilege of playing in the dirt. They say there's some nice old beadwork and a few old squaws out there."

"I suppose it don't hurt to dig them up if you can make money at it," Bob agreed, not really sure how he felt. "Any idea whose graves they are?"

"Well, if you can keep a secret . . ." Warren began. "They're supposed to be graves from that old man Mesabe's family, but don't you go tell anyone because I don't want any of those Indian drunkards coming after my scalp."

As Bob watched Danielson leave and walk to his pickup, his thoughts jumped back thirty years to the incident with Lucy St. Clair. His father never noticed the knife scars on his stomach, but his wife did, years later. He told Jane they were from a farming accident, and it was the only time he had ever lied to her. Then he remembered seeing Lucy St. Clair in town a couple Saturdays ago, and she looked as beautiful and as distant as ever—and she only looked through him as if he were invisible. He thought then of the graves of his own grandfather and grandmother who had worked to carve out the family's farm on which the title was now in dispute. This trouble with the land hurt him, and he suddenly had a sense that it must hurt the Indians too. Originally, it had seemed to him that if white people wanted the land and the Indians wouldn't have that, then the Indians had to be the bad guys. That seemed strange. He didn't truly hate Indians the way Warren Danielson or even his own father did, and he couldn't say he ever had, but then he didn't like them too much either. And, then, there was something else wrong too. It didn't seem right to dig up graves. No matter who or why or where, the dead should be left alone.

THE OLD ONES
1989

Moose Hanford was a man with little regard for the American concept of private property. It wasn't that he was unable to read the signs that said No Trespassing or Keep Out, it's just that those signs made no sense whatsoever in his particular order of things.

Hanford came from a Marten Clan family from Naytahwaush, a village named after an old man who lived there at the turn of the century. A long time back, his father's family had lived there and cared for one of the Big Drums. His father's family's trapline was over in the Buckboard Hills, and they spent a third of the year or so on that land. His ma's family were Pillagers from Cass Lake. They had land just south of Mesabe's folks on Many Point Lake. Most years, they trapped and hunted near the Buckboards, but about every three years or so, they would let the land rest and go to the "southern" trapline, as they called it, near Many Point and Round Lakes. This was about twelve miles as the crow flies but more like two days by horse, which was how they used to travel.

His old people knew every bit of that land. They knew exactly when to go to a stream in the spring for spearing, when the berries were ripe in each area, where the deer would go and how many to take. They knew both of their traplines because their lives depended on it. Eighty years ago, his great-grandfather, Namaybin Minnogeeshig, would reach right into those beaver houses and count the beavers and their sizes so as to know how many to take each year. That was why things sustained for all those years and also accounted for why they knew when to give the land a rest.

Namaybin Minnogeeshig was something like a "tally man" or hunting boss. He kept a count of all the animals taken and still remaining on that land. He also made sure that things were done properly and that all of the families had enough food from their land. If someone came up short, his grandfather would always find a way to help them out. That's the way things worked then. No one really owned it, they more or less shared the land, even after the government said that this certain piece here belonged to that certain family. Things never worked the same on the land as they did in a government plat book.

It was on account of all this that Moose did not have much understanding of how a man in Minneapolis who came up two or three times a year to his summer cottage could say he owned the land and could post No Trespassing signs on it.

It was October of 1989 when Moose found the old people. He had set up his pop-up tent camper on the Camp 7 Road, south of Many Point and within someone's enclave of No Trespassing signs. Moose wanted to get an early start hunting. He was a man who did not like his meat with a stamp on it and that meant hunting was his only option. This time he brought his nephew, Elijah. Like most Indians on White Earth, they went out a few weeks before the white man's deer season began, simply because no one wanted to get shot by a crowd of city boys driving deer through the reservation.

Yesterday's thin blanket of snow had disappeared in the late afternoon warmth. Now a sheet of frost greeted the hunter. Moose awoke first and reached to the stove to turn on the gas burner for coffee. He listened to the short, even breathing of the teenage boy and saw his own breath billow as a cloud of mist in the early morning. As he heard the sound of water boiling, he sat up and quickly threw on a flannel shirt and pants over his long johns.

"Damn cold," he told himself. He pulled on his rubber boots, carefully poured himself a cup of coffee, and sat back down. He pulled his hair out of his eyes and smoothed his braid from yesterday. It would need to be re-braided. He sighed and went outside to look at the day.

A flicker sat on a branch above him, peering down. He acknowledged the bird in turn. He took three steps down and said some prayers of thanks for hunting. He placed a small mound of tobacco under the flicker's tree and then took a long pee.

Frost dusted the leaves, and he felt the cold against his face. A slight wind blew from the northwest. He reached inside the camper door and pulled out a tin pail. He wet his hands to wash his face. Then he returned inside to rouse the boy.

The man and boy walked deer trails toward the east and then cut back to the north looking for more signs. They finally found tracks of a big buck and followed him through a slough where he had intended to hide from them. Most hunters, the deer figured, would not bother with an animal in a foot and a half of water. Indians crossed all that and more, especially Moose, who had stalked through rice paddies in Vietnam.

On the edge of the slough, Moose noticed the tracks of an all-terrain vehicle. As far as he knew, no one had trapped or hunted back there for years and few Indians would use a three-wheeler in the woods.

"You stay here and keep an eye on that deer. I'm going to check these tracks," he said to Elijah, adding, "Don't take a shot until I get back." Just for precaution.

"Alright," said the boy, noticeably disappointed but obedient to his uncle.

Moose turned down the tracks. "Damn white people," he whispered bitterly. "I wonder what they're dumping in the woods this time."

About a hundred feet farther, a clearing was cut in the brush, revealing around fifteen or twenty *jiibegamig* or gravehouses used for old people. The small pine houses were the length of the bodies and approximately two and a half feet high. He estimated the houses were around eighty years old and most of them pretty well broken down. That is, the ones that were left. Someone had dismantled ten of the houses. They were each piled on the northeast corner of the clearing in a specific order.

This was something no Ojibwe would do; Moose was sure of that. For a few seconds he debated the options and consequences and then decided to take a closer look. He reached into his shirt pocket and took out some tobacco and a medicine to keep away any evil. The tobacco he held in his hand, the other medicine he put in his mouth. He did not fear that a *jiibay* or ghost would come for him, but the disturbance of the dead was a serious violation in the order of things.

Near the violated graves, his heartbeat quickened. A number had been cleared off entirely, and in three graves, the contents had been removed. In these graves, the beadwork, medicine pouches, and other items were gone. What remained were bones, bleached and in a jumble with clothes, leather scraps, and tattered material still on them.

All three bodies lay from east to west. Judging from the size of the remains, he was looking at a woman and a child. Next to each grave were the grave markers, each about two feet high with clan signs imprinted on them. The grave markers indicated that one women was Bear Clan and the small child was from the Sucker Clan. A third had a horse carved into its marker, but there were no Horse Clan on White Earth. He wondered. Then he looked closer: There were two long braids of hair laying separated from the body that was in the process of being excavated.

The tools and excavation equipment looked professional, and a series of numbered stakes marked off the various locations in the site.

Moose had seen enough. He took his tobacco and placed it near the faces of the women and the child.

Then he tried to comprehend what he saw. This was not a simple looting. Obvious care had been taken of the bodies and the contents. That left government or university researchers. Then there was the question of who approved it. The diggings were not on public land; this was private land. The boy scout camp was near here, but this also could be Warren Danielson's so-called property. That he could determine from a map.

Finally came the question of who those ancestors were. He hoped they were not his family: His family told of Bear Clan, but they knew of themselves as Marten Clan. They might be his relatives, but he hoped not. He swallowed hard. No one spoke of where his own great-grandmother, Ishkwegaabawiikwe, was buried. He hoped now that he had not found her. This property was due north of his great-grandfather Namaybin Minnogeeshig's allotment.

His chest hurt now, a deep ache, something that was not merely physical. He felt a tear swell in his eye. Then the ache again. Slowly, he walked back to the boy in the woods.

"*Ambe,*" he said softly. "No hunting today. We'll let that buck rest."

The boy looked disappointed but then saw his uncle's face. He knew something was wrong.

"Are you OK, Uncle? You look different."

"I am different," Moose said. "I'm changed. I've seen death before, but not like that."

The boy looked frightened. "What did you see?"

"Some *Chimookomaanag* took those ancestors out of their graves," he said using the old terms and then translating, "The white man is digging up our old people and disturbing the past."

"*Howah*, you're kidding!"

"I wouldn't joke about a thing like that, my boy. Not something like that."

THE REZ WAR
1990

Lucy St. Clair's glossy black jingle dress shimmered in the hot sun of the June fourteenth powwow. As she moved rhythmically, the silver cones sang her name and punctuated her steps. A graceful dancer, she fully enjoyed the celebration that was *niimiidiwin*, the powwow.

While other Ojibwe jingle dress dancers demurely carried large eagle-feather fans behind which they modestly observed the other dancers and the crowd, Lucy would have none of it. Her dance outfit, dreamed of and made from her own hand, included a lavishly quilled pouch for a skinning knife and a small hatchet with an intricately beaded handle. This she would often raise aloft, and on occasion, whirl as she slowly revolved in her small steps. An imposing figure in her everyday clothes, her dance outfit was daunting. No woman of sanity would cut in front of her, and only the lovesick or a brazen idiot would catch her eye as she circled the arbor.

Lucy St. Clair had always been theatrical. If an unwelcome suitor tried to court her affections, she could just as easily ignore him as she could flaunt her skinning knife. If an unwitting soul slurred her family, they might receive a black eye. And when she had grown sick and tired of the tribal politics and plans to begin new logging on tribal land and erect a state-of-the-art paper mill, she simply filled the gas tanks of the logging truck engines with Crystal sugar and torched the brand-new thirty-five-thousand-dollar pickup truck that was the pride of the tribal chairman.

After all these years, Lucy was still one of the most striking women on the reservation and attracted a tenacious flock of admiring men wherever she sauntered. She called White Earth village home and came from a poor family of the housing project known as Hungry Hill, overlooking the relative opulence of the tribal office building. This was as opposed to those few who had tribal government jobs or had "succeeded" by intermarrying with non-Indian farmers. Lucy's resources for survival were her beauty and her brains.

Her wit kept her alive through the public schools and ensured the ongoing wrath of corporal punishment. Indian kids needed extra discipline, the white principal decided, and Saucy Lucy needed an extralarge dosage. The lockups and corporal punishment administered by the principal only made her hatred more intense. Then, when farm kids would taunt her, she retaliated and beat the shit out of them, just for good measure. After more than one attempted dog pile, she emerged torn and dirty, but the only one standing.

As she grew older, she excelled in the use of her looks to get what she wanted. Men circled around her like moths near a light bulb. They would shamelessly chase her until she decided if she would offer part of herself to them. She would draw them close, and then when the proximity became too much, she would lash out and send them reeling toward any refuge they could find.

By the time she was twenty, jackrolling became her specialty. She and her cousin Juliet had moved to the greener pastures of Minneapolis, staying in the upstairs of their Auntie Hilda's bungalow. At first, they worked the usual bars. Lucy and Juliet would find the best-dressed and best-looking white men and saunter over. Within the next hour and a half, the women would have lulled the prey into submission with the promise of Indian bliss. The men would order up high-class drinks to impress them, and in the process, lose their senses while the women let the ice cubes melt in their own drinks as they grew warm and stale. At an appointed time, Lucy and Juliet would escort the intoxicated men outside, and as the men fumbled with their clothes, the girls would grab their wallets and run.

If Lucy was good, she could make two hundred dollars a night, especially at the beginning of the month. As their bravado and wardrobes amassed, Lucy and Juliet moved to higher-priced bars and richer white men. To the girls, jackrolling was a game as well as a good living, and it became a steady job until Auntie Hilda caught on to the girls' new clothes and late hours. In March 1975, Auntie Hilda packed them both up and sent them back to the reservation via Greyhound.

Lucy was hard and fearless. Life had taught her that white men control power and money in society, and that society made sure she stayed in her place. Since her place was poor and lacking in control of her own destiny, she came to hate the whole system. Life had also taught her that survival was intimately linked to how one used what one had, and to brute force. In most cases she would alternate between these tactics, and thus she managed to succeed in most of her pursuits, that is, within the realm she was able to work. Over the years, the experiences formed her view of reality, and as a result, she often overreacted to situations and came out with both guns blazing when she only needed to jackroll, or perhaps to leave the situation well enough alone.

When word got around of new clear cutting on White Earth, Lucy's response was typically theatrical.

For the past year, the tribal government had been lavishly entertained by a number of large corporations interested in logging the land and building a pulp plant expansion on the reservation. Finally, Potlatch, a British conglomerate, leased almost half of the tribal land from the tribal government and entered an agreement to build a new mill.

After years of having trees and land stolen out from underneath their feet, giving away reservation land for logging and milling was the final straw. A group of people concerned about the government's dealings met one evening at the elders housing unit and formed a group called the Protect Our Land Coalition. In a quick vote, Elaine Mandamin was made its leader. The coalition wrote a letter to the tribal government demanding an open meeting about the logging proposal. The reservation government never bothered to answer.

Lance Wagosh was the tribal chairman. He had been in office for going on sixteen years now, running the reservation with an iron hand based on *Patronage, Privilege, and Punishment*. Wagosh knew that the tribal government needed the money the logging and new mill would bring, and that most people on the reservation would welcome the work the mill would offer. He also knew that the contract meant long-term income, and since jobs equaled votes, he liked the political implications for his administration. Neither he nor any other tribal officials had any interest in opening up negotiations to a public forum.

A month after the permit had been granted, a regular meeting of the tribal government became a battleground. Everyone from Protect Our Land was there along with numerous others, some asking for plumbing and electricity to get fixed, some looking for jobs, some lamenting the lack of education funds or requesting funeral expenses, others worried about what the new logging would do to their cemeteries, their hunting and trapping lands, and their medicine plants. But the meeting was a typical council meeting. Few of the issues people wanted to talk about were addressed, the tribal leaders tabling most of the them.

Lucy was sitting on a folding chair near the front of the room as Elaine addressed the council: "We have tried for decades to get our land back from the land stealers, and now you want to simply give away more of it?" But the tribal government was paying no attention. One councilman was asleep, two were talking and giggling, and the chairman was daydreaming of better days and his summer golf tournament. Finally, Lance Wagosh interrupted Elaine and decided simply to adjourn and take up discussion of the timber leases and land issues in private the following morning.

Lucy went from angry to furious to theatrical in a matter of minutes. Without a moment's hesitation, she grabbed a full pitcher of ice water from the council's table and threw it on three of them.

"Wake up, you stupid bastards," she screamed as they abruptly returned to the present. "We're talking to you, and you'd damn well better listen."

Lance Wagosh called for a security guard to remove Lucy, but she promptly slapped the guard across the face.

"I am happy to leave, and on my own," she announced and trotted out.

Her theater had already shown.

Protect Our Land worked over the coming weeks to try to stop any further negotiations with Potlatch or the start of issuing mill permits and construction. The group organized demonstrations in front of the council offices and at the state legislature's environmental quality board in St. Paul, demanding an environmental impact statement. They appealed to the tribal court process and were denied a hearing. In turn, all administrative remedies in the Bureau of Indian Affairs had been either exhausted or ignored by the federal government; a short, terse letter addressed to Elaine stated that the BIA was "washing its hands of an internal matter of sovereignty." And, from what Elaine and the others could see, their own council was not likely to listen to the community anymore.

Money and favors for approving the new mill's permit were already beginning to roll into the council. Lance Wagosh bought a brand spanking new, fully pinstriped, turquoise-colored Chevy extended-cab four-wheel-drive pickup truck, and a new sparkle-finish bass boat with a 150-horsepower Mercury outboard motor appeared on a trailer in the driveway of another representative's house. Relatives of other councilmen began bragging of coming jobs and big paychecks. A couple weeks later, yet another council member bought a bass boat. Their license plates read Chief 1, Chief 2, and Chief 3, underscoring their modesty and estimations of worth.

Again it was Lucy St. Clair who changed the course of events. It was only a rumor that she was involved in any way, of course, but Elaine knew the secret. Lucy had been busy that night.

Her first stop was in the Buckboard Hills where the skidders and logging equipment were stored for the night around the first lease site. The Potlatch workers had the foresight to lockup all of their machines, but where there's a will there's a way. While the loggers slept free of worries, Lucy poured a couple of cups of Crystal white sugar into the gas tank of each and every skidder, bulldozer, and logging truck.

Her second stop was at the Shooting Star Casino in Mahnomen. While Lance Wagosh was inside holding an unofficial council meeting over mixed drinks, Lucy found his pinstriped pickup in the parking lot. She waited in the shadows until no one was about, quietly smoking a cigarette, biding her time. Then, under the glare of the parking lot lights, she emptied a gallon of kerosene over the hood of the truck and tossed her lit cigarette into the puddle.

The whole truck did not go up in flames, of course, but most of the front end did. Someone leaving the casino noticed the flicker of the flames, and soon those whose arms weren't stuck to a slot machine emptied into the parking lot. Lance Wagosh was swearing and stumbling around his truck as someone else ran for a fire extinguisher.

Any leads as to who might have ruined the logging equipment or torched the truck were either carried away from the scene or went up in smoke. Elaine sensed who was the perpetrator, though. Lucy had not divulged her secret—she was not the type who needed to brag up her actions or to seek approval from others—but Elaine knew. *"That's OK,"* she said to herself. *"It might have just taken Lucy to get them to sit up and listen. And no one else had the guts to do it."*

Lucy's theater became a source of inspiration, but it also divided the sides even further. Lance Wagosh ordered a new hood and other new parts for his truck, and the bass boats disappeared into garages. All of the council members begin locking up their other assets cultivated from tribal coffers.

The logging equipment was soon back in action, and new locking gas caps fitted to all the machines. But three weeks later, the equipment was torched just the same. Mimicking the style flaunted by Lucy, someone had drenched the machines in gasoline and set them ablaze. This time, however, the effect was final. The trucks were left as charred ruins, and the skidders were burnt-out hulks.

Elaine knew that Lucy was not responsible this time. The Mahnomen County sheriff found George Ahnib walking down Highway 200 with a shit-eating grin on his face and the smell of gasoline all over him. He had done in a million dollars worth of equipment and walked away without a scratch. As the sheriff loaded him into the back of the patrol car, George began howling at the moon.

George sat for two days in the Mahnomen County jail before Elaine, Kway Dole, and others raised enough bail money to get him out. The sheriff's people would not have let him go at all, but they discovered in short order that George had a few cards missing and did not relate well to white people. Besides that, George had a tendency to howl and then break into hysterical fits of laughter. All of this weighed on the district attorney's decision not to oppose bail, and Elaine and attorney Karen Ordstrom successfully argued that George could do no more harm and would be safe on the reservation until trial.

After the fires, the Protect Our Land Coalition attempted once again to meet with the council, but this time Lance Wagosh tried to take a swing at Elaine, only to be stopped by George Ahnib, who quick as a cat, had intervened and admonished the chairman for his crew cut, saying, "Real *ogichidaa* have long hair." When the coalition met the next time, they agreed they had only one way to make themselves heard: They decided to occupy the tribal government offices.

The coalition members had gathered at the elders housing unit once again. Each of the elders, including Mesabe, Charlotte Oshkinnah, and others, had spoken. The old people said that the land needed to be protected and that the logging and new mill would desecrate the water and their sacred places. A young man stood up and said that he would fight to the death to protect the land. Lucy St. Clair, who sat next to Elaine, whispered in her ear that the young man was a drunk. George Ahnib was at the back of the room, swaying to some imagined drum and then beginning his slow men's traditional dance. A few of the young men such as Moose Hanford and Willie Schneider, both Vietnam vets, began to talk about how the takeover could be organized, and George Ahnib interrupted to point out once again that "Real *ogichidaa* have long hair," just in case they needed some clarification. Only a few expressed real fear of the situation.

Together, they had carefully deliberated deep into the night, and finally had come to a consensus agreeing to occupy the tribal government offices. As Elaine looked around the room at Lucy, George Ahnib, Moose, and Willie, she knew it was the right decision, but also knew it was a hard decision with which to live.

MANIDOO DEWE'IGAN
THE BIG DRUM
1990

It was several days later when the four women crammed themselves into their war pony of the day, a 1976 Nova sedan. Their natural form of communication was usually a series of giggles, but they stifled the laughter today and concentrated on the solemn nature of their journey. They had been preparing for this journey, and the time was now. Their minds were clear, hearts set on their task.

Elaine's grandfather, Mesabe, had given her detailed instructions. Then the old man sat with the four women, telling the stories of the drum's arrival to White Earth, the story of Ishkwegaabawiikwe and Situpiwin, the old ones like Chi Makwa, Minnogeeshig, his own grandmother Mindemoyen, and others. He told how the drum spread to the other reservations, and then how it had been sleeping at White Earth. He instructed them next on a drum song, and how to greet this relative of the Anishinaabeg. "You can't talk about the history of White Earth without telling the story of the drums," he said. "The drums are the history of White Earth." That Mesabe was clear on.

They all listened. The tall, thin young woman with tattooed knuckles was his granddaughter, Elaine. Kway Dole was her contemporary since grade school, and today was a muscular and beautiful army veteran. Maggie Jourdain, the eternal caretaker, was the plump matriarch of White Earth village. Danielle Wabun was the outspoken daughter of Indian leader Warren Wabun. They were the mothers of their nation, like it or not.

"The Episcopal church rafters?" Kway Dole gasped and placed a hand over her mouth in a mixture of astonishment and wonder at the gravity of the sacrilege.

Maggie quickly crossed herself.

"No, it's ingenious," said Danielle. "Your grandpa is a genius. No one messes with the church."

True to form, vandals and bored teenagers had struck many a building and house on the reservation through the years, but not the church. Amidst the chaos of the times, that institution still had a hold even the most rebellious elements of the community would respect.

The sage burned, a pungent odor carried to the trees by a stiff breeze of spring. Embers smoldered and burned again. Smudging themselves with the sage, they prepared for the mission. Tobacco loaded in the pipe, Mesabe made a prayer for them and blessed them again, proud of the young women.

Now, finally, they drove toward town, stopping their war-pony Nova in front of the small white clapboard building. Elaine turned the key off, but the car continued to sputter until it finally quit. Elaine looked at Kway. "What an entrance."

"I sure hope it starts again," Kway responded. "Hate to have to call for a ride."

The four women crawled out of the car, mounting the stairs to the church. Elaine stepped forward, knocking boldly now.

The janitor, an old Ojibwe man named John Brown, shuffled to the door, opening it and looking with surprise at the women. His puzzled look gave way to a quiet smile. He had rarely seen these women in church, so he suspected their motives were different. He sized them up again. He smiled.

"I suppose you're here for that drum," John Brown said in a whisper.

The women looked at each other tentatively and then nodded in unison.

"Eh heh," he said and smiled again. All of the women smiled now at the old man.

"It's here," he said. "I make sure it's OK. Never touch it. Just make sure it is OK. Never let anyone else touch it either."

The old janitor winked at the women.

"*Biindigiin.* Come inside. *Ambay.* Follow me, I'll show you."

The old man pointed to the attic stair. "*Iwedi. Ishpeming.* Upstairs."

The stairs creaked under the janitor's weight. The women glanced at each other, their faces marked with both trepidation and anticipation. Then they followed the janitor.

They came into the darkness of the attic. The janitor turned on a hidden switch, and yellow light from a solitary bulb dimly lit the room. It was filled with moldy prayer books and tattered Bibles, memorabilia of past priests, deacons, funerals, and weddings, all a chronology of their village. The path meandered through the generations, until in the back corner the janitor stopped.

"Here it is, here it is," the old man said excitedly.

The women looked about them but saw nothing but mouse droppings, spider webs, and dustballs. They feared the old man was mistaken and the drum was gone. Elaine was overcome with sudden sadness.

Then the old man looked upward.

Elaine followed his eyes and looked up as well.

"*Aniin Dewe'igan. Aniin Oshkabewis. Aniin Dewe'igan,*" the janitor said in a reverent whisper.

Elaine let out her breath, not realizing that she had been holding it. Slowly relaxing, she inhaled the scent of age. Her eyes got used to the dark above, and she saw an old cedar box nestled in the church rafters.

"Look," said the old man, "look, here it is."

The four women gathered close while the old man proudly looked up at the drum and then at the women. Kway found a chair and pushed it toward Elaine. Maggie ushered forth another and passed it to Kway. They all looked at each other again. They took a few deep breaths, and it seemed like an eternity as they stood between the old and the new.

"*Ambay, Ambay,*" Maggie Jourdain urged them on.

Elaine stepped onto the old chair and carefully tested it for her weight. She stood and slowly raised her arms to touch the cedar box in the rafters, gray with age, still solid. She touched it again carefully, and whispered, *"Aniin Odewe'igan. Aniin Odewei'gan."*

"Help me," she said, looking toward Kway.

Kway climbed onto the other chair and raised herself next to her friend. With great care and determination, they lowered the drum from its hiding place.

"Aniin Odewei'gan."

They carefully placed the box on the floor, then reassembled around it. Slowly, Elaine opened the lid, turning the latch on the top, then pulling back the creaking door until the box stood open before them.

The drum face was gray with age and slightly concave. Beneath the dust, a faded yellow and blue face was faint yet present. Yet it was clear that nothing, not even rodents or insects, had encroached on its sacred space. The old man had kept his word. The beads on the black velvet stood out clearly, and most of the beadwork was still tight. Old greasy yellow beads, translucent purples and reds, clan signs, bears, thunderbirds, fish, and the floral patterns told the stories. Silver cones adorned the skirt of the drum. It was beautiful and the women were breathless, hesitant to touch it. But they could not hold themselves back. They carefully placed their tobacco on the drum face, tracing it gently with their hands, touching the signs and symbols. They could not help touching the velvet, touching the women from a century before.

Together they began to hum the song Mesabe had taught them, a traveling song, intended to safely move the people from one place to another. The traveling song resonated from the rafters of the Episcopal church, the ribcage of the beast.

Back at his house, Mesabe sat in his chair, knocking his cane against the table leg in a slow rhythm. Then he raised his voice in the traveling song.

PART III

The
Occupation

THE BEAUTY
OF JUNKED CARS

The strange doings of White Earth village were observed with interest from the nearby housing project of Hungry Hill. The people leaned in their doors or perched on porches throughout the spring night, drank coffee, called across to their neighbors, and discussed from the sidelines the reconfiguration of their village.

Most of Selam Big Bear's junk car lot had been relocated to the perimeters of the tribal government offices during the night. The takeover had been swift and orderly, the logistics of the operation organized by a group of Vietnam veterans led by Moose Hanford. Mesabe's pipe ceremony to bless the *ogichidaaweg*, or warriors, earlier that evening had launched the offensive. They moved in at eleven on a Monday night, politely excusing the tribal government's security guard and borrowing from the maintenance room the keys to the bulldozers and tractors. With the efficiency of a tightly run military maneuver, the heavy equipment hauled the junked cars from Selam's collection and deposited them at the tribal offices. Like a settler of old circling the wagons for defense, Willie Schneider drove the tribal bulldozer, nudging the old sedans, crashed vans, immobilized pickups, and a few charred remains of unidentifiable war ponies into a circle around the office building to create a perimeter. Moose had theorized that strategically positioned junk cars and pickups would make excellent sentry posts.

Selam Big Bear returned with a few truckloads of his winter fire-
wood, and the logs, as well as sandbags, were packed in between the
junked cars. The *ogichidaaweg* had completed a barricade behind which
the Indians could now make their stand. Elaine, Lucy St. Clair, and
Kway Dole arrived soon after in Elaine's Nova, the car riding heavy in
the rear due to its trunk load of deer hunting rifles and boxes of
cartridges happily loaned to them by friends and neighbors across the
reservation.

This had been one of the most organized occupations in recent
history, although it too had its share of complications. They had come
up with a steering council consisting of traditional elders and representatives from the different villages. And, in this instance, they had
the luxury of a week or so of prior planning and the benefit of a
number of previous takeovers of tribal offices and the BIA building in
Washington in the 1970s from which to draw experience. Meetings
leading up to the occupation had laid the groundwork for most of the
logistics, and this time the White Earth people were prepared.

Moose flipped through his notebook now. His planning map of
the site had been largely realized: four sentry posts, junk cars and logs
for a border, and two entrances, one large enough for cars and another
the back way up to the housing project for people and emergencies.
The command center was located in the tribal offices where they
inherited the council's phones with direct WATTS lines, fax, radios,
computers, office supplies, television set, and kitchen.

Moose was satisfied. From atop a crashed Chevrolet Impala that
served as a sentry post, he radioed Elaine in the command center that
all was ready.

The night was still and quiet. The tribal government's bulldozers
and tractors were parked amongst the cars in the barricade, and many
of the coalition members, as well as the housing project inhabitants,
were sleeping, waiting for morning when the excitement would begin. Only a handful of sentries kept watch, sitting on the trashed vinyl
seats of wrecked cars with their .30–06s in one hand and a cup of hot
coffee in the other.

At eight in the morning, the tribal council secretary would arrive
to unlock the office and discover the occupation. She would probably
call Lance Wagosh, who would call the Becker County sheriff, who

would call the FBI. By eight-thirty at the latest, police officers and sheriff's deputies would be everywhere, and the FBI would be on its way. The media would turn out, and the bureaucrats in Washington would go crazy.

But for now, all was silent. It was a beautiful, peaceful night, the moon shining down on the perimeter of cars, illuminating the peeling paint, rust, and dents in luminous blue light, reflecting off the starred windshields and pitted chrome. Moose stood on the roof of the junked Ford and watched the stars.

DENVER—
NINGAÀBII'ANONG
(THE WEST)

The wire machine quit printing, and Alanis Nordstrom picked up the first page of the Associated Press story. Her breathing stopped short when she saw it was about Indians, *her* Indians.

White Earth, Minn. (AP) — Indians today on the Minnesota White Earth Reservation took over the tribal government offices, burnt cars and trucks, and are holding hostages inside. The sky was filled with the black smoke of the burning vehicles as FBI and federal troops amassed on a hillside nearby. The Indians are reported to be armed and dangerous. They have issued no demands as of yet. . . .

At her desk was a note from her editor telling her to get on the story *now*.

Alanis was the "Indian reporter" for the *Rocky Mountain News*. The large Denver newspaper was one of the few papers that had decided Indians, at least light-colored ones, could cover Indian stories fairly. Other major newspapers still believed white reporters were more objective and knowledgeable in covering Native issues than Indians themselves. Either way, Alanis was qualified enough. She had a degree in economics from Stanford, two years of journalism school, and four years of experience when the paper hired her. She was a safe bet.

Alanis made several phone calls, and then booked a flight to Minneapolis and on to Bemidji. On her way from the newspaper building, she spoke briefly with her editor to get out of covering the Miss Indian America contest so she could concentrate on this story.

Professional experience and her own personal background taught her to start with Indians when researching Indian stories. She pulled her Saab into the parking lot at the Native American Rights Fund building. NARF was involved in a slew of Indian lawsuits across the country concerning hunting and treaty rights as well as other issues. For outfits like the *Rocky Mountain News*, the law firm was the "authority" on Indians. Alanis also had a good friend in the NARF library with a list of contacts.

By the time Alanis reached the library, the librarian had already pulled several files for the reporter in response to Alanis's earlier phone call.

"Hello, how's my best source?" Alanis said appreciatively to the other woman. The librarian looked up from her papers, then smiled. Almost opposites in color and shape, Linda Chavez was a Pueblo, short, and the brown of a walnut shell. She was dressed in a floral polyester outfit highlighted by turquoise jewelry. Alanis on the other hand was five foot nine, lanky, and some three shades lighter.

"Nice to see you," Linda said. "You gave me a run for my money this time."

She reached for a folder and began reading.

"Well, Alanis," Linda said, obviously pleased to be of help. "It seems that there is a big problem with the land up at White Earth. According to our files, they've had about fifteen federal investigations into the land situation since the turn of the century and almost as many pieces of legislation. In the end, they still don't appear to have gotten any of that land back; non-Indians still have ninety percent of it. Unfortunately, it looks like our records are short for two reasons. First, they aren't our clients, and second, if anyone was a client of ours, it would probably be the tribal council. Between you and me, I've heard they're a big part of the problem up there."

"What do you mean?" Alanis asked, sensing a possibility.

"Well, you know my husband, Buddy. He's from White Earth, and according to his relatives, the council is at the center of this current mess."

"Is this about Indians and casinos?"

"No, not exactly. See, the White Earth people have been trying to get their land back for years, and now suddenly the council signed some big leases with a logging company. This logging deal has pushed it all over the edge. The council is getting rich and flaunting it. Rumors are that last year the chairman made over two hundred fifty thousand dollars, while most of the reservation is dirt poor. Buddy says that the council acts more like white people everyday."

"So the council is corrupt?" Alanis tried to simplify the story.

"Well, I wouldn't really say that; but you should check it out."

"Well, you're a wealth of information," Alanis said gratefully, remembering why she came. "It must be that small world that is Indian country, or maybe you just have one of those strategic inter-tribal marriages."

Linda blushed and smiled, "Mergers and acquisition, you know how that goes. And here's my husband's cousin's number if you need it."

Alanis saw that the name was Elaine Mandamin. She tucked the number into her notebook.

Alanis piled everything into the passenger seat of her Saab and took a deep breath. She needed to see her friend Browning Teaman at the Indian Center before she caught her flight. She had a good sense that there was more than one story here.

Alanis had gone to school with Browning. He was the original Comanche renaissance man: a bureaucrat, father, traditional dancer, and one of the best-known emcees at powwows nationally. At the powwows, the multitudes were punished with his never-ending humor. And, by traveling nationally, he was a gold mine of information. He probably knew more about Indian communities from California to Chicago than anyone else.

The big man looked up as she entered his office.

"Well, howdy there, Alanis," he said as his brown hand reached across to her.

"Hello, Browning," she said, with relief. Somehow, he always made her feel secure. "Thanks for seeing me on such short notice. I see you've got another one of your beautiful ribbon shirts from your wife, *heh?*"

Browning was an impeccable dresser, thanks in part to his wife, who painstakingly prepared his wardrobe for business and socials. "You know those Otoes," he said, referring to his wife. "They're such perfectionists."

"Lucky for you," she said. "Maybe you know an Oto man for me; I could use some help like that myself."

"You're OK, Alanis—although over time, we expect you to stop looking like a yuppie," he chuckled. "Anyway, I can't gab. You know I'm a busy Comanche today. So what is it you are after?"

"Browning, the funniest thing is that here is a Chippewa to ask you about Chippewas. You know my family is from White Earth, but having only been there a few times, I don't really know much about it. And now that all hell breaks loose, I need some help."

Browning smiled. "Chippewa are strange people, and all of this illustrates that. I have been at the White Earth powwow for the past two years now, and I am still not exactly sure what is going on there. Your family is from Pine Point, right?"

Alanis nodded. "And some of my folks still live there. Just a couple of branches moved out during the relocation days."

"Well, those folks are Pillagers and others are Mississippi with a few Pembinas mixed in. They all got put together at White Earth. Anyway, from what I hear, this stuff has been going on a long time. Those people all got screwed by the feds and the white folks, and now some of their own are screwing them too."

"That's kind of what I figured. The old 'lateral oppression,' *heh?*"

"Well, that's about as basic as you get. Now all I know for sure, is that the council puts on a pretty good powwow, with dancers from all over. They pay well and on time; but besides that powwow, not much else is holding up. I got some friends who live there, pretty good dancers and all. Two of those brothers were in 'Nam with me. I don't think they side with the council, and I think you could talk to 'em. Let me find a number."

Alanis relaxed. It always paid off to see Browning; he seemed to put things into order. Browning extracted a number from his meticulously organized address book and passed it to her. Alanis looked at the perfect boarding school penmanship and found the names, Moose Hanford and Willie Schneider.

"Moose was a point man in 'Nam. He's a good dancer. Willie was also in 'Nam with me. Say hello to him for me and be careful of him, yourself. If Willie's not snagged yet, you're just about his type."

"Miigwech," Alanis said, adding, "for all the prospects."

"Giga-waabamin miinawaa," he said and laughed when a puzzled look spread across her face. "That's Chippewa for 'See you again.'"

As Alanis boarded the Northwest flight to Minneapolis, she looked at all the tired businessmen in their tired suits. She settled into her seat and kicked off her shoes. She pulled a Tony Hillerman mystery out of the side of her bag. She read a few pages and then stated to nod off, too tired for even Detective Jim Chee. She lapsed into that space between dream and wakefulness, and her mind wandered to White Earth. Her memories were dim. *Smell of wood fires, old cars, old women who pinched her cheeks.* She touched her cheek now, and her hand slowly dropped. She awoke in Minneapolis.

The Bemidji flight was a small commuter, and the airport seemed distant. In the darkness, she looked down at the lights of Bemidji and felt both excitement and exhaustion at the same time. She mustered enough of the former to get into a hotel.

It was her greatest fear that she would return as a ghost, haunting the remotely situated motels of Indian country border towns, credit card in hand, seeking refuge from the howling winds and blizzards that blanket much of what is left to Indian people. Arriving in a billow of snow, the innkeepers would look suspiciously at the ghost when asking, *"How many people will be staying tonight?"* The innkeeper would invariably look over her shoulder at the car outside, peering to see if this Indian ghost woman would be harboring a swarm of insurgents and wild children in the meager motel room. Then the innkeeper would give a look of surprise when the ghost produces a credit card, one that will hold the charge.

This scene repeated itself tonight in Bemidji. She surmised that the Holiday Inn would be accustomed to Indians, especially since three reservations bordered the small town. Tonight her flight arrived late, and she rummaged through her notes for the hotel and rental car information. After a few calls and a wait, she finally arrived, somewhat disheveled, in the lobby to register.

"How many people in your party?" The large, freckled reception-ist looked over Alanis's shoulder to the rental car outside. Alanis smiled, acknowledging the ritual.

Alanis pulled a credit card from her billfold, placing it on the counter. Her maroon fingernails clicked on the card, and the woman looked up at her hand, her rings, and the credit card. Alanis wondered about the freckled mind. A large chubby hand reached for the credit card, running it through the electronic billing device. A hesitation, then after a few moments, the key changed hands.

Finally accepted into that bastion of American luxury, Alanis un-loaded her car and straggled exhausted to her room.

GIIWEDAHN
COMING HOME

On the White Earth Reservation border, a signpost held a handmade sign that read simply, "This is ours." Alanis Nordstrom smiled at the sign as she turned her car due west on State Highway 113.

Pines slowly gave way to marshlands and beaver dams. Willows and cattails bordered the lakes with maple and aspen stands rising behind them. As she passed a large maple grove, Alanis peered into the woods at the remains of spring's maple sugar camp. The fifty-five-gallon drums were still there, as was the collection of tin coffee cans. She remembered the smell of wood fires, and for an instant, she could taste the sap, fresh from the tree. The tire tracks into the woods were raw from thaws and rains, but the sap collectors were gone. The maple syrup season had passed.

Above a marsh and adjoining pasture she saw a flock of Canada geese flying north. Alanis eased the car onto the shoulder and stood looking at the birds. There were hundreds of them in an undulating formation, dark against the overcast sky. She rested on the hood of the car and took in the air and the sounds of the geese. The wings made a sound like waves against a wooden boat, their calls breaking the gentle rhythm. She watched as they moved further from her, and then remembered the tobacco in the side of her purse.

Now is the time, she thought, reaching for a pinch. She held some in the warmth of her hand and walked a few steps toward the side of the road. She stood, watching the geese overhead, and thought of safe travels and a good life. She put the tobacco at the foot of a pine tree and returned to her car.

She turned on the radio to hear the voice of a reporter named Tim Harvala on station KAXE's morning news. The account broke into her thoughts of childhood as the reporter described the scene of the takeover: ". . . on the edge of White Earth village with the tribal chairman and his attorney." The reporter paused. "Chairman Wagosh, how do you feel about the present situation?"

Lance Wagosh was tense, but vigilant. "These people are terrorists. They are destroying federal and tribal property." He paused. "They have never clearly presented a grievance, and all we know is that they're violating the law."

"Do you think the tribal council might have avoided this situation by meeting with the protesters last week?" Harvala interrupted.

"We can't meet with everyone. They only represent a small fraction of the community."

Harvala seemed challenging. Alanis smiled. Someone had some guts. Now the reporter responded, "But they've had hundreds of signatures on their petitions. According to the protesters, they just want a meeting."

"Sure, they asked to meet with us, but we've tried that and ended up with a virtual riot. We can't be expected to meet under those circumstances." Wagosh dug in to justify his position.

"The point is," the tribal attorney broke in, "they are breaking the law. You can see that for yourself, and you can't expect us to defend them."

"No," Harvala agreed. "But do they have any valid points? After all, isn't the controversy over community input into any decision regarding the logging and mill agreement?"

"*We* are the *elected* tribal government," Wagosh huffed, emphasizing the words "we" and "elected." "*We* represent the people in these decisions, and there has been quite a bit of debate on the proposed project for the past few months. We feel secure that the proposal is the best offer possible."

Harvala let them go. This story would carry him for the next few days, and undoubtedly, things would always change. The reporter spoke now directly to his audience. "The council seems set in their position, and as of now, there has been no new word from Protect Our Land. Will they negotiate, or will they continue this armed occupation of the village? We will keep you posted in our up-to-the-minute coverage here in White Earth village." Harvala signed off.

Alanis was pleasantly surprised by the coverage. She had looked over the newspaper clippings from NARF this morning and anticipated this position from the tribal government. The reporter was far better than she had expected. KAXE was a border town news station and most reservation border towns were notorious for their racism. Press coverage was rarely an exception. Harvala seemed to be a few steps above the norm.

As Alanis approached the outskirts of White Earth village, the peace gave way to disorder. She stopped the car at a roadblock as a county deputy motioned for her to roll down the window. The deputy's face hardened when he saw she was an Indian, although she flashed him her press credentials. He spoke briefly on the radio, looked quizzically at Alanis again, and to the person on the radio he said, "You sure?" His face still hard, he directed Alanis to a trailer up the road.

The trailer was the federal command center. It was a typical enclosed trailer on wheels such as used by engineers and surveyors at construction sites. Parked haphazardly around the trailer were four identical federal vehicles, all with South Dakota license plates. TV-station vans encircled the trailer, each van bristling with antennas as hustling technicians unrolled cables in a spider web of wires, and reporters freshened their makeup and hairdos. A gathering of white farmers and townspeople stood off on the side armed with placards and banners denouncing the Indians. Meanwhile, a group of FBI agents sat at a picnic table unconcernedly and blissfully eating monstrous frosted donuts and drinking coffee. The men stiffened at the approach of a stranger, an Indian woman. They looked her over as she emerged from her car.

Alanis looked like a reporter. Even if she was Indian, at least in part, she was still a reporter. Her camera hung from her shoulder alongside a bag that held her laptop computer and cell phone; she carried a tape recorder, notebook, and pen in her hands. After their careful examination of her as she exited her car, the men now ignored her.

"I'm from the *Rocky Mountain News*, and I'm covering the story for the paper and United Press International," she offered. "I would like to talk with whomever is in charge here."

A burly man with reddish hair spoke without looking up at Alanis. "I'm Agent Simpson," he said simply. Simpson did not look impressed at or approving of Alanis's credentials. He wore a camouflage down vest, a brimmed cap emblazoned with the letters "FBI," and a holstered pistol. He took another bite of donut and spoke with his mouth full. "I suppose you know what your getting yourself into, Miss, but we can't vouch for those Indians."

"I've taken that into account, thank you." She tightened her jaw. No question the FBI was uptight, but what did she expect? She could play hard ball, too. "Who *is* in charge here?"

The agent spoke over his shoulder without looking her way. "Agent Cope's in the trailer."

"Might I speak with him?" Alanis said, in her most polite voice.

The man motioned toward the trailer and said, "You go on ahead, Miss, but I don't think he'll be in much of a mood to speak with the press right now."

"That's alright," Alanis said, thankful to at least be changing agents. What was worse than being uptight was to dress poorly as well.

Today, Alanis wore jeans, a denim shirt and a leather jacket. As she turned her back, the men at the table turned their heads to watch her walk to the trailer. She was, Indian or not, by any standards an attractive woman.

Before she could knock on the door, a tall man wearing another FBI baseball cap leaned out. "Can I help you?" Agent Cope put on his most congenial smile for the pretty reporter. Alanis extended her hand.

"I'm Alanis Nordstrom from the *Rocky Mountain News* and UPI." A freckled hand grasped hers. A stiff, formal shake. He did not invite her inside. She continued, "If you're Agent Cope, I'd like a little briefing."

"I'm him," he said. No change in expression. His smile tightened slightly. *"An Indian, damn it,"* he thought to himself. He would have to make the best of it.

"Tell me what's going on, Agent Cope." Alanis started her tape recorder and held it up.

"Well, Miss Nordstrom, it's like this. These Indians have broken the law."

She raised an eyebrow and thought about the frequency of law-breaking in Indian country by white men in Italian suits.

"They burned up about a million dollars of equipment owned by a logging company that we understand had been negotiating in good faith with the Indians. And they destroyed federal property, including a truck or two owned by the BIA. Not to mention whatever they're doing inside with the council's equipment."

"Is that why the FBI is here?"

"We're here because we were called in. This is way out of the league of the local sheriff, and those people are heavily armed. They're playing hard ball." He motioned with his arm toward the housing project and tribal offices.

"Now, tell me about the layout," she said, "and how you think I should go in."

"Go in?" Agent Cope asked.

"I plan on interviewing this Elaine Mandamin from Protect Our Land. That's the organization here, right? She's expecting me shortly. I just wanted to let you know that I plan on going in."

Agent Cope's reply was curt. "Well, suit yourself, Miss Nordstrom."

The agent finally moved back inside the trailer, and Alanis guessed that was an invitation to enter. He stood before a map and an aerial photo of the village laid out on a table littered with empty paper coffee cups and the crumbs of more donuts.

"Are you from Rapid City?" she asked.

"As a matter of fact I am," he said, taken aback. "How'd you know?"

"Plates." She motioned with her head out the door toward the fleet of cars.

He shifted somewhat uncomfortably and turned toward the map.

The agent had been imported from South Dakota, she thought to herself, that region of the FBI that specialized in Indian uprisings. Northern Minnesota might have to grow some *local* specialists, she mused.

"Here's the playing field," he said, looking at the aerial photo-graph. "Here's our team and there's their team. And this is the scrimmage line." He pointed with his index finger at the barricade of cars. "This," he traced with his hand, "is the vehicle entryway."

"Show me outside," Alanis motioned toward the village. The agent and the reporter walked to the porch of the trailer. The other FBI men looked up from the picnic table at their leader.

"Over there." Cope pointed to a line of wrecked cars and logs protruding from the site. "Between all those Indian cars, that's how you go in." A pause. "They really did a pretty damn good job at making a mess."

He continued, "I think this afternoon should be safe for you to go in. We're just watching it close right now. You'll be OK. I'll notify my men of your trip."

"*Miigwech.*"

A questioning look.

"That's 'Thanks' in Ojibwe."

"Oh," he said.

"*Giga-waabamin miinawaa.* I'll see you later."

He muttered something, and then she was gone. Cope watched her walk away, a long single braid down her back. *"Pretty woman,"* he thought to himself. Then he shook his head. "I must have been on these reservations too damn long," he said, and sighed.

THE AK-47

Under the watchful eyes of both Agent Cope and Moose Hanford, Alanis maneuvered the rental car through Selam Big Bear's barricade extravaganza. Her adrenaline was elevated knowing that there were probably a hundred binoculars and rifle scopes trained on her as she crossed the line. She edged the car into a parking space near the tribal council offices. Two camouflage-clad men appeared from the door of the tribal headquarters and ran at a crouch toward her car, motioning for her to get out. Taking a deep breath, Alanis opened the door just as a dark hand reached out to help her.

"Can I carry anything for you?" Willie Schneider asked the reporter.

"No, I can manage, thanks," she said, surprised by his politeness amid the surroundings.

"*Weeweib.* Hurry. We don't know what the feds or the rednecks are gonna do."

With her camera and bags in hand, Alanis Nordstrom obediently followed Willie Schneider and Hawk Her Many Horses back into the office, mimicking their crouched run.

Once inside, Hawk took what remained of her belongings and asked, "Can you move over here please, *duga*? I need to check you out." A shy smile, somewhat apologetic.

She looked at Willie and Hawk Her Many Horses, both clad in their old army fatigues with "White Earth Warrior" painted on the back in large white letters and carrying deer rifles strapped over their shoulders. Hawk Her Many Horses was a slight man, half Lakota, half Chippewa. Judging from the number of scars on his face, it looked like he was a veteran as well, either from Vietnam, or from Minneapolis's Franklin Avenue. Willie examined her laptop, tape recorder, cell phone, and camera while Alanis waited impatiently. Hawk took it upon himself to do the frisking, running his callused hands over Alanis's arms.

She grimaced and said angrily, "Is this really necessary?"

"Uh huh, sure is. There's a war going on, lady." But he stopped and winked at her. "Can you remove your shirt now, Miss?"

"Fuck off!" Alanis jerked herself away. "Go find yourself a date."

"Give it up, Hawk," Willie scoffed. He handed Alanis back her equipment. "He was just kidding," Willie offered gently.

Just then Elaine's tall form appeared in the doorway. "What are you guys up to? She's a reporter, not an idiot."

Elaine extended a hand to Alanis and welcomed her to White Earth. "Thank you for coming," she said in a voice both strong and strained. Their eyes met. "I'm sorry about Hawk. He's really kind of a sleaze, but he's a good guy."

Alanis nodded. "I won't take it personally."

"So how was your trip, and how were the feds?" Elaine asked, mostly interested in the latter. She led the reporter into the tribal offices.

"I tell you, it wasn't as hard as I expected to get in, but I'm a little worried about getting back out," Alanis said. "I think they consider me one of the enemy twice over."

"That's OK," Elaine said with a straight face. "We've got both some white flags and an extra .30–06, depending on how things go."

Alanis felt a sense of this woman as she observed both the strain on her face from responsibility and the ability to keep laughing. Her lanky frame looked like that of a teenager, but when close, one could well see the twenty eight years on the reservation. Even her hands were a testimony, a series of tattoos covered the back of her knuckles, highlighted by a scar from a windshield she had gone through at the age of twenty.

"So, what exactly is going on?" Alanis said, stiffening slightly as she remembered her task.

"Let me show you around and you can see for yourself," Elaine replied. "This is the third day of the occupation. We've got our people behind these barricades and most of Hungry Hill up there." She motioned with her hand toward the housing project overlooking the tribal offices. "The housing project ended up being cordoned off with us whether they like it or not. I guess the feds decided there were some pretty dark Indians up there in the project, and it was better to have them inside the danger zone rather than behind them."

"You mean the whole housing project is blocked off?" Alanis was incredulous.

"Yeah, it sure is, except the tribal employees that live there. They got out before the feds came in. But the rest of the people, they ended up sticking it out with us."

"Between the feds and what looks like the vigilante crowd, there are a hell of a lot of guns out there. And there must be a bunch of children in that project."

Elaine noticed that Alanis had skipped the usual part about "women and children." She smiled to herself. She might like this woman.

"Actually, there are whole families up there, twenty-five or so. Plus, there's the elders housing unit, too. So all in all, there's people that it'd be bad public relations to shoot. Somehow, those agents must have decided that all us Indians are dangerous. You know, cowboys and Indians."

Alanis remembered back to the original Associated Press wire story she read about the takeover. "But the newspapers are reporting that you're holding hostages . . ." It was half a question, half a baited query.

"Really? Well, there's no one here who doesn't want to be here. That probably came from the FBI who wanted to dress us up as the bad guys—and because they didn't want the world to know how many people are standing behind this action. These elders are real *mindawe*. They're mad as hell about this land too and sure don't want to see any logging up here. A bunch of them have been at the center of this struggle pushing the rest of us along."

"Oh, I see, revolutionary elders," Alanis said, surmising the feds' position. "If I were a fed, I'd make sure those elders were in the enemy camp, too.

"Right. And here's one of the radicals right here. This is Mesabe, my grandfather," Elaine explained as they walked up to an old man. He wore sunglasses, a plaid flannel shirt, Levis, and an "Oka is OK" baseball hat, referring to the Quebec Mohawk occupation of 1990.

"Goshkozi Mishoomis," Elaine bellowed to a minimally operational set of working ears. The old man slowly opened his eyes. "There's a war going on here, and you can't be sleeping." She laughed and helped him straighten up his blanket.

"Ikwe Giiwanaadizi," he said, but he smiled.

"This here is Alanis Nordstrom. She's a reporter for a paper out west. She is from White Earth but lived out west with the Sioux and the Navajo all her life. She's Bear Clan too, like me."

Alanis was surprised. How Elaine knew her history, Alanis was not sure, but it was all true.

"Eh heh, mino, mino," the old man said, nodding his head. He smiled, and mostly gums showed. "So you're going to make us famous."

Alanis smiled at the old man. He reminded her of some of her father's friends in Denver with whom she frequently sat at the pow-wow.

"You're already famous, sir. I've been reading about all of you in the newspapers. I just had to come and see for myself. *Boozhoo.*" She extended a hand which he took.

"Write about my granddaughter," he said, obviously proud. "I'm the *ogimaa* here, but she's the *ogichidaakwe.*"

"I'm sure I will write about both of you," Alanis told Mesabe, then turned to Elaine. "Looks like you folks got a real revolutionary here."

Elaine chuckled as the old man wondered what a "revolutionary" was.

Elaine spoke to her grandfather. "We're going to get some food and coffee. She's probably sick from the airplane and eating all that *Chimookamaan miijim.*" Now she placed a hand on his shoulder. *"Buckaday ina, Mishom?"*

"Bring me some coffee when you have time. I'm just going to have a rest here so I'm ready for the action." He pulled out a can of Copenhagen and stuffed a small pinch behind his lower lip, then receded back into the chair and pulled the visor of his cap over his eyes.

"So, how'd you know what clan I was?" Alanis was curious.

"Well, I asked around. Then I did a little research on the old rolls and confirmed what I'd heard. I just wanted to know who you were and how you fit in here. It's like an Ojibwe security check."

"I guess I never thought of it that way," Alanis said. "Although it's not as if I didn't notice you have tight security. That frisking I got was telling. Hell, I'm glad I was wearing a bra—and not a padded one."

"Watch out for Hawk. He's got those Oglala eyes."

"Oh yes, those Oglala eyes," Alanis acknowledged knowingly. "I'll be sure to look the other way so I don't get bewitched."

The two women made their way back to the kitchen where Elaine introduced her to Georgette Big Bear and Lucy St. Clair and a third woman, Claire St. Clair. The three women comprised the cooking contingent, and they had hot coffee, corn soup, and fry bread ready for lunch. Alanis followed Elaine's example and filled a plate. Elaine said she would be back later to check on supplies.

"Don't worry about supplies," Georgette said, obviously delighted with a discovery. "We just found about four thousand pounds of commodities stashed in a closet back here. We can stay for months."

"Leave it to the tribal council to keep a hoard," Lucy said, shaking her head.

Elaine led Alanis into a room of phones and maps that looked like a command center for the occupation. "This is our planning room," Elaine gestured into the air. "And this is Selam Big Bear, the representative from White Earth and one of the point men of this occupation. And hopefully our *next* tribal chairman."

A small, dark man held out his hand to Alanis. He had long braids carefully wrapped in red flannel strips at the bottom.

"Selam loves interviews," Elaine said, "so when I have to do some business, I'll leave you with him for the briefing. There's one more person for you to meet," she added, nodding to a man typing into a computer. "This here is Reverend Lee Swenson, the spiritual leader of the progressive white people on the reservation."

Reverend Swenson waved happily from behind the computer. A big blonde man in stark contrast to the other occupants of the tribal office.

"So what's going to happen?" Alanis queried Elaine.

She nodded to a map of White Earth village illustrating housing, sentry posts, barricades, and the various federal, state, and county men. Alanis looked at scribbles designating who was in charge at what times, what radio frequency they were on, as well as similar notes about each of the feds.

"We're not sure at this point," Elaine said. "It's up to the feds. We've issued a series of demands and so far there's no response. They're still trying to wait us out."

"This is the first time I've heard of actual demands," Alanis said. Somehow, she wasn't surprised, either at the fact that demands actually existed or at the lack of media coverage.

"That's typical," Elaine sighed. "The issues are always too complicated for the media to explain in fifty words or less so they just breeze over them. And the FBI isn't interested in letting our demands get out because public opinion might side with us. They prefer to just paint us as crazed terrorists."

"So what are you after?"

"Let's see if I can find the official list," Elaine said as she began shuffling piles on the center of the table. "Oh good, I found one," she smiled as the minister passed her a paper. "Here's the background part. Our documentation on how we lost the land and the legislation, the deal with Potlatch, the burial ground desecration, and what we know about the tribal government's collaboration. These are just the highlights. We have a full report here," she said as she thumped a red-covered document on the desk.

"There's been no response to our demands, right?" Elaine looked over at the Reverend, wondering aloud. Swenson was the liaison between the federal officials and the Indians. He had also set up a team of religious observers to watch the perimeter of the occupation and observe any negotiations. So far they had done a lot of the first, but none of the second.

"Just this fax," the Reverend said. He handed Elaine a sheet of paper, which she read and passed to Alanis: "The Federal and State forces will not consider negotiations until all weapons are handed over and all individuals have vacated the tribal council offices."

"That's productive," Elaine said, irritated at the tone of the response. She had hoped they would negotiate, not let it get worse. "We'd better call a press conference and make a statement. I'll go get people. Lee, can you call on the radio to get the others in here?" With that, she was out the door, leaving Alanis and the others behind.

Five minutes later, they had all assembled. About two-thirds of the committee were men, mostly younger, but a few elders as well. She recognized one or two seasoned Indian movement people, Warren Wabun the most obvious, and saw a few others she thought she recognized from the news. Alanis and the two non-Indians stayed outside, the minister and a white lawyer named Karen Ordstrom. Fifteen minutes later, Tim Harvala, the reporter for the local radio station appeared, having successfully negotiated the perimeter. Reporters from the Minneapolis and St. Paul papers and TV stations chose to follow the proceedings from behind the safety of the FBI lines and get the official story.

Warren Wabun emerged from the conference room, a towering man, with long braids and a booming voice; he stood proud in front of the meager press assemblage.

"In response to the government's decision to invade our community, we're issuing a statement," Warren began. "Ninety percent of this reservation is held by interests other than Native People. Our people have been forced into desperate poverty, and yet we watch our natural resources and wealth flow off this reservation, without any benefit to us. Now, the headwaters of the Mississippi River are threatened by contamination. This is our survival. We are not willing to surrender until there is some meaningful intention to negotiate. The federal, state, and tribal governments have been given a clear and reasonable set of demands. We await a response. We are prepared to defend our land and future generations by any means necessary."

The two reporters made notes and asked questions. Then Alanis asked Warren if she could take his photo. He was obviously pleased. He asked her to wait a moment and then ran from the room. He returned five minutes later with his hair rebraided and holding a monstrous, lethal-looking assault rifle.

Alanis stepped back, surprised. "Excuse me, Mr. Wabun, do you want to be photographed with the gun?"

"Of course, this is *the* AK-47."

"What do you mean, *the* AK-47?"

Warren Wabun quieted as he prepared his remarks in his mind. The towering war veteran hoisted the big gun and held it to his chest. The camera snapped, shutter closed. *Mazinaakizigan.*

Warren Wabun was a representative from the Twin Cities Indian community and a veteran of tribal political wars, numerous rallies, marches, and takeovers—as much as anyone who can claim to have been party to five armed occupations in their short time on earth. Wabun had perspective to contribute to the occupation, and local reservation people were pleased to have a nationally known Indian in their midst.

"This, Miss Nordstrom," he paused again for emphasis and began, "is Commemorative Memorabilia. There is an honoring tradition of sorts between various nations engaged in these occupations to defend our people. This tradition involves this special AK-47. A legendary weapon first seen at the Wounded Knee occupation in the possession of Bobbie Ankar, another Vietnam veteran. Photographs of the weapon were circulated by the John Birch Society as 'proof' that the Indian occupation was communist backed. Ironic isn't it? Actually, Bobbie brought it back from 'Nam, captured from the enemy.

"Since that time, however, this weapon, the one here, *niin bakizigan,*" he emphasized, "has become a sort of traveling honor tradition. Passed from one nation to another as occupations graduate to a level of legitimacy." Now he continued, a matter-of-fact historian. "The AK-47 was reported by the Canadian Broadcasting Corporation in a video produced by the Canadian Armed Forces at the Mohawk Occupation of Oka in 1990." He stopped again. "Of course, it was there," Warren said with authority. "Any credible occupation would get the AK-47 Award.

"When the White Earth occupation entered it second week, the coalition was also awarded the AK-47, which was brought in by a support contingent from the Six Nations Confederacy. This award signifies a national regard for the strategy and commitment of the White Earth people."

A pause. "Well, got to *maa jaan,* Miss Nordstrom. Let me know if you need help to get that photo out to the press and wire service. I can *always* get through the police lines."

A few photos and questions later, his mission was complete. Warren passed the press release to the Reverend Lee Swenson and his own daughter, Danielle Wabun, who sat in position by the fax machine.

"Thank you Great Spirit for the fax machine," Alanis heard Warren Wabun whisper in passing, and he was gone.

VETERANS OF DOMESTIC WARS

Armed Occupation of Tribal Offices
Demands Halt to Logging

By Alanis Nordstrom, *Rocky Mountain News* Staff Writer

White Earth, Minn. — Hidden behind a barricade of junked cars and armed with deer hunting rifles and a single, prized AK-47 assault rifle, two dozen Native American protesters have occupied the White Earth Reservation tribal offices for six days now. International attention is focused on the occupation by the group striving to stop the planned logging of sacred reservation lands. . . .

Alanis had adopted a survival strategy, one that suited her well: Alanis was conveniently Indian. Powwows, yes, but from the bleachers. Political events and rallies, yes, if the weather was nice and if interesting speakers or her friends were attending. Ceremonies, only when she was really in a bind. Occupations, definitely not. While she remembered well the Indian takeover of Alcatraz in the early 1970s, she was not about to go out of her way to break the law, or make herself uncomfortable.

As she filed her first story from inside the occupied council offices, Alanis was struck by the difference between herself and her distant relatives, those she had come to report on for the newspaper. *She had a choice.* She could live anywhere, work for the *Rocky Mountain News*, or the London *Times*, for all it mattered. The people of Hungry Hill and Protect Our Land lived on this reservation, and if they wanted it better, they had to work at it. Maybe even break the law, something that made Alanis uncomfortable.

And the weapons too made her nervous. Alanis had been an urban Indian most of her life, and while she had dim memories of her father's gold panning and squirrel hunting in the backwoods of Santa Barbara, she had never seen so many guys in camouflage. *And so many guns.*

White Earth was fortunate to have a good share of Vietnam veterans who returned home. Most had somehow maintained not only an arsenal of offensive weapons, but also a collection of defensive equipment. Today, Moose was making an inventory of the gas masks that Willie Schneider had bought at an armory garage sale a few years ago. Moose believed it likely that the federal forces would resort to tear gas at some stage.

Alanis wandered over to Moose and Willie's post, wondering aloud what was next.

"I sure hope to shit that they don't fire anything up at the elders housing," Moose said anxiously, ignoring Alanis and talking to Willie. "That would pretty much do in some of those old people." Alanis found herself shuddering involuntarily. She braced herself.

She regarded Moose. He stood almost six and a half feet tall and towered above her. With a beaded baseball cap and hair down to the middle of his back, he had a physical presence that made her feel secure. His confidence enhanced those feelings.

"We should send some equipment, just in case," Willie suggested. Schneider was a tall, lanky man with a sheepish grin. He had done a short tour of Vietnam, and after that, a stint in Stillwater Penitentiary, but now he had been straight for a decade. He was second in charge of security.

"It looks like we've got about fifty or so masks here," Moose checked his notes again. "We should keep around thirty or so here, and then send what's left up to the project to make sure people are covered. I don't trust the feds at all, and I sure don't want anyone getting hurt because of this."

Willie looked at Alanis now, after ignoring her in the conversation. "Miss Reporter, you'd better prepare for the worst. We are," he said with some authority.

"Georgette and I will take some of the masks up," Moose continued, still ignoring Alanis. "She knows all those people in the project, and we can get people prepared. Willie, check around here." Now, he looked at Alanis, and referred to the other reporter, Tim Harvala: "Both of you reporters, get it together. I doubt you'll be getting out of this for at least the night."

"Thanks for the advice." Alanis was unsure how to respond to the news. She was grateful to be informed, but displeased with the promise of a hard floor and a gas mask.

Alanis had been taking notes and a few photos as the men checked the gas mask supply and now found herself backing up as the two men started loading the gas masks into backpacks.

She backed herself to the side of the hallway and caught her breath against the wall. *"It's going to be OK, it's going to be OK,"* she repeated to herself inside her head. *"I am a reporter. I am not a member of the takeover committee. This is my job."* She repeated it again to herself, cutting into her nervous edge.

She watched now as Willie helped Moose load the gas masks into a couple of backpacks. Georgette appeared from the kitchen and wiggled her rather ample frame into one backpack while Moose deftly threw the other over his shoulder.

"If Georgette had to haul ass, she'd have to make two trips," Moose grinned over his shoulder.

"Tsssss," Georgette responded. "Just remember, you need me."

The two went out the back door and started running for the housing project about one hundred yards up the road.

Alanis felt herself getting uncomfortable and edgy, but she was too proud to admit it. Elaine was nowhere in sight, and the last thing she needed to do was be in someone's way. She decided to collect her things from the car. She stopped Willie Schneider to ask if it was dangerous to go to the car now.

"I'd take the door by the daycare. It's close, and about half sheltered," Willie said. "Besides, they probably know who you are, so they won't worry you're smuggling anything in."

"Thanks for the reassurance," Alanis said as she shouldered her camera.

"Here, I'll show you the way," Willie added, happy to spend time with the reporter.

Outside, it was quiet. But then, almost as if in response to the silence, the agents' radios began. Inside, Elaine heard them. It was dusk. That may have accounted for why the shot was fired.

"Holy shit," Alanis screamed as she heard the whine of the bullet shrieking past. She dropped her bag and ran as fast as she could toward the door that Willie held open for her. A second shot rang past her, hitting the wall to her left. She fell through the doorway onto the concrete floor, tears in her eyes.

Willie picked her up, and she stammered at him, half angry, half hysterical, telling him what had just happened as if he did not know. "Why did they shoot at me?" she demanded of Willie, who looked blankly back at her and saw a face flushed with fury and fear. "Why did they shoot at me? I am not . . ." she almost said *I am not one of you*, and then caught herself.

A moment later, Elaine appeared at her side. "Those sons of bitches," Elaine said under her breath. "They know better than to start shooting."

"I doubt they were trying to hit you," Willie said, trying to be soothing. "They're just trying to put the fear of the white man's god into you."

Selam was listening in to the police frequency and heard a lot of swearing and accusations flying back and forth. The Becker County Sheriff disclaimed responsibility, as did the police department. The FBI said they would never order anyone to fire on a woman, and some other voice jumped in and said, "Well, who the hell did?"

"It sounds like no one knows who fired those shots at you," Selam said to Alanis as Elaine led her into the control room. "I'll bet one thing, though. They probably thought you were Elaine, you two look close enough alike. I can't imagine them wanting to fire on a reporter, but I know Elaine doesn't have many friends."

"I *had* been planning to use you as a decoy," Elaine said and smiled. "This is a little early though."

Just then, Willie returned with the bag Alanis had gone to retrieve at the car and handed it to her. She took it, looking at Willie with surprise and gratitude.

"What a gentleman!" Elaine said to Willie, who beamed and then grew red in the face. Everyone else in the control room laughed.

But Willie turned to Alanis. "May I suggest that you stay here and don't try to go out again for awhile?" he ventured, obviously shaken up as well by the shooting. "Girl, you're Indian first and a journalist second, according to whomever was behind that gun. You'd better stay here with us Indians."

But Alanis was not listening. She was still shaking, wiping the tears from her cheeks, and trying to get her breath back. She did not hear a word they said to her.

The bullets had not hit her, had not torn into her physical body and shattered bones and spilled blood, but the bullets had hit her just the same, hit her somewhere else deep inside. She was in shock as she stood still, silently fighting to regain her composure. *I am not one of you*, she had almost said, yet obviously to whomever had leveled the rifle to his shoulder, closed one eye to sight it, placed his finger on the cool steel of the trigger and pulled, obviously to that person she was *one of them*. And that person—whether he had tried to kill her and missed or merely had tried to scare her with a close shot—had taken away a part of her. And now her image of herself as the objective, professional newspaper reporter became confused with her image as the gunman saw her, as an Indian, as an enemy, as someone to shoot. The bullets had destroyed the boundaries in her mind, and the ricochet reverberated through her very soul.

THE WHITE MAN'S WAR

Agent Cope paced the floor of his trailer like a football coach in deep deliberation on the sidelines of the big game. He had called together a meeting of the leaders of the military and the police for a pep talk.

"First things first," he announced, "I want to know who fired those shots at the reporter."

His assembled team erupted into denials and accusations. Becker County Sheriff Buster Parisian, his chief deputy, Kevin Bennert, and National Guard commander Major John Traversy all began talking at once, each denying responsibility, each pointing a finger at the other. Cope stood still and silent. He looked over at his assistant, Agent Simpson, and shook his head. Finally he raised his hand and quiet reigned.

"Obviously, no one seems to want to take responsibility for firing at the reporter," Cope said, stating the obvious. "But let me make one thing absolutely clear: We can't have any shit like that again. We know those Indians are heavily armed, and we need to use that for the media. We can't be shooting at them, or we're seen as the bad guys."

Deputy Bennert spoke up: "I believe, sir, that the shooting was most likely done by a member of the Equal Rights Congress, the white protesters. They started out just waving banners and signs but they seem to be getting out of control."

Cope sighed and shook his head, speaking slowly now to remind his team of their strategy. "This whole operation should be a slam dunk: We wait them out, then just when their guard is down, we blitz, and pass out the handcuffs. That's the game plan."

The National Guard representative was antsy about the whole affair. Traversy was ready now to send in the tear gas canisters. "We should blast those Indians while they're still reeling from the shots," he suggested, thinking practical and strategic. He commanded the biggest force of the Guard in the region. An older man, he was well seasoned with weekend training sessions at Camp Ripley and ready to see some action.

"Not yet," Cope said, repeating the "wait them out" part of his game plan for the hard of hearing. "But in the meantime, let's look at our options."

The men gathered around their maps of the village, clearing away the day's coffee cups and donut crumbs to look at various estimates of weapons and people. The census data had been invaluable, telling them how many people were in each housing project home and what their ages and sexes were. The elders housing unit glared with the bright red alert of a "political liability." But no one would blame them if they roughed up Hungry Hill; it was full of known sympathizers.

Traversy suggested that they allow an evacuation of the elders, women, and children. "We should get all of them out of there before we try any tear gas. I wouldn't want that on my conscience."

Cope had to agree: the elders housing unit was dangerous ground. They would need to evacuate before there were any maneuvers.

Then there was the problem of image.

"We don't look so good right now," Cope said woefully. "The evening news says we opened fire on the tribal offices. We need a response."

"How about a short video on the kind of equipment the Indians have in there that we can release to the media?" Agent Simpson suggested. "It's worked before, putting the fear of God in most good Americans. We show some bazookas, some heavy firepower, a mound of bullets. That gets people onto our side right quick."

Cope nodded, amused at the tried-and-true tactic.

"What exactly do you think they have in there?" Sheriff Parisian asked nervously. "All I've seen is some deer hunting rifles and a couple duck hunting shotguns. I know some of those guys are vets, but I doubt they've got anywhere near what they'd like to have." He knew what guns most people had in town because he made almost regular raids into the housing project, looking for "fugitives from justice."

"According to our sources, they are loaded down with heavy artillery," Agent Cope said with a half-smile. "Assault rifles, M-16s, Uzis, probably a bazooka or two, shoulder-held surface-to-air missiles, the usual."

"I'll take charge of the video," Simpson said, taking Cope's list of the Indians' firepower as approval for his filmmaking. "We have samples of most of that equipment, so we can make something up. We'll have a video cassette to distribute at tomorrow morning's press briefing."

"OK, now what about the evacuation?" Cope said. "We release the video to make people see how well-armed they are and convince more of those people in the housing project and the elders project to evacuate. We can plan for an evacuation tomorrow afternoon. Then we drop the gas before dawn on the day after."

"That sounds fine with me," Traversy said, obviously pleased to have an action plan. The sheriff concurred and Bennert nodded his head vigorously.

"Fine, it's settled," said Cope. "I'll call the radical reverend and tell him he's got eighteen hours to get those people ready to evacuate, and this is their last chance."

"He should like that," said Parisian.

"Let him tend his flock; he chose it," the FBI agent responded.

FACING THE ENEMY

As the word came in of the government evacuation plan, people lightened up. It appeared that the feds weren't planning an assault until at least the next day. Lucy St. Clair relaxed and started in on Jim Vanoss, her classmate from Mahnomen High School.

"Hey, here's Roy Orbison himself," she announced when she saw him for the first time since the occupation had started. He appeared mysteriously from Hungry Hill where he'd apparently been resting for battle. Vanoss was about fifty years old and had recently returned to traditional spirituality with a righteous fervor. No one held that against him, but it was just that he was so human that they couldn't take him seriously. After all, he acted pious now that he'd cleared things with the Great Spirit. But it was only six months before that he'd fallen off the cross from his two-year stint as a born-again Christian.

And then there was his hair. At fifty, he had a full head of mousy-gray hair. He wore it in two braids, meticulously coifed into place with Brill Cream. Rumor was he fancied a twenty-five-year-old woman who was indeed taken by his charms. No question, he was impressive. He did know a lot about most things, and enough to lecture about most others. She was bewitched by him, and he was foolish for her.

In an overnight miracle, he discovered the Grecian Formula Traditional Indian secret, sauntering into the occupation limelight with a full head of jet black hair. He looked younger, there was no question. He also looked ridiculous.

"So, we've even got an entertainment committee," Lucy giggled as she gave him a friendly push on the shoulder. "Roy Orbison is back from the grave."

"Hey, don't be violent with me, sister," Vanoss said defensively, "now is a time to come together and make peace."

"Right, like make love, not war," Lucy said sarcastically. "Well, we're all happy you found someone to do that with; maybe you'll quiet down with all this sacred stuff for awhile. The rest of us imperfect human beings need a little rest while we find our way."

"You will find your way. I have seen it," he said. "This is a new beginning for all of us, including yourself. The Red Road is here in White Earth, and it starts now."

"Good," Lucy said, mocking. "I assume it's around the block from the long and winding road the rest of us are on?"

"That's enough," Moose Hanford said abruptly. "Be irreverent about white people, not Indians."

Jim Vanoss looked relieved. He passed Lucy a cigarette as a token of peace, and she hungrily took it.

"Speaking of that Red Road," Warren Wabun interrupted, arriving with a mission. "You and I had better head down it pretty soon here," he said nodding to Vanoss. "I've got an eight-thirty plane out of Fargo to catch, and we won't make it if we don't leave now."

"Where are you going now?" Lucy asked, aghast.

"Well, I've got a speaking engagement in St. Louis," Wabun said, apologizing with embarrassment. "I made the arrangements a few months ago, so I can't get out of it."

"Right," Lucy said and rolled her eyes, obviously not impressed. "And you, Big Indian Vanoss, you're going along to help him out."

"Yeah, but I'm just going as far as Fargo. I'll be back tomorrow to help out. Someone has to watch that 'war horse' for him," Vanoss laughed, referring to Warren's new Lexus.

The two men slipped out the back door as Lucy peered out the window. It was uncanny. Warren had all the mannerisms of a movie star. And, the truth was Jim Vanoss looked just like Roy Orbison with braids. She put out a tobacco offering for them, just to make sure that they traveled safely, and watched the car as it edged toward the barricade. She could hear the grass dance songs blasting on the stereo system as they passed.

★ ★ ★

As the road warriors arrived at the perimeter, they realized their mistake. The barricade was occupied by the Equal Rights Congress protesters, with a handful of sheriff's deputies half-heartedly attempting to hold them in check. The white farmers and townspeople had successfully amassed a throng of forty or so protesters near the perimeter with twenty cars and pickups parked in a hodgepodge fashion. The protesters were mostly men, although a few women in flannel coats and baseball hats had joined their ranks. They spoke quietly in groups, with occasional rough laughter and coughing punctuating their conversations.

On the first day, Bob Grist had been one of the leaders, and the people gathered around him to hear his speech: "We just want to make sure that no Indians get out of here with any guns. We live here too, and we don't want them running all over this reservation like an army."

But things soon turned bad. The crowd had taken on a life and will of its own that paid no mind to speeches and leadership. At night there were six-packs passed around and more than a couple protesters hinted to each other that they had their .30-30s stowed at the ready in the trunks of their cars or behind the pickups' seats "just in case."

Tonight the crowd was feeling mean and ready for action. It was almost dark, reducing visibility, but Warren Wabun and Jim Vanoss could tell from the way the protesters walked and yelled that the men had been drinking. Behind the steering wheel, Vanoss started to feel edgy, spotting Warren Danielson and the big farmer Miles Spaaker coming through the crowd to the approaching car. But Warren Wabun was a veteran of confrontation and thrilled in it. Vanoss slowly edged the Lexus toward an opening in the crowd.

As they got closer, the stench of beer was overwhelming. Vanoss realized that most of the white men were incapacitated. Warren unrolled the window and the grass dance songs resounded over the crowd.

"So how do you like the music?" Wabun prompted in his loud Crane Clan voice.

Warren Danielson glared, and Miles Spaaker looked taken aback at Wabun's choice of question. Both men were intimidated more by the big Indian than the music but didn't want to admit it.

Vanoss sensed an opportunity. As the exchange continued, Jim Vanoss nudged the car forward into the crowd that was now closing in on Warren. He desperately wanted to get out of this situation.

Warren Wabun eased up. "No, really folks, I just stopped by to say hello and share one of our top hits with you." In his best Casey Kasem voice, Wabun explained the grass dance songs: "This one's been a big hit for the past thirty thousand years or so. I hope everyone enjoys it."

Miles Spaaker didn't know what to think and sensed the Indian was making fun of him, so he gave him the finger. A few of the more intoxicated protesters began to hoot and jump around, playing Hollywood Indians, drumming on the roof of the Lexus. Warren seemed unconcerned, but Vanoss urged the car forward. Warren Danielson began swearing at Wabun in a long, evil stream of curses. Wabun turned up the grass dance music until it filled the car and the night, calling out, "Maybe you could sing something from your culture instead, like say 'Ninety-nine Bottles of Beer on the Wall'?"

One man who could barely stand up threw a beer can at Wabun and started singing the bar song. Warren snickered, then his laugh caught on, a big barrel of a laugh. Jim Vanoss panicked and gave the car gas, sensing that now would be an opportune time to leave. The crowd parted before the Lexus, and they were through to the other side of the barricade. Vanoss kept his foot on the gas all the way out of town, Wabun still laughing along with the grass dance music.

THE EVACUATION

Evacuation of Elders May Be Prelude to FBI Assault
By Alanis Nordstrom, *Rocky Mountain News* Staff Writer
White Earth, Minn. — In an effort to end the three-week occupation of White Earth Reservation tribal offices by protesters, FBI officials arranged an evacuation of Native American elders from the barricaded buildings. Inside those buildings, the move is being considered as a prelude to an assault. . . .

The old people did not plan on leaving. The more Elaine and Moose tried to persuade them, the less inclined they seemed to go. They had been passing their time watching the events through infrared night-sight binoculars, comparing this occupation with other takeovers around the country, and playing bingo. The pay-off was a red beret with an eagle feather attached that had previously belonged to Hawk Her Many Horses before Elaine sent it to the elders. Each winner sported the hat for the duration of the next game, until another "bingo" was called.

Elaine interrupted a bingo game a second time to plead with the elders to leave.

"Hell, no. I'm gonna stay and fight," seventy-year-old Charlotte Oshkinnah announced obstinately. "I've got nothing to lose."

An old man named Cheo waved his carved walking cane menacingly at Elaine and said, "Besides, they want us out of here so they can do more of an attack. If we're in here, they'll look bad."

After an hour of discussion and a disrupted bingo game, eight elders were convinced to evacuate.

The same discussion was held in the housing project, and although forty people agree to go, it was not without debate. The remaining one hundred and fifty or so residents of the housing project and elders units decided to throw their lot in with the protest.

Reverend Swenson made arrangements for observers to assist in the evacuation, since Moose wanted to keep the Indians' cars at the tribal offices for security. Swenson rounded up vehicles from sympathetic church people in the area and also volunteered the loan of the church's mini-van.

"We'll be ready to move at daylight," the Reverend said, pleased with the organization.

No one slept easy that night, but they rested. Willie Schneider led the night watch, keeping in radio contact with his other sentries stationed in their junked cars. It was a silent night, punctuated only by an occasional howl. Alanis lay in a borrowed sleeping bag between Elaine and Claire St. Clair, a woman of obvious Christian faith who whispered Novenas into her rosary beads. Claire, it happened, was Alanis's second cousin on her father's side. On the occasion of a series of particularly lonesome howls, Claire sat straight up and called out "Praise the Lord." Alanis nudged Elaine, puzzled.

"George Ahnib is his name," Elaine said matter of factly to the reporter.

"What is he doing?" Alanis wondered aloud.

"What he always does." A pause, and a sigh, "He's a huffer."

"What?"

"Someone who sniffs too much gas, or whatever else he can get near his nose. Go to sleep."

"Easy for you to say."

"Just remember he's on our side. Kind of like our mysterious edge, our secret weapon."

At first light, George Agawaateshkan began to pray, turning as he spoke. His wispy gray hair gently moved in the breeze as the fire licked at some kindling near his feet. Selam Big Bear carried a braid of sweet grass, the scent of which wafted through the circle. Alanis had been invited to the morning offering, and she too now carefully motioned with her hands to pull the stream of smoke over her as Selam held the braid.

"*Miigwech,*" she whispered. Selam nodded, then moved to her right. George Agawaateshkan continued praying until the other man had blessed each person with the sweet grass. The two men nodded to each other, George carefully placed his tobacco in the fire, and the circle disbanded. The ceremony was over.

At seven, the church people and their cars approached the barricade. Reverend Swenson was exuberant, assuming yet another role in changing history. A parade of Oldsmobiles, Buicks, and mini-vans rolled into the compound. Reverend Swenson shook hands with his congregation and directed them up the hill to the housing project. In the distance, he could see Agent Cope and with him, Sheriff Buster Parisian, looking down from a second hill through binoculars. The Reverend waved in acknowledgment.

As the cars parked in front of the housing project with their engines running, Willie Schneider caught the Reverend and spoke to him with obvious embarrassment. "The elders have made a final demand. They want to drive the cars out themselves, otherwise they're not going."

"Oh, that shouldn't pose a problem," the Reverend responded. "That's probably because they want to keep their dignity as they evacuate."

Willie replied, "Well, sort of."

"Or maybe they feel more comfortable if they are driving, instead of a white person they do not know?" the Reverend offered.

Willie examined his feet for a moment before responding. "The real reason," he said, "is because most of them have never been in such nice cars, and they just want to try them out."

But the elders were still not ready to leave. The morning news was on and ten or more old people gathered around the TV. Cheo knocked his cane against the side of the television and cursed the newscasters. The National Guard video had apparently been hand distributed to the regional television stations. It was now showing, with a full display of advanced weaponry. "Just like the gospel truth," Cheo said bitterly. Then he looked sheepishly at Reverend Swenson. The Reverend smiled, then grimaced at the TV.

"What a crock of shit," Charlotte Oshkinnah said, not caring what the Reverend thought.

Cheo added, perhaps encouraged, "We don't have any of those damn weapons down here. What are they trying to pull?"

"If we did, we'd already have won the war," Charlotte Oshkinnah replied.

Lee looked closer at the TV. Then he radioed Elaine.

"Are you watching this?"

"Of course," came the response. "They're trying to make out that we're a whole army."

Alanis watched the news report standing alongside the Reverend. For the first time, she found that she was angry—angry both at the way her fellow news reporters were covering the events and, with a troubling anger shared with the protesters, at the turn of events. She was irritated by her political anger, a feeling that threatened her role as an objective reporter. She struggled to quell it within herself, but still it was there, lurking.

The coverage was improper: It was essentially a National Guard PR piece and no self-respecting journalist would run something like it without checking it out. She waited to see if there was a commentary or any rebuttal. None came.

"I'd say they're trying to make you guys look pretty bad," she said, stating the obvious to Swenson. "I think that's a bad sign for negotiations," she continued, catching herself as she suddenly realized that she actually felt concern at how things would turn out. She told herself that even if she could not stop herself from feeling this way, she had to remain objective, had to do her job.

The old people were furious. Cheo swung at the TV with his cane. They all knew that there was no way that Moose, Willie, Elaine, and the others had all that artillery in there. Even if they had wanted it.

"Well, all we can do is issue a rebuttal," the Reverend said, shaking his head. "It's just hard to believe they're so unfair."

The National Guard ploy had worked, but only partially. Now

only ten elders wanted to leave, most of whom needed constant medical care. The rest planned to "stay and fight," as Charlotte Oshkinnah said. The people from Hungry Hill walked carefully down the hill to the cars, and the grownups, elders, and children loaded themselves into the nice American cars. Most of the faces behind the steering wheels were Indians. They took their time adjusting the power sideview mirrors and seats.

Reverend Swenson radioed to Lieutenant Traversy, second in command. "We're sending out a caravan. Which exit do you want to send them through?"

Swenson waited while static took over the line. After a few tries, the lieutenant got through to the Reverend. "Send them out the northeast exit, there are no troops over there."

"Isn't that where the Equal Rights Congress people are?"

"Yeah, but I'll send some people over there to watch. You'll be fine," came the response.

"OK, over and out," he said as he walked outside to the cars.

The Reverend's wife, Jane, sat nervously behind the wheel in the first car. Swenson leaned inside and patted her on the shoulder. "It'll be fine," he said. Then he gave her directions. "Just close your windows and drive. Be careful and go slow."

The Reverend walked down the line and repeated his advice. Then he made the sign of the cross and watched through his binoculars as the cars move down the hill.

Alanis trained her telephoto lens on the cars for a photo as they moved through the exit. At that moment, a premonition struck home.

The assembled throng had formed a gauntlet. As the cars approached, the crowd opened up enough to let the cars in, but not enough to let them pass. Alanis saw the flash of a rod iron at the same time as a brick flew toward one of the cars. A woman in a flannel shirt screamed, "Fucking Indians," and a protest sign slashed the air by the car window.

Reverend Swenson's radio came alive with the voices of FBI agents and deputies simultaneously screaming at each other and yelling for backup: "What are those rednecks doing?" "We need help!"

For his part, the Reverend was frozen in place, watching his wife trying to lead the caravan.

As she saw that she was trapped, Jane Swenson started to speed up. She gunned her engine and moved the car forward enough to evade most of the crowd. A big man jumped on the hood, still drunk from the previous night. Jane panicked, hitting the gas and knocking him over the top of the car. As he rolled off the back of the car, she saw in the rearview mirror that he was injured.

"Oh Jesus, oh Jesus," she gasped. "Did I kill him?"

An old Indian woman in the back seat said, "He's OK. Just drive. He probably would have killed us if he could."

Jane watched through her rearview mirror as other protesters helped the man up and then the rear window erupted into a star of broken glass as a brick landed square in the center. A face appeared out her side window as a woman shook her fist at Jane and screamed, "Indian lover!" She saw bricks flying at the other cars, thrown rocks, and swinging tire irons. Warren Danielson was screaming into a bullhorn and placards were shoved against the car windows, reading, "Spear an Indian, Save a Fish" and "Timber Niggers." And then the crowd thinned out and she was through the gauntlet. She gunned the engine toward Ogema.

The radio was still crackling with voices. Alanis heard Agent Cope barking out orders: "Who the hell are these people? We arrange an evacuation for women, children, and old people, and someone takes to throwing bricks and tire irons at them. These people are fucking insane. Get them the hell out of there!"

Gunshots sounded, and Alanis looked to see a pistol waving in the air amongst the crowd. The Reverend turned as white as a dead man. Hatred smelled on the bullets.

Just as the last of the evacuation cars cleared the crowd, a trio of county sheriff cars roared up to the crowd, their lights flashing. Deputies began chasing the protesters away.

Alanis and the Reverend ran to the tribal offices where Hawk Her Many Horses opened the door for them as they dashed inside. Swenson was still pale as he shouted to Lucy St. Clair at the radio, "Are they out? Are they OK?"

"They're alright," she said, shaking the anger out of her voice to calm them. "They made it out, and none of them were hurt."

"How about the guy she hit, whoever he is?"

"Unfortunately, he's fine," Moose said bitterly as he walked back inside behind from his sentry post. "It was one of those Spaakers from over by Mahnomen. The guy regularly picks fights with old drunk Indians just for the hell of it. Dooring is his second favorite pastime."

"What's dooring?" Alanis asked innocently.

"Dooring is when you drive down the highway and see someone walking on the shoulder that you want to get," Lucy said. "You swing your car over by them and then open your door as you go by and knock 'em flat on their ass."

"Dooring can kill ya easy," Moose added. "It's something some of these guys practice just for the hell of it. That's how Elaine lost her mother."

Agent Cope was beside himself. He called Traversy on the radio. "Get your butt over here and bring along that Becker County Sheriff."

Cope paced his trailer as he waited for the men. When they had finally gathered, he turned on Sheriff Parisian.

"OK, time for the post-game locker-room chat, and I ain't a happy coach," Cope said. "I don't suppose anyone was arrested for that fine display of racial hatred," he asked, looking directly at the sheriff.

Parisian shook his head helplessly. "Well, actually, I didn't see any-one do anything in specific," the sheriff stammered, on the defensive. "But I've got some idea of what happened."

"Great. It's always good to know who fumbled the ball after we've lost possession," Cope said sarcastically. "So I don't suppose you can arrest anyone without direct evidence, is that right?"

The sheriff felt suddenly relieved. "That's right, Agent Cope."

Cope persisted, "Well, there's no instant replay to watch. I suggest you go out there and find out who pulled that end run on us. Find out who their quarterback is, and sack his ass. This makes us look like rookies."

"I'll try," Parisian said, looking puzzled at what he interpreted as a betrayal. He had counted on the FBI not to side with the Indians over the white people.

Traversy jumped in: "I think we should move in with the tear gas, sir," he said, still anxious to make use of his equipment. "Things might get worse if we don't."

"You're right. We don't want to give them any time outs," Cope returned quickly to the offensive. He preferred the position. "Are your men ready with those canisters?"

"We're ready."

Cope looked at his watch. "OK, kickoff time at dawn."

DIBIKAAG
NIGHT

The darkest of skies was filled with stars shining brilliantly against the backdrop of the northern woods. Agent Cope looked at the sky, clear after an afternoon of northwestern winds. A wind whose power came regularly to the people of White Earth, bringing most changes of weather each season in succession. The silence tested Agent Cope's nerves; he distrusted the quiet in this foreign land. He felt precisely the same fear as his generations past had felt in outposts to Indian territory. He was uneasy, relentlessly struggling to resolve the silence with sounds familiar and remembered: sirens, shouts, radio music, a combustion engine.

A dog barked now, somewhere in the housing project. He looked again through his binoculars: Nothing moved. All was still. He was waiting, but he could not remember what for, and he wondered what this was all about. Finally, he sighed, walked back to the trailer that was his home more often then his true house was his home. He opened the creaky door and looked at his men as they played a game of poker at the Formica table of a relocated tribal employee.

"Guys, I'm gonna grab a few minutes of shuteye. Keep a look out and wake me at four."

"Sure, no problem." One man raised an arm to acknowledge his boss, and Agent John Cope entered a fitful sleep of the warrior in battle, as slowly the night took the FBI men, one by one.

Several hours later, Agent Cope was dozing on the couch. Two other FBI men snored peacefully in the chairs in the small living room of the trailer, while one sat at the table listening to the scanner and looking over an old *Sports Illustrated*. The TV was in static mode. The Becker County Sheriff had some men watching the encampment who were in contact with the FBI, giving the agency a little breathing room before the assault at dawn.

The trailer shook, then lurched suddenly to the side. Agent Cope rolled off the couch and crashed to the floor. The whole trailer teetered again onto its side. Books, maps, plates, paper coffee cups, and stale donuts slid and fell to the floor. "Holy shit, what is this?" Cope yelled as the trailer landed again on its proper footing. He scrambled toward the back door, tripping over other rudely awakened agents struggling to their feet. Cope swung open the door to see Kway Dole's face gleaming through the windshield of a Ford pickup as she backed the truck up and worked the gearshift.

Kway cackled out the driver's window, *"Heh, heh, heh."* She finally got the shifter into first and spun the tires in the sand in her haste to get the truck going again. "How do you like being Dorothy?" She screamed as the pickup took one last lunging run at the trailer. Agent Cope dug for his service revolver as the truck slammed head on into the trailer and his whole world tipped over onto its side. Tires spun again in the sand, and just as suddenly as she had appeared, the wicked witch of the west was gone.

The Hungry Hill housing project, it seemed, was not as asleep as Agent Cope had originally thought. As soon as the trailer toppled over, lights went on everywhere and whooping yells filled the quiet night. The truck careened past the project at seventy miles an hour as Kway leaned on the horn. She wanted to share the moment of glory.

In the pickup cab, Kway Dole smiled.

"A good night's work, eh, sister?" she said to herself. *"Maajaan. Let's hide this baby before the posse gets their panties out of a bunch."*

The pickup raced toward Naytahwaush and was out of sight before Agent Cope could even find his way back to the doorway.

THE GILL NET

Kway Dole was lesbian. It was a well known, uncloseted fact, part of the intricate, social fabric of White Earth. Stories told of times past, remembering women who took wives, lived singularly or fought as well as any man—true *ogichidaakwe*, in the true sense of the word, and Kway was cut of that cloth.

She lived alone now, in a small cabin on White Earth Lake. Her woman friend of before had moved away from the small community, back to the amenities and luxury of a city in which she found the peace of anonymity, not the openness of a forest people's culture. Kway had replaced her affection. She had assembled a collection of *awakaanag*, domesticated animals. Her menagerie of dogs, cats, parrots, and others inhabited the ecosystem of her house. For some, it was unconditional love; to others, she was their meal ticket. And for Kway, they provided her with a companionship and more importantly, a constant love she could count on.

Kway lived a life contemporaneous with most of her community, working as an administrator for the Tribal Health Program during the day. She lived the glory of her life in the early morning hours when she would set her gill net for whitefish or walleyes, check her trapline, or pick off a deer two hundred yards away without a scope on her rifle. This occupation fed her soul. It was a cleansing of all the awkwardness she remembered, the teasing, lewd remarks, the pain of humiliation in her childhood, and those who continued it in their own sly way now in her adult life.

If there was anyone on the reservation preoccupied with her sexual orientation, it was Fred Graves, a tribal councilman, who occasionally made offhand remarks about her in the hallway, barely audible, yet enough to catch her ear. Graves would never say a word publicly, to whatever extent one could say the tribal council meetings were public as most meetings were held in executive session. But that was because Kway Dole was a star employee. Her pristine public image was, perhaps, due to her work performance. Her department management was consistently under budget and with few personnel problems, all concerns of a tribal government scraping by with meager resources. No matter how hard she worked, however, Kway still judged herself harder. She wondered why the Creator had given her a different path to follow and where she might find a road map.

She parked the now infamous F-250 Ford pickup behind her mother's garage in Naytahwaush and went inside. Her mother, a small round woman with gray hair, sat at the kitchen table, coffee cup in hand. It was eleven, and the scanner blared:

"Authorities are looking for an unidentified, navy or blue pickup truck reported to have been involved in an incident outside White Earth village. A single woman is believed to be driving. Some damage was sustained to the truck body from impact. The suspect is at large and is considered extremely dangerous."

"You OK?" her mother asked, her eyes surveying her only daughter.

"Fine, just fine. I feel a lot better."

"How's the truck?"

"Good. I think." A pause. "Probably smart I left that snowplow on."

Kway poured herself a cup of coffee and leaned against the counter. She pulled a pack of cigarettes out of her jeans pocket, lit one, and looked out at her mother. Her mother's face was brown and wrinkled— she had been easy on the cold cream. Her face was kind, yet hardened by years of circumstances the Oil of Olay woman would never see or dream of.

Her mother had always been understanding, Kway considered, especially after all the challenges she had put her through. In spite of a social history in the Indian community of tolerance to the different, and in fact valuing diversity, coming out as a lesbian brought families and individuals face to face with the imposed intolerance of colonialism, churches, and "American values." The resulting confusion ran like a raging river through small villages and trickled down to the families. Her mother had weathered the flood and stood by her daughter.

"I'm gonna head back out, ma," Kway began slowly, looking to reassure her mother of her best-laid plans.

"Those FBI men sound pretty mad at you."

"Embarrassed, more like it. A woman and a pickup truck turned their sorry butts over."

Kway's mother giggled, and her eyes sparkled.

"You be careful, honey; don't get into it with them. I don't want to know what you are planning to do." A pause, she surveyed her daughter again. "I'm sure it will be good."

"The net in the other truck, ma?"

"Last time I checked, but I ain't got much use for it. You just bring me the fish. Right?"

"Right."

"I'll listen for you on the scanner." She patted the police scanner with her hand.

"I'm sure you will. *Nan giige.*"

Her mother watched as Kway turned and walked out the door.

In the other truck, Kway sat and spun the radio dial to listen for news. The reports were still on, saying much the same. Angry Indians, angry white farmers, lots of federal cops. No background explanation of why the Indians were angry, still. Kway sighed. She flipped through her tape collection, powwow tapes, Michelle Shocked, Steve Earle, Indigo Girls, picking the last. She drove in the darkness, an occasional deer, porcupine, or raccoon wandering into her sight.

She slowed, arriving outside the village, and pulled her truck into an old farmstead and got out. She paused for a few moments to pray once again. Absent a road map, she relied heavily on guidance from outside. Satisfied, she walked to the pickup and grabbed up her gill nets. Two of them spanned one hundred feet by six feet each. Then she picked a smaller net, one she occasionally threw to catch fish in a smaller spot. She put the huge mass of nets over her shoulder, and with a flashlight in hand, began her surreptitious walk back into the White Earth village.

At 5:45 A.M. there was a hiss, then the gas. From his fort of broken dishes, Agent Cope looked through his night-viewing binoculars at Hungry Hill, the crown jewel of White Earth. It was dim and foggy and he could detect no movement whatsoever. A dog barked again and two ran free through the housing project. The old-model sedans cozied up to pastel houses, lawns littered with children's toys. The people seemed oblivious to the invasion. Five minutes later, flares went up on the south edge of Hungry Hill as a diversion as national guardsmen advanced toward the north side of the tribal offices.

Eight guardsmen, practiced in the weekend exercises of warfare, stealthily edged into the housing project. They crouched, sprang, and ran between the HUD houses trying to get close enough to launch some tear gas canisters on the tribal headquarters and "flush out of the key players," as Agent Cope had briefed them. Watching through his infrared binoculars, Agent Cope was already giving himself a high-five for this slam-dunk mission.

Too late did he realize the folly of his action.

The gill nets were invisible in the dim light of dawn. With ingenuity as his chief tool, Willie Schneider had worked in the darkness to rig the long nets on poles near the council offices. Springs on the ends of the nets kept them taut and ready to ensnare unwary guardsmen. The gill nets were set like a giant spider's web ready for prey.

A black guardsman on point was the first to walk into the invisible web. "Shit!" was all Agent Cope heard through the guardsman's radio headset as he whispered under his gas mask, the net collapsing on him and springing closed around his team, entangling their guns, equipment, and arms in the nylon mesh. The guardsmen tried to extricate themselves, and it got worse. The point guardsman fumbled for his knife.

In the early fog that had settled on Hungry Hill, women's voices yipped in a high-pitched shrill, the sounds of counting coup, a successful capture. The point guardsman hurriedly extracted the knife blade from his scabbard and began cutting furiously when a heavy boot kicked the knife from his hand, sending it spinning through the fog and tear gas. He heard the sound of it landing far away and looked up to see an angry Kway Dole hidden behind a gas mask.

"Don't mess with my net, buffalo soldier," she growled. He cringed and held his hand, his fingers feeling broken. He grit his teeth, determined not to let her know he was injured.

The high-pitched shrilling rang through the morning, blurring the commands issued to the guardsmen over their radio headsets. "Regroup! Regroup!" turned into "Retreat! Retreat!" and the guardsmen turned tail and ran. Housing project dogs barked and set chase. Overhead, flares lit the scene through the fog and tear gas. Running in crouches, Indians appeared through the mist and dragged their catch into the tribal offices.

Inside, the glare of fluorescent lights blinded the guardsmen as they squinted their eyes, trying to get their bearings. Indians with gas masks encircled them.

"Give me the guns and the masks," Willie Schneider ordered the two ensnared guardsmen.

The guardsmen hesitated.

Kway lifted a .30–06 deer hunting rifle and shouldered it. "Better move, guys, we ain't kidding." A pause. "Do it, buffalo soldier."

The black guardsman wished she hadn't taken such a special interest in him. He sighed, took off his radio headset and mask and passed them with his rifle and pistol out through the holes in the net. The other guardsman followed the leader. He started choking on the remaining tear gas fumes and Kway passed him a wet towel to cover his mouth and nose.

"I'm gonna go check the others," Willie said, as two more Indian women appeared behind him. "See you at Chi Makwa's."

Kway and the two women stood and watched the men for a few minutes, while the gravity of the situation dawned on the government forces. Clothed completely in camouflage, Kway held her deer rifle at the ready. Georgette Big Bear and Danielle Wabun wore gas masks and red bandannas over their hair. Danielle Wabun was dressed for the occasion in a black leather jacket and pants she had found at a rummage sale. The Indian women herded the stumbling guardsmen toward Georgette Big Bear's basement in the housing project. George Ahnib yipped and howled, occasionally joining in and prodding the soldiers with a big stick.

"George," Kway Dole said softly to him, "*Real* Indians count coup and don't have to hurt their enemies."

George nodded, knowingly, and used his stick less vigorously.

The Big Bears' basement had been designated as the holding area. Kway led her two guardsmen into the basement and was soon met by Willie Schneider with two more guardsmen in separate gill nets. The Indians had successfully harvested four hostages, but no one was exactly sure what to do with them.

Danielle Wabun peered down at the guardsmen who sat crouched on the basement floor. "You guys sure look young," she observed.

"And scared," added Kway.

The women shuffled slightly back and forth now, wondering what to do, a little bit like a high school dance between unsure, hormonally charged teenagers.

The black guardsman glared, still holding his fist.

"Suppose your hand's kind of sore, buffalo soldier?" Kway asked. No response.

The women stood and looked at their prisoners. Finally Danielle said, "Listen, guys, we'll tie you up a little so you're more comfortable, and we don't got to baby-sit too much."

"You're too fucking nice," Kway said. "These guys are the enemy."

"Yeah, sure. But not really," Danielle said. "They're lackeys of the enemy."

"What's the difference?"

"Listen, girl," Danielle said firmly, pulling her aside. "We're probably stuck with these lackeys for the day at least, maybe longer after that. Let's get this set up so we can get our work done."

"Alright."

"Then we leave George to watch them."

"Good one."

After an hour of work, each man was deftly tied to a chair. Danielle had decided they should be fed, so an arm was left undone. Buffalo soldier's sore hand was left free and there was enough distance between the chairs that no one figured they could get into too much trouble.

"Are you hungry?" Danielle asked. The men looked at each other in disbelief, mute.

Georgette Big Bear appeared with four bowls of macaroni and meatball soup. "Special government issue commodities, you should be used to that," she said as she carefully placed the bowls in outstretched hands.

Kway watched with dismay. "For Christ's sakes, this is not a dinner party. These assholes were trying to gas us and arrest us, and now you dames are caretaking them."

Georgette sashayed by. "It's my house, Kway. Even the enemy gets fed here." She smiled triumphantly and turned on the television to Bugs Bunny cartoons. At the sound of the TV, George Ahnib returned downstairs with a bowl in hand and took up his guard post on the landing, looking down on the guardsmen and watching Elmer Fudd.

"Alright," Kway sighed. "You hostesses take care of our guests here, and I'm gonna go see if our people are OK." She glared at the soldiers, slowly walking by each and nudged them with her deer rifle.

"You, buffalo soldier. Get your loyalties straight." A pause. "After this is all over, *if* I let you live, you better not suck up to no fucking white cop."

He set his jaw and glared back at her.

She flicked her rifle over her shoulder and walked neatly up the stairs.

Agent Cope stood in the bathroom of his trailer and placed his head in his hands. The trailer was a mess, his men were shaken in morale and stunned, and he was miserable.

"I hate Indians," he said again and again, repeating his phrase like an empowering meditation mantra. Repeating it four times, he emerged from his respite and faced his men.

The radios were buzzing with arguing agents and policemen and guardsmen. By midday, Agent Cope summoned his inter-agency colleagues for a meeting. He was wishing for negotiations.

"Well, maybe we could see if anyone from the Justice Department would think again about refereeing this thing out between the tribal government and those Indians," Agent Cope told his war council. "We've tried to scare them out, chase them out, and flush them out, but nothing seems to be working." A tone of resignation. "It's fourth down and time to punt. I'll call Washington again to see if we can get some help."

As a policy, the FBI was not keen on negotiations, and to be truthful, the Bureau had a special ax to grind when it came to Indians. Everyone knew it. Especially since the shoot out at Oglala in 1976, which had left two agents dead. Although the FBI had succeeded in sending one Indian up to prison, the whole affair left a bad taste in the Bureau's collective mouth. Then there was the *Crazy Horse* book. That made the agency look worse. Despite some six lawsuits, they had been unable to stop the book's publication.

Agent Cope was intimately aware of the Indian problem. He did not like this position, and he certainly did not like this particular take-over. At this point, however, it did not look like the FBI was winning, and no one wanted to be a loser. The circumstances led him to opt for negotiations as the only way out. He telephoned Washington.

"We've been playing this game for almost three weeks now, and we're beginning to stink. If we stink, so do you," Cope tried to explain the situation to Washington. He was sure Washington was more than a little out of touch. Cope was exhausted and wanted to be honest.

"We'll take your position under advisement," Washington responded.

TRAVELING SHOES

**FBI Assault of Occupied Tribal Offices
Turned Back by Protesters**
By Alanis Nordstrom, *Rocky Mountain News* Staff Writer
*White Earth, Minn. — Under cover of night, National Guardsman directed
by the FBI failed in their attempted assault on the occupied White Earth
Reservation tribal offices. . . .*

"It's the bottom of the eighth inning. The white guys are up to bat
with guns, pens, bats, and cellulars. Schneider tosses a low curve to the
right. Cope takes a hit . . . starts running . . ." Moose Hanford's voice
trailed off on the intercom as he chuckled, *"ho wah!"*

Using the tribal council's fax machine, Alanis managed to file her
story and several updates for the *Rocky Mountain News* and UPI. During the evacuation, one of the drivers from Reverend Swenson's church
agreed to courier Alanis's rolls of film to the local newspaper, where a
darkroom aide developed them, printed the best images, and got them
on the international news wire. With a little persuasion, Alanis's editor
gave her a reprieve from Miss Indian America and let her stay on the
story. Alanis was sure the newspaper would get mileage from it.

It took the Indians about two days to return the guardsmen. Their
captors, the *Ogichidaa Ikwewag*, or the Women's Warrior Society, decided that the men were dangerously young and inexperienced. They
might be irrational. Besides, no one really wanted any "hostages." The
soldiers were sent back unceremoniously in an ex–Tombstone Pizza

truck Selam Big Bear had owned into a few years back. The guardsmen were certainly no worse for wear but incredibly relieved to be
free.

Following the botched attempt to storm the tribal offices, the
FBI had apparently decided to wait things out. There was little sign of
activity at their trailer. Even the white protesters seemed to have gotten bored.

Remarkable as it was, things remained relatively calm at the White
Earth tribal offices and in the villages. It was as if the state of siege had
waned and waxed for one hundred years, and this was just one more
phase of war.

Sweat lodges were constructed near the tribal offices, and on a
number of occasions different *Anishinaabeg* spiritual leaders came in to
lead ceremonies. There had even been talk of the return of the Big
Drum and *Midewiwin* ceremonies. Those, however, would come in
their own time.

Besides that, people were cooperating. The occupation team had
developed a good network in advance, and Lee Swenson and the
Lutherans had done a good job in mobilizing their people. Warren
Wabun and a few others volunteered and were dispatched for public
events. Between those speeches and frequent press releases and updates, they generated a great deal of support. The result was that fifty
to a hundred calls daily were going in to the Minnesota Congressional
delegation and the State Legislature's offices, putting pressure on the
elected officials to negotiate with the Indians.

As things started to ease up a little, more subtleties became apparent.
The first and probably most interesting thing Lucy St. Clair noticed
was that Moose Hanford and Elaine were having an affair. She had
ascertained this notable fact since Elaine wasn't in her bedroll at night.
And she noticed how Moose watched her. Elaine had started to hum
a little as she ambled around, and Moose had lost a major crabby streak.

"They're perfect for each other," Lucy gasped with pleasure as
she reported this important liaison to Georgette Big Bear. "They're
young, lovely, and committed. I think they're perfect," she noted ob-
servantly again a day later, this time clasping her hands together as if
she had made the match herself. Georgette, of course, agreed. It was

true that Elaine and Moose seemed like a perfect pair and they both deserved someone nice. Besides that, she thought to herself, *"Who wanted to argue with Lucy?"*

As Lucy's curiosity mounted, she investigated further. That night she tracked the new lovers to validate her suspicions. *"Sure enough,"* she whispered to herself as she carefully listened at the door of the tribal chairman's office to the two sets of snores. *"It's got to be them."* Lucy padded back to the women's sleeping area and curled up in her bag. Content, she slept hard and well.

There were, of course, a series of other possible romances that blossomed during the occupation but none so interesting as the romance of Elaine and Moose. "Intrigue is the essence of life," Lucy divulged to Alanis, informing her of the new and interesting information.

"I guess there is something about crisis and Indians," Elaine observed philosophically when Alanis approached her a few days later. "We just get romantic in dangerous times. I think it's in our history, and by now it's downright traditional."

In the middle of this came the shooting. It was a Wednesday night, cold and crisp. Thinking back on the events later on, Elaine Mandamin suspected that Hawk knew his number was up. He had asked her to make him some "traveling shoes" a few weeks before the occupation. She remembered it now, but she honestly thought at the time he that had meant for the new ceremonies he was attending, especially since he had just completed making his dance outfit a few weeks past. "Just in time for the June fourteenth powwow," he had said when he mentioned it to her again and passed her some tobacco. It was strange, though, how he prepared both to celebrate life and walk toward death at the same time

Moose knew the occupation was going too easy, and someone was going to blow it. His people were in order, and he knew it. But ever since his tour of Vietnam, he never again would trust the feds. And the redneck protesters were always a wild card. When he heard the shot, heard it hit metal and glass, he shivered as a cold chill crawled up his back.

"What the hell was that?" He glanced at Willie Schneider and scrambled for a radio.

"You there?" he broke into Selam Big Bear.

"Yup, no problem here, check Hawk."

"Hawk, you there?"

No response.

"Shit! I may have a man down." Moose lumbered toward the back door, ducked, and ran low to the ground toward the brown pickup Hawk sat in. The radio waves were jammed with the FBI and Becker County Sheriff volleying questions back and forth.

Moose was scared now for the first time during the whole occupation. Willie was almost climbing over him by the time they got to the truck. The driver's window was shattered by a bullet from a high-powered rifle. Inside, Hawk's head rested against the steering wheel. Blood dribbled from his temple. Moose grabbed his hand and looked at Hawk's eyes. His spirit was already gone.

"Shit, shit, shit!" Willie screamed into the radio. "Those sons of bitches killed Hawk!" Elaine and Lucy scrambled for a stretcher.

Moose grabbed Hawk's still-warm hand and whispered, "I'm sorry, bro, I'm sorry. We'll do it. We'll take care of you."

He kept mumbling softly. Then he stopped. Paused and pulled some tobacco from his pouch, placing it in Hawk's hands. He folded Hawk's fingers over the tobacco, stood, and tried to remember what to say.

They finally got Hawk back into the tribal building as Elaine, with a shaking voice, called Agent Cope on the radio. "One of our guys just got killed by someone out there. You better figure out who." She slammed the radio down.

There was a sheriff's deputy named Kevin Bennert who had it out for Hawk, and Moose suspected Bennert immediately. He would have a rifle that could take out someone at that distance, and he had a motive. Hawk and Bennert hated each other since junior high when they rode the bus together to school and Hawk used to scrap with Bennert, usually getting the best of him. Over the years, Hawk had forgotten the details but remembered that Bennert didn't like Indians much. And now Bennert was a cop.

Hawk had thought he was a lousy deputy, who only liked Indians in certain circumstances. Hawk had been doing his own investigation into police brutality and sexual assault cases on the reservation, and a number of the complaints traced back to Bennert. The complaints usually involved Indian women in the backseat of a patrol car, two or three of whom seemed to be of special interest to the patrolman. It seemed that he would pick them up for questioning and then return them much later. In any case, Bennert's name always came up, and Hawk had his suspicions. Besides, Hawk's own weakness for an occasional binge would invariably end him up with his own trip in the back of Bennert's patrol car, a night in jail, and a lot of cursing. Hawk had been close to pushing on Bennert hard when the occupation had happened.

Elaine too remembered Bennert and his little personal grudge against Hawk. That grudge might be relevant and might not. It wouldn't bring Hawk back but it might get him some justice. It was all strange, though. Hawk's fate, more than almost anyone else's, seemed to be driven by intensely opposing forces. He would do amazingly well for himself, then he would fall into drinking. He had finally gotten his dance outfit together, and he would talk about dying. He would be a true warrior, and he would get jailed.

Elaine caught Moose and led him to a private room, then burst out in tears. "Hawk was trying so hard, he almost had it together," Elaine said as she sobbed on Moose's shoulder.

"Hawk was a good man," Moose said. "I don't understand why he had to die."

And Elaine could feel the big man tremble with tears.

"Who fired that shot?" Agent Cope bellowed into the radio. The radio waves erupted with a static of voices casting blame, denials, more accusations, curses, and arguments. It was then that Cope realized the game was over.

He simply turned the radio off and hung his head. Looking down at his empty hands, Major Traversy stood across the command table strewn with maps, ashtrays, and the colored sprinkles from too many donuts.

Cope finally spoke. "It's out of control," he said, pausing. "The sheriff is running his own show, the rednecks are out of hand, there's no way to coach this thing."

He motioned to Traversy for the cellular phone, and the major skidded it across the table to him. Cope pushed the first programmed button and waited for the phone to ring.

"This is Cope," he told Washington. "We're negotiating."

And he hung up.

It took three days to prepare the negotiations. Helicopters ferried in the federal negotiating team, and then the four identical federal cars packed with government officials, bodyguards, and observers drove solemnly into the barricaded tribal government grounds through the northeast entrance to the encampment, arriving at the elders housing unit, the appointed site for negotiations. All of the white protesters had gone home, the local police were sent away, and the site seemed quiet and still. Moose, Willie Schneider, and Kway Dole stood by with their rifles on their hips, watching the federal cars parade up to the council offices.

The federal negotiating team consisted of two dour-faced men in dark suits from Washington and Agent John Cope. White Earth tribal leader Lance Wagosh and representative Fred Graves trailed behind, Wagosh trying to look like he was in control but appearing simply uncomfortable. They were met by Elaine, Selam Big Bear, Warren Wabun, and George Agawaateshkan, and everyone sat down at a dining room table borrowed from one of the housing project's families. The discussions were held in full view of some forty interested people from the occupation and the elders housing unit. Mesabe and Charlotte Oshkinnah sat side by side and stared angrily at the suited government men until the men began to shift in their seats.

"First of all," Elaine began, "we want a full investigation into who shot Hawk Her Many Horses and immediate prosecution."

Agent Cope stirred uncomfortably.

"This is not just another dead Indian," Elaine continued. "He was shot with a government bullet."

"You don't know that," Cope stammered.

"Well, you figure it out," Elaine interjected. "Do it!"

Cope leaned back, paused, and then nodded.

Lance Wagosh jumped in, changing the subject back to the original issue at the root of the takeover. "We have the authority to negotiate and sign leases," he said stubbornly, repeating a frequent position.

"We know you have that authority," Elaine said emphatically. "We just want you to cancel them."

Federal eyes focused on Wagosh. The tribal chairman would not waiver. Elaine stared back at him, keeping her voice even as she looked now to the federal officials and repeated the demand. Warren Wabun spoke now, talking calmly and directly: "That logging equipment will never be safe."

It was an understatement that everyone understood.

The negotiations continued through eight that evening. And although there had been little movement on any side, everyone agreed to return the next morning to recommence.

"Keep a stiff upper lip," Moose whispered to Elaine during a recess the next day.

"Does that mean no kisses?" Elaine asked as she returned to the negotiating table.

After three days of talks, the federal men began to look at their watches. Finally, returning from lunch with the government men on the third day, Lance Wagosh gave in, agreeing to cancel the logging permit and mill construction lease. An agreement in principle conceding to Protect Our Land's term was drafted, adjusted, rewritten, and then signed. Everyone breathed a sigh of relief, although none more so than Agent John Cope.

NIIMIIDIWIN POWWOW

Two weeks later came the annual White Earth Powwow commemorating the signing of the 1867 Treaty of Peace. Alanis had returned to White Earth for the powwow after filing her Miss Indian America story. Now she rested in the bleachers, sitting with Elaine. Together, they admired the dancers. She felt more at home than she had in a long time, her eyes resting on Browning Teaman in the emcee's box. Wearing an exquisite red-and-black ribbon shirt, he appeared, as usual, every bit the showman. He looked over at the two women and waved.

For Protect Our Land, the powwow seemed to be a true celebration, marred only by the loss of a warrior in the face of victory. Moose, Elaine, and the others all joined in the honoring of Hawk's family, as four veterans led the dancers out in one last dance for Hawk. His newly completed bustle fluttered in the wind that brushed through the arbor. Moose was the head men's dancer, and he couldn't help but dance almost the whole three days. That was his way of giving thanks for the gift of peace. Sometimes through the corner of his eye, he thought he saw Hawk dancing too.

PART IV

Oshki Anishinaabeg

LEECHING CAPITAL OF THE WORLD
1994

"This here reservation is the leeching capital of the world. There ain't no place like it," Moose proudly told Willie Schneider, his partner in most things requiring two people except sex. "And this here is one great leech pond."

The men had cut down the Buckboard Hills Road to a logging road. The underbrush was thick with thistles and small popples from where it had been cut over. Flies buzzed in his ears, and a woodtick crawled up his leg. Moose walked in front of Willie carrying a backpack filled with turkey kidneys and leech traps. The kidneys came cheap from the turkey packing plant in Detroit Lakes. He also had a small bag on his shoulder with a lunch and a thermos.

Leech ponds are usually shallow and have no fish. "If there were fish, there would be no leeches. They'd already be eaten up," explained an ever-patient Moose more than once to a white supporter of the land rights struggle. "I know you don't believe this, but a bunch of us make half our money on collecting these bloodsuckers to sell to sports fishermen," Moose added.

This had been a good leeching season. They had leeched for two weeks on some ponds north of Rat Lake and then moved on to the so-called state land in the Buckboard Hills. They had already leeched two ponds there, and Moose had now found the third.

The best season lasted from May until July, when the leeches were most active. After that came dog days, and the lake water was too warm. The leeches got lazy and retired, taking siestas toward the bottom of the murky ponds.

When it was still cool but sunny, the *Anishinaabe* men would go out and bait up their traps late in the afternoon. The traps would be full by morning, and at seven dollars a pound for jumbos and four dollars a pound for smaller ones, Moose and Willie could make a lot of money on a good day. Leeching was also a hell of a lot better than a casino job, waiting on retired farmers or schoolteachers dumping their nickels into the slot machines in a trancelike state.

This had been the land of Moose's great uncle. The old people had had a trapline out here. Because of that, Moose often thought about trapping here in the winter to give his other trapline a rest. For now, though, he figured they would bait their traps and then take a look around for animal signs.

Moose pushed the canoe off the shore. Willie was already in the canoe, his wet rubber boots making a growing puddle. As the canoe inched forward, Moose gingerly hoisted his two-hundred-and-fifty-pound body into the boat, while the other man hugged the opposite side of the aluminum canoe. The boat tipped a good fifty degrees toward Moose, then abruptly plunged back.

"Almost," Willie gasped as the boat tipped back to level. "You'll drown me yet."

The men towered above the canoe as they paddled it from shore. With an incredible agility, they maneuvered the canoe between stumps and water lilies, until they found what appeared to be the best spot to set their line of traps. Willie was the first to begin unrolling his line.

The leech traps consisted of a series of small black plastic bags tied onto a nylon rope. Each bag had a small rock in it to weight it down, and between every few bags was a plastic pop jug to keep the line afloat. Inside each bag they placed a turkey kidney to attract the bloodsuckers.

"How's the bottom feel here?" Moose asked Willie, who put his paddle down deep into the murky water.

"Mino ayaa," Willie responded, "good."

They stowed their paddles now and began to ready their traps.

Moose watched Willie as he opened the plastic bag filled with several pounds of turkey kidneys. Willie was quiet today, Moose noticed, as Willie passed him a handful of dripping wet kidneys. Moose drew his hunting knife and began slicing the kidneys in half, chasing them around the cutting board as they slipped from his hands. Willie still didn't say anything, seemingly intent on cutting his own batch of kidneys.

"So," Moose began.

Willie did not even look his way.

"So," Moose said again. "How those kidneys look?"

Willie paused now. *Working up his nerve,* Moose realized. He wondered what was coming.

Willie broached the subject by asking Moose about Elaine, Moose's new and most promising love interest.

"So," Willie began, "how is it living with that woman?" A pause. Willie continued to look straight ahead, nonchalantly. "Is the honeymoon over yet?" Willie paused again. *"Ehhh?"*

"Well, aside from the fact that she hits the road like a bat out of hell six days a week, it's great. She's good company—and never boring, that's for sure," Moose grunted, looking at Willie's hunched-over back.

"So, married life suits you?" Willie wondered if it was possible.

"This kind of married life suits me just fine. As long as I can be in the bush, I'm real happy. She stays pretty busy, and so do I. It's good," Moose offered willingly. He had been a bachelor for five years, give or take a few weeks with various wives. So, all in all, he was a man used to his space.

Moose now sensed Willie's line of questions. It was an excellent time to discuss women, being that it was just Moose, Willie, and a few thousand leeches. Moose opened the door to Willie's heart. "You seem to have quite an eye for that woman Alanis," Moose ventured as he pulled another handful of kidneys out of the bag. He looked up again at Willie's back, to see if his friend had indicated any interest.

With his fingers, he worked to separate the pieces he had already cut with the knife. The kidneys were stringy, unwilling to split easily.

Willie had been with a woman a couple of years back. She had left him for a guy in the cities, a guy with a desk job and a powwow van, one painted with that ghastly *End of the Trail* logo in sunset colors on the side. He was a city man who didn't leech. It took a special kind of woman to like leeching, and Willie was on the lookout. This new woman who had visited White Earth, Alanis Nordstrom, was something else. Not a leecher, however.

"She sure is pretty," Willie said wistfully, "and smart."

Then Moose knew what was troubling Willie on such a fine day for leeching.

Willie fished out a few cut kidneys now and carefully opened a small black plastic bag. He dropped one in and looked at Moose for the first time, his face inquisitive, seeking answers.

"She's a city girl, Willie," Moose observed, adding hopefully, "but maybe she'll come back to visit now and then; maybe she could make it up here."

"How would you go about getting a woman like that, *Niij?*" Willie stopped now and wiped his kidney-covered hands on his pants. He glanced over his shoulder at his friend again. Then he looked at his immense palms.

"Carefully," Moose said slowly. "You have to get good bait and be real patient."

"I can do that." Willie's lips pursed with determination. His mind was optimistic, more so in reference to his food gathering than *nooji'ikwewe*, the act of actively seeking women. He looked straight ahead at the woods, his eyes searching the shore.

"I think she might, somewhere deep inside, like an outdoors kind of guy, a rez boy," Moose volunteered.

A hopeful look spread on Willie's face, turning to a rather sheepish grin.

Willie returned to baiting traps, his mind clearly focused on this woman.

Moose looked more critically at Willie again. He rarely noticed the actual physical appearance of his friend, considering him more on the practical side. From behind he wasn't that bad. Willie's hair was frizzed out in a number of directions outside of the confines of his hot pink hair tie. Borrowed from his niece, Moose surmised. Willie had also developed a modest frybread gut, now protruding over his Wranglers. His friend, however, had a nice face. *And* an earnest expression.

Not learned. Earnest. If Willie, his best friend, was set on this woman, there would be challenges ahead.

Moose sighed.

The men continued to bait their traps. Willie maneuvered his buck knife to separate the kidney pieces.

"A lot of Indian women like those tight Wranglers you got on," Moose reported, knowingly.

"Maybe I should take up rodeo," Willie said. "Bull riding. That would definitely get her attention."

"No, *really*." Moose said.

Willie looked up at him.

"Go to the library," Moose suggested. "Read a few books. Subscribe to a magazine or something. One of those fancy Indian ones, or maybe . . . maybe, a yuppie, hip one. Like that one from the cities . . ." Moose paused now, groping for a name. "Utne," he said triumphantly, "like the insurance company."

"OK, whatever that is." Willie was unfamiliar with this intellectual arena. Maybe insurance company guys were interesting.

Moose continued with his advice. "Then after you read a little more, go talk to her."

"About what?"

"About what you read, and—hey!—about life on the rez. Tell her some really terrific stories about your family, your old uncles, war stories. . . ."

Moose sat up straight now and took a breath. Leech baiting was stinky work. However, advice giving was hard, especially in such a far-fetched case.

"And if that doesn't work, there's always medicine."

Willie raised his eyebrow.

"Who knows that kind of medicine?"

"There's folks," Moose spoke slowly, hesitating. Lowering his voice, just in case a stray spirit was listening. "Christ, old Lucy St. Clair for sure. How do you think she keeps those young guys?"

"Fear, I thought."

"Yeah, that too, but love medicine for sure. Lots of it."

Now Moose slowly paddled the canoe forward as Willie continued to set the line. In total, he set about forty traps in a small area. As

Willie finished, he took up his paddle to move the canoe toward a small channel that flowed into the next pond. Moose set his leech trapline in a second section of the pond that was about six feet deep.

"Good enough," he said, as his eyes searched for a place to beach.

They found a landing of sorts and pulled the canoe up to shore. Seeing a small creek, they walked about fifteen feet to the water, and washed their hands and faces.

"That kidney smell's gonna stay with you all day. I can tell already," Willie noted with a grin. "Are you sure you aren't skunk clan instead of Marten?"

A grunt. *"Shhhhhh, ehhh."*

Willie was laughing to himself at his own joke but Moose was serious, still trying to think of helpful advice, sort of like a rez Dear Abby.

"Just remember," he told Willie, pointing a kidney-covered finger at his friend, "you got to have the right bait in the right trap to catch you a woman like that."

Willie halted his laughter. He nodded his head seriously now, scrubbing the leeching kidneys off his hands with renewed energy.

OGICHIDAAKWEG
THE WOMEN'S WARRIOR
SOCIETY
1995

Two matches burned at once, while the oil popped and cracked in the flat cedar needles. The flames jumped with each sound, and almost as quickly as they erupted, they died, leaving a glowing edge. Georgette Big Bear pulled the smoke over her head with each of her hands and whispered to the cedar. She pulled the smoke over her body and began to turn around.

Elaine picked up the eagle feather with her right hand and the small pan with her left. She bathed the feather in smoke and pulled the smoke over Georgette as the older woman turned clockwise. Georgette then helped Elaine pull the smoke around her.

Elaine returned to her seat in the northeast of the circle as Georgette continued to smudge each woman in the circle. When finished, she sat down on the east of the circle. Georgette made full moon prayers. She blessed the water and sipped from the bowl. Then she passed it to the left, clockwise. Elaine, the last, completed her prayer and placed the water back in the middle of the circle. As she prayed, the women listened intently, occasionally punctuating the rhythm of her voice with exclamations of support.

This was the third season of the Full Moon Ceremony.

It was Kway Dole who brought forth the story at the Full Moon Ceremony in November. She started to talk about Frances Graves, the eleven-year-old daughter of one of the tribal councilmen, Fred Graves.

"I watch that girl in school, and there is something going on at home," Kway said. "She cries most days and is gone at least once a week. The truth is, she's got bruises on her too, mostly on her wrists— or at least that's all that I can see. It looks like she's trying to cover them up, but she's such a nervous girl that she ends up fidgeting with her sleeves, and then I see those bruises again."

Kway looked around; the women were listening. "I found her in the bathroom at the clinic crying more than a few times. She won't talk to me much, though." A pause. "You all know that her mother is in Minneapolis a lot, and Frances's got the job of taking care of those two young boys and cooking for her dad. Everyone knows that her dad has a lot of power, but that's no reason to turn our heads."

Then Georgette Big Bear spoke up. She was a guidance counselor at the school. "I talked to her one day in my office. The girl told me that she respects her father a lot and that he's a good man. I asked her if her dad treats her all right, and she just kind of looked down. 'It's hard for him,' the girl mumbled, saying, 'With my ma gone, I sort of take care of all three of them.'"

"I came right out and asked her then," Georgette continued. "I said, 'Does your father touch you in private places?' That girl really looked sad then, but she said 'no.'"

The truth was that Fred Graves abused his daughter. It was an awful secret women spoke of in hushed voices and men pretended did not exist. Graves had been on the tribal council for three terms now and had a firmly entrenched base of power. He controlled most of the jobs in his district, and people depended on those jobs for their families. Speaking out meant losing your job. "Besides," most people figured, "the girl seemed OK, and she wasn't the only one who had been through it." Most had survived, and some men actually said that "the experience was a rite of passage." As far as the Graves family was concerned, it was said that the father had been abused by his own father, Boodoo Graves. Fred Graves was passing on the sickness.

Georgette did not think abuse was a right of passage, and neither did Kway or the other women. There had been a suicide a year before. A fourteen-year-old girl who had been molested by her uncle had blown off her head with a shotgun in a shack behind their house. There were other girls too. For one of them, people said, her grandfather and her father were the same person.

The women all listened to the stories and thought about their own lives and experiences. Everyone acknowledged that the sickness existed, but that did not make it right. It was even worse if they let it continue. They prayed, rested, and planned.

Bawa'iganaak oog, *the ricing stick, is carved from soft, light cedar, and is used to coax the* manoomin, *the wild rice, from its stalks. In the fall, the sound of the sticks hitting against each other and on the rice makes a soothing sound of harvest. This winter night, the sticks would make a different sound.*

Kway ran her hands over the smoothness of the ricing sticks. She was crouched in the dark behind Elaine's war pony, the 1976 Nova. Alongside Kway there were five others, including Lucy St. Clair, Georgette, Danielle Wabun, and Elaine. In other parked cars along the street, Charlotte Oshkinnah and a few determined elders waited at the ready. Each woman listened to her own breathing as she waited.

The sound of an approaching car came through the night. Kway peered over the hood of the Nova and watched Fred Graves park his car in his driveway at 115 Amik Street in the White Earth housing project of Hungry Hill. When he climbed out, Kway could see he was a big man, twice her own size. He took a last drag on the butt of a cigarette, tossed it to the ground, and crushed it out under the toe of his heavy work boot.

The girl sat frozen in the front seat. Kway kept her eyes fixed on Frances. The burly man walked around the front of the car and opened the passenger door. "Get out and go inside," he said. She reluctantly emerged and walked toward the house. Her body was mature for an eleven year old, but she was still a frightened girl. She waited for the man outside the front door. He followed her inside.

Lucy shifted her weight from one haunch to another as she braced herself against the cold. Tonight the moon was almost full, one of the coldest nights of the month. It was clear, and she could see the northern lights dancing over the edge of the house. One light appeared in the kitchen and another in the bedroom. Lucy tapped the ricing stick against the palm of her hand and waited.

Danielle saw the man retrieve two beers from his refrigerator, pause to open one and take a long drink. He was facing the window, and Danielle swore she could smell the alcohol and smugness. He flicked off the light and went toward the living room. The television came on to a late-night rerun of *Dragnet,* and the man sat on the couch, a beer in one hand and glowing cigarette in the other.

Maggie watched the girl in her room. The pink walls were covered with posters of rock stars and cartoon characters. A few stuffed toys and knickknacks were packed against the window on a corner shelf. The girl closed her door and now sat fully clothed on the side of her bed. She carefully removed her shoes and walked to the window, scratching the frost to better look outside. Slowly she turned and walked back to switch off the light. Still fully clothed, she lay down and pulled her blankets around her.

It was twenty minutes later that the living room went dark. The man walked away from the TV, which was still droning. As he opened the bedroom door, Lucy saw he was clothed only in his shorts.

The women were up and running. Maggie made her way toward the girl's bedroom window and carefully placed the small step ladder near the window. She climbed and listened. She could hear the man swearing at the girl and the girl crying as she tried to push him away. Maggie waited a few moments and then motioned with her arm for the women to move forward.

Lucy used a key she had extracted as a favor from an old boyfriend at the housing maintenance office. She put the key into the front-door lock and turned the handle. Lucy and the other women slipped inside and moved toward the bedroom, their steps concealed by the monotone of Sergeant Joe Friday on the television.

Elaine pushed open the door to the bedroom and flipped on the light switch. Suddenly the darkness of the room was banished in the glare of the overhead light. Elaine was stunned for a moment at the sight of the man as he tried to force himself inside of the girl. His body was heavy against her as he held her arms down and pushed apart her legs. Her pants were on the floor and his shorts were to his knees. As the light illuminated Elaine's face, the girl looked up at her and shame crossed her young face. The man was too intent to notice until Elaine's ricing stick struck him across his back.

"Get off her!" Lucy screamed as she rushed into the room and pushed at the man. He looked up and gave a small cry. The women surrounded the girl's bed. The man lifted himself up slightly, and the girl broke free, running from the room. Georgette quickly grabbed her underpants and followed her into the bathroom.

As the man attempted to stand, the ricing sticks began to fall on his back, head, and butt. He managed a cry and reached to pull his pants up. Danielle grabbed them with her ricing stick.

"Howah!" she yelled and yanked them off his legs, twirling them on her ricing stick.

The women herded him toward the front door, raining down blows and prodding him with their ricing sticks. Lucy signaled with the porch light, and as she did so, Charlotte Oshkinnah, Kway's mom, and another elder, waiting in their cars, switched on the headlights, illuminating the housing project block.

"Get moving!" Lucy screamed at him as she kicked the naked man out his front door. The man stumbled toward the snow, covering his head from the blows as the women herded him into the street.

Fred Graves was greeted by the car lights and the sound of car horns. The residents of the project were awakened by the light and noise and appeared on their front porches, wrapped in blankets and coats. The women chased the naked man through the housing project with the might of their ricing sticks. As he ran down the street, each family came out to look at their tribal council representative.

It was December of 1995. A young woman cried in her bathroom and was comforted by an older friend. As Georgette helped the girl into her clothes, she whispered, *"shhh, shhhh, shhhh, shhhh, shhhh, shhhh,"* just as if she was calming a baby. "It's OK, my girl. It's not your fault. It's OK. We will take care of you." Finally dressed, the girl sobbed again, and once more Georgette drew her close.

The *Ogichidaa Ikwewag* had had its second war party.

THE LONG WINTER

BIBOON 1995

Moose was the fireman for the ceremony. He started the fire around six in the evening, carefully building the fire around the rocks until they glowed with heat. There were thirty rocks tonight, exactly the number the old man had requested.

The sweat lodge was out on the west of Rat Lake at a site that had been used off and on for this ceremony for the past one hundred years. This lodge was freshly constructed of willow covered by canvas tarps, old sleeping bags, and army blankets. Moose and Selam Big Bear had rebuilt the lodge that past summer, and they had been using it on a regular basis since the occupation.

It was almost eight when the men gathered around the fire and put in some prayers. The old man, George Agawaateshkan, was leading the ceremony tonight. He softly made his greeting, then ducked inside the lodge. He entered from the east and moved clockwise until he seated himself near the door on the other side of the entry. The old man inhaled the smell of sage as it covered his body.

Then the old man called for the other men to enter. Willie Schneider made a greeting, then crawled inside. He was followed by Selam, George Ahnib, Jim Vanoss, and several others. Most of these men had taken to having the ceremony on the new moon, or when someone felt the need. On this night during the new moon of *Manidoo Giizisoons*, the Little Spirit Moon of December, the sweat was a healing ceremony for George Ahnib.

Once they were all inside, Moose carefully extracted the rocks from the coals and gingerly carried the glowing stones one by one to the sweat lodge. As each "Grandfather" came inside, George greeted the stone, saying, *"Aneen Mishomis."* Then, with two deer antlers, he maneuvered the rocks into the pit at the center. With each subsequent stone, the small lodge became warmer and the greetings more accentuated. After Moose had moved fifteen of the stones from the fire to the lodge, the old man motioned for him to stop. Moose carefully closed the flap and slowly circled the lodge. He heard the old man begin his prayers, and then he walked back to watch the fire.

George Ahnib had never been in a sweat lodge, but everyone had agreed that it was time. It was risky to bring him into the sweat on account that he was half crazy, but George trusted Selam, and between Selam and Jim Vanoss, they had prepared George over several weeks for the lodge.

Moose heard the songs start within the lodge and knew that George would calm down. The old man, George Agawaateshkan, was using a small hand drum to accompany his prayers. His singing was high pitched and fast, keeping time with the quick beat of the drum. Now other voices joined in, *"Way yah hey hey, way yah hey hey."* Then the old man led again. Four times the song and drumming came, each subsequent round louder and more urgent. Moose listened to the song and to the barking sounds that came from the lodge. The song ended, and George Ahnib howled. In a low voice, Moose could hear the old man talking to his helpers, *"Oshkabewis . . ."*

As the old man prayed, George Ahnib alternated between a soft whimper and a wail. Finally there was silence.

The old man made a knock on the flap. *"Nee dah way mug in nug."*

Moose opened the flap and let out the spirits. The first round had ended.

George's trial date was set for December twentieth, and there was little question as to his guilt, only to the length of time the state would put him away. Elaine and others wanted him sent to a new treatment program near Kenora, Ontario, that was culturally centered and would do him more good than the state mental institution. Unfortunately, while the Ojibwe did not see the U.S.-Canadian border as a barrier in their own community, the government did, so it would take a lot of work.

George's trial was less of a media focus now, however, although Alanis Nordstrom had flown back to the reservation again to cover it as a follow-up to her stories on the occupation. Following a federal investigation, the grand jury had indicted four tribal council members, including the chairman, for embezzling federal funds.

After Councilman Fred Graves finished his grand jury trial, he faced a sexual assault trial for abusing his daughter. Owing to his own smugness, Fred Graves made a crucial mistake of underestimating his daughter. He thought Frances would never testify against him, and as such, had tried to get the charges reduced in a plea bargain. Unsuccessful, he opted for a plea of not guilty, which inevitably meant he would face a jury—and his daughter.

By the time the case was scheduled into court, Frances Graves had been to counseling and ceremonies for six months. The counseling helped her work out her loss of self-esteem and trust and relearn right and wrong, while the doctoring ceremonies drew the poison from her and sent it back to where it had come from, or at least, away.

It was at this particular time that Fred was reminded that one of the unfortunate things about Indian country is that everyone is related. As a consequence, when he entered the courtroom, the front three rows of observers were filled with women who were related to the family. Charlotte Oshkinnah was his father's second cousin; Georgette Big Bear had successfully petitioned for temporary custody of his daughter; Danielle Wabun was his wife's first cousin; and worse yet, Lucy St. Clair was his daughter's godmother. The women sat and watched Fred, and they watched the judge.

Each day the women came to the courtroom and watched. The trial took four days, and the jury took only four hours to decide he was guilty. Two weeks later he was sentenced to five years in prison. Everyone could agree that there is no worse crime than stealing innocence.

It was on the third round that Moose noticed the sweat lodge was vibrating. He had just brought in more rocks. The old man was singing what sounded like a *Midewiwin* healing song now. Moose could hear the hand drum and what sounded like a rattle. As the singing got louder, the sweat lodge began to shake. Over the old man's voice a wolf barked again and again, and then there were voices talking in what sounded like old Ojibwe. Words that were rarely used today. Moose could no longer hear the old man's voice. Twenty minutes later, the old man's drum re-emerged, then silence.

"Nee dah way mug in nug," said the old man, knocking on the flap. Moose opened the door and felt what seemed like a wing brush against him as the hot air escaped.

That winter was one of the coldest people had ever seen on White Earth. From January to March, the thermometer never moved from fifteen below, and the winds from the Dakotas swept in without mercy. Each day Charlotte Oshkinnah would look out her window at the sundog around the sun and know that this day would be colder yet. The Ojibwe called the sundog *waawiyaasenagweyaab*, a round light rainbow.

"Look at the dream net on the window," Charlotte said to Kway, pointing at the spider web–like frost formed on the pane. "There's a lot of spirits here now. They've come inside to keep company with us and stay warm."

Some of these spirits were in the sweat lodge with George Ahnib. It was almost quiet now as the old man prayed. It was the fourth and final round. Whatever battles had been fought were over, and some sort of balance had returned. All that remained in the lodge were the seven men and the protector. At first Selam smelled the wolf, and then he felt the fur between George and himself. George howled and the wolf answered.

THE OLDEST WHITE
MAN IN THE WORLD

"Kaginig minokumini
minwa bigoninig
me eta go ni nibowin
Kebish kage makug
Kichi Misawinagut su
Iwidi agaming
Oma ondas nakakegam
Onza bundjigeshig. . . ."

"Amazing Grace
how sweet the sound
that saved a wretch like me.
I once was lost
and now I am found. . . ."

"There was a wake and those Ojibwe hymns. That was about all that made sense at Grampa's funeral," Frances Graves reported with clear disappointment to Georgette Big Bear.

"What was wrong this time?" Georgette understood the girl like no one else. She too grieved the passing of the old man but knew it was time for a rest.

"Everything," the girl continued. "They buried him in a box that looked like a Cadillac. The white men from the funeral home hovered around like we were gonna steal their damned rug or the casket was rented."

Frances's grandfather was Boodoo Graves. In a drunken stupor, he had shot himself with a hunting rifle. It was tragic, but not surprising. A widower, he could not reconcile his own loss and what remained of his life. People said he was tormented by his own demons as he wandered endlessly from the cross to the gutter—or, in the case of White Earth's dirt roads, from the cross to the ditch.

Frances mourned his passing, but secretly thanked the Creator for allowing him to rest. She had placed tobacco on his casket before they lowered it down.

"Worst of all," Frances complained to Georgette, "was that beastly priest, Father Thomas. He must be the oldest white man in the world. They probably sent him back to be put out to pasture."

Father Thomas had insisted on burying her grandfather, eulogizing from the pulpit about his favorite student from boarding school forty years before. But the ancient Father scared Frances. There was something about him that unnerved her, but she did know what it was. She shrank away from his handshake after the funeral, and her grandfather's passage did not bring her peace. That came only after the oldest white man in the world passed away, three days later. Whatever it was that had frightened her about the Father went with him silent to his grave. Somewhere in her subconscious, Frances hoped closed gates awaited him.

FOR THE PATRON SAINT OF HOPELESS CAUSES

1995

In the years just before the Great Depression, in a time when everyone, not just Indians, was dirt poor, Claire St. Clair was born, a second cousin to Alanis Nordstrom's father. It was on account of this relationship that Alanis, during her return visits to White Earth, came to know her relative and the nature of her devout and peculiar ways.

Claire embraced Catholicism as the center of her life and as the long-term salvation from the misery of deep poverty. She had made plans to be a nun, but found herself sidetracked by an Irishman who farmed on the Ponsford Prairie. With him, she joined into twenty years of marriage and virtually as many children. A woman of ample size and heart, Claire's zest for life grew with age.

The second passion in her life emerged after the death of her husband and followed on the heels of her children as they left home for the cities. In 1983, Claire St. Clair encountered bingo. Operated by the tribal government, the Golden Eagle Bingo Lodge generated almost a quarter of total operating revenues. More importantly, it served to provide the folk of the community with a hope that they too could be rich, or perhaps just foolishly spendy. Claire played bingo feverishly, not out of loyalty to the tribal treasury, but with a sincere religious belief that Jesus instructed her in card selection and that winning was an affirmation of her faith. In recognition of this affirmation, she split her winnings fifty-fifty with the church. And she won with relative frequency.

Claire St. Clair was loyal, attending Monday and Friday nights in White Earth, Tuesday in Pine Point, and Thursday night in Naytahwaush. Occasionally feeling cashy, she would round up her friends and together they would drive to Cass Lake for higher stakes bingo. And on visits to her children in the Twin Cities, she frequented the Little Six Bingo Parlor at Shakopee, where she occasionally won a small jackpot. In total, she had several thousand dollars worth of earnings and a Ford Escort to show after ten years of resolute commitment.

As a consequence of a history of repeated crisis, Claire suffered from a chronic spiritual anxiety. This propelled her into copious servitude. In the year after her husband's death, Claire aligned herself with the charismatic Catholics, embracing the church with a consuming passion. She attended daily mass, took communion, and dutifully confessed once a week to divulge whatever sins she imagined had occurred during that brief period. She found that she could help spread the word by contributing to the various missionary efforts she had read about in the Catholic periodicals at the church and those she received at her home. This eased her conscience and, over time, her pocketbook, of a great weight.

She became the head of the reservation Altar and Rosary Society and followed in the footsteps of her grandmother Philomene St. Clair. On her knees, she scrubbed the church after each Sunday service and took it upon herself to wash the altar linens, keeping them spotless, well pressed, and creased. She swore at times that she could hear her old relative's whispers and instructions, and occasionally the pages of her hymnal would fly open without explanation. On those days she sang those hymns from sunup to sundown. This she did not only to save her own soul but to fend off the evils that she saw encroaching on her village.

Alcohol was only the tip of the iceberg. She saw tribal politicians adrift in deceit, men beating their wives, and saw children who had no respect for anyone. Most disturbing, however, was the lack of any faith whatsoever in much of the community. There were a diminishing number of parishioners, not only at the Catholic church, but in all of the other fourteen denominations who had come to save Indian souls. There seemed to be no commitment to God and no belief in the Savior. There were many things she disliked, but she felt she had no direct power to change them. For this she prayed to Saint Jude, the Patron Saint of Hopeless Causes.

In retrospect, it was most fortunate that a vision redirected Claire's spiritual focus. There was, of course, some question if it was a vision or a spirit sighting, since a number of other people on the reservation had been witness to the same apparition. No others, however, had been able to stand their ground.

It was said that at the White Earth Powwow in June, Deer Woman would sometimes appear. Usually adorned as a woman's traditional dancer, but sometimes as a jingle dress dancer, a devastatingly beautiful woman with an elongated neck and deep, mysterious eyes would weave her way through the intertribal dancing. She would appear for the duration of the dance and disappear when the drum stopped. In the flurry of fringed shawls, sinewy grass dancers, and hundreds of moccasins, her tiny hoofed feet were scarcely noticed save by an occasional child who would pull repeatedly on his or her mother's sleeves and point, while the mother would continue talking incessantly to a neighbor. When the mother finally turned to her child and listened to the child's observations, the drum would stop and Deer Woman would be gone.

There were also a few late-night drivers who reported seeing her on the highway to Naytahwaush or Cass Lake—a tall, lanky woman in jeans and jacket, long braids and deep eyes. Two women once pulled over to offer a ride only to watch her bound into the deep woods, leaving only deer hoof tracks in her wake. She was the siren of *Anishinaabeg* culture, and all who saw her counted their blessings at the sighting—and more importantly, at her departure. To be lost in her company was to be lost forever. Except for Claire St. Clair, who clothed herself with disbelief.

Claire St. Clair was so thoroughly indoctrinated with Christianity that she deemed herself safe from the spirits and powers of the woods and remained confident in her rosary beads and confessions. What she knew about her own culture and history, she had dismissed, and what she did not know, she had forbidden to enter her thoughts.

It was perhaps because of this obsession that her fate would collide with her culture.

Driving home from White Earth bingo in the early spring of 1991, she rounded the corner past Adam's schoolhouse and saw what appeared to be a woman standing by the road. She flicked her lights so as to divert the person from the road and slowed down. It was then that Claire realized this was no ordinary person. A woman clad in jeans and jean jacket, with the deepest of eyes and no apparent feet whatsoever, approached the car. As Claire slowed the vehicle, Deer Woman sauntered slowly in front of the car and looked straight at her. Out of reflex, Claire grabbed the cross hanging from her rearview mirror and began to recite the Lord's Prayer. To her dismay, Deer Woman continued to stand unmoved and undaunted by her actions.

Then, for some reason beyond her comprehension, a voice, a memory, flickered through her mind: *"Don't forget your* asemaa.*"* Claire reached into her purse and extracted a Lucky Strike cigarette. Breaking off the filter, she opened the cigarette and emptied the tobacco into her shaking hand. She unrolled enough of the window to push through her large arm with a fistful of tobacco. *"Aneen Wayway skayshee kway. Aneen Manidoo Oshkabewis,"* she gasped in the singing tones of the Ojibwe language and dropped the tobacco on the road.

Deer Woman approached the car and looked down at the tobacco; her nostrils flared. A few moments seemed eternal. Deer Woman looked at Claire, nodded, and slowly walked off the side of the road, down the shoulder, and then bounded away, disappearing into the brush.

Claire waited in the car, breathless. When she had regained her composure, she gingerly stepped outside to peer at the footprints. Her fear was realized when only hoofprints remained. She scrambled back behind the wheel of her Ford Escort and gunned the motor for Naytahwaush.

That sighting marked her for life. There was no explanation on the path of Christ for what she had seen. The occurrence left her totally bewildered. Only with the help of Selam Big Bear, a born-again pagan, was she introduced to George Agawaateshkan, a leader of the *Midewiwin* Society, who counseled her in the traditional healing practice. According to George, the sighting had meaning not only for herself but for the whole community. *"This is about our need to remember and re-engage in our relationship with this Earth, our Mother,"* he explained. It was most probably true, he acknowledged with appreciation, that her demonstrated spiritual commitment had opened the doorway for this vision. To Claire, for whatever reason the vision had occurred, the effect was a spiritual transformation.

Christianity played less of a role in her life. In the face of a community-wide scandal, she left the church. But she fortuitously retained the practice of sending her bingo winnings into the coffer, out of both habit and a true conviction that Jesus taught her to play and to win. Claire was still loyal.

In 1993, she began to play the Minnesota State Lottery on a regular basis. Each time she would buy a ticket, she would offer tobacco to the Deer Woman and patiently await the results. In retrospect it was most fortunate. Alanis, her distant cousin, would say that nothing occurred until something good could be done about it. They were words she had learned from her father.

These words had meaning for Alanis as well. Ever since the shots were fired at her during the occupation, she had felt the emergence of a side of herself she never knew existed. She began to have a dream: An old Indian woman with a straw hat talked to her in the Ojibwe that she did not understand. And then she found herself, even though awake, dreaming while writing at her office computer, dreaming of the life her father had left behind, White Earth. She wished herself back among the trees and the rice, and whenever she could take a long weekend off of work, she cashed in the frequent flyer coupons she had saved from her reporting trips and flew back to White Earth. As her father used to say, nothing occurred until something good could be done about it.

Over the years, many tribal members had been lost to the relocation programs and were scattered now across the continent. As living in the city had grown desperate and dangerous and as prosperity had not come in the promised lands, people had been drawn back to White Earth both for its refuge and for the signs of promise now blossoming on the reservation.

In 1994, the White Earth *Anishinaabeg* government was rebuilt with a melange of traditional tribal structures and new administration to manage relations with federal and state bureaucracies. A center-piece to the new authority was land consolidation, managed by Elaine and a committee of traditional people. As a result of the Occupation of 1993, almost a third of the land had been returned to the White Earth people. This included those lands held by various absentee government and private owners.

What remained a challenge was the financing of the re-acquisition or the buy-out of the non-Indians who were private landowners on the reservation and who wanted to leave. This had been a major challenge for the new tribal government since the market value for land in 1995 was considerably more than it had been when it was taken from the Indians. Claire St. Clair would soon come to the aid of White Earth.

In August of 1995, Claire St. Clair won the Minnesota State Lottery, hauling in an amazing fourteen million dollars in one fell swoop. Elaine thanked the Creator that Jim Baker had done time, Jimmie Swaggert had been caught twice with his pants down, and that Claire had seen the Deer Woman. With her first installment check from the state lottery, Claire St. Clair had her hair done into a monumental beehive, bought new, floral-pattern linoleum for her kitchen floor, and set up a trust fund in the name of White Earth and Protect the Land. It was Claire's financial gift that secured the buyback of almost a tenth of the White Earth Reservation for the *Anishinaabeg* people.

GIIWOSEBIG
THE HUNTING PARTY

When D-Day laughed, he sounded as though he was on the verge of death as he brought forth the wrath of thirty years of smoking, chewing tobacco, and alcohol. Inevitably, his heartiest of laughs ended with a long coughing and sputtering spell. The point was to laugh anyway.

D-Day was a short, sturdy man who watched the world from behind thick glasses set in ancient horn-rims. He carried in front of him a belly that had settled like a gunny sack of potatoes. His white, crew-cut hair glistened against his dark skin, his weathered hands whispered of years in the woods peeling pulp for logging companies, and his tongue spoke mostly Ojibwe. He preferred the nuance of his own language, and over time, age and amnesia had taken most of the English he knew and returned it to its source, a shelf of yellowing books in a boarding-school library somewhere faraway.

D-Day had been on the beaches of Normandy on June 6, 1944, one of the few Indians on the front lines of the invasion. The victory had stayed with him through time, as had the name and an incredibly shiny uniform, which he extracted from a cocoon of plastic for ceremonies, powwows, village events, and Veteran's Day each year.

Although Veteran's Day was over and done with for this year, the celebrations were still going strong. D-Day, Mesabe, and John Brown were silly, although not *waawaashkeshi*. The old men sat on the porch of the elders housing unit in White Earth village. They were all upstanding veterans of various wars, foreign and domestic. D-Day had his victory to brag about. Mesabe was a World War I vet, but he had returned without all the decorations that D-Day carried pinned on his uniform's chest. Now ninety-seven years of age, Mesabe had simply the honor of having lived. John Brown served a short stint in the Korean War and returned home to the safety of the reservation and his family. Each year for Veteran's Day, they gathered again, celebrating their wars and their own longevity.

Tonight they had been talking about a long time back, before any of them were born, but well within the stories of their parents and grandparents. It was Mesabe who was speaking: "I'm telling you, store-bought buffalo meat tastes different. It's not right, not the same."

D-Day and John Brown nodded their heads in time to his words.

"Long ago, buffalo roamed over the flat, western part of the reservation—before it was a reservation, remember. And in the late summer each year, the herd grazed the grasses of the Red River region. That was a good time. And that was good meat. Real live meat. Not like now."

"Not like now," D-Day echoed.

The old men were silent for a moment, all remembering the succulent taste of meat roasted over a fire.

"That was meat with spirit," said John Brown, licking his lips without thinking.

Mesabe continued: "The hunting parties were honored and important. The men were gone for days, traveling by horseback to find the buffalo herds. Then, after a successful hunt, two to three buffalo were cleaned, butchered, and brought home by horse and canoe. That was how we used to go. Remember, *ina*?"

"Now all the meat comes from the feed lot and is wrapped in paper," D-Day said, shaking his head, "paper with a stamp on it at Country Market. That's how Indians got to eat now."

Summer had slowly eased into fall. Warm days lingered as long as they could until a crisp damp wind and a mist of rain fell on the land as always. Then a last dance of summer, one week of southern winds, sun, and a soft rain returned for that last, sweetest of memories.

It was late in the evening when Willie Schneider drove by with Alanis Nordstrom in his extended-cab pickup. The old men were still on the porch, still deliberating over the taste of buffalo and the virtues of different morsels. Mesabe waved them down. When Willie stopped, D-Day commandeered the pickup with Willie and Alanis as their chauffeurs. "*Equay, Ambe maajaa weesnik biziki.* Will you drive us?" D-Day asked as he pulled open the truck door. Before the surprised Willie could nod his head, the old men stumbled into the back seat, and the odor of aftershave, chew, and cigarettes filled the pickup. Alanis noticed that D-Day was carrying a rifle half hidden under his coat and Mesabe had a set of wire cutters held behind his back. John Brown's pocket bulged with the weight of a flashlight.

"What are you doing back in these parts?" Mesabe queried Alanis.

"I am just back to visit," she responded. "I had some vacation time due me and wanted to come see you all."

At that, the old men in the back of the truck giggled. Willie looked straight ahead, shyly watching the road.

"So, where are we going, *Mishom*?" Alanis asked, looking in the rearview mirror at their set faces.

"Lets head out by Mahnomen; there's plenty there," D-Day directed to the designated taxi service.

"Plenty of what?" Willie questioned him.

But the old men were silent, as if they had not heard him. They were all looking intently out the front window of the pickup.

"So where have you been tonight?" Mesabe finally said, as crafty as a fox.

Willie and Alanis professed that they had come from a late meeting at the land office when they had been flagged down. The tribal land program, with the hefty donation from Claire St. Clair, had managed to purchase a number of farms. Indian families from the HUD housing project in Minneapolis and the reservation were now moving into the farms. Willie served on the land committee, and Alanis showed up to watch the proceedings. Willie had been happy to see her there and offered her a ride home.

"This land's all ours, you know, Alanis," Mesabe pronounced from the backseat, reaffirming Indian law as he did each day.

"Sure is," said Alanis. It was land these old men had known forever, but land until recently not owned on paper by Indians.

"No, I mean this land's really ours. Never mind the paper," Mesabe said.

Alanis looked into the rearview mirror as Willie drove and saw Mesabe's eyes meet hers, glowing with ferocity even in the dark of night.

With the changes in land ownership wrought by the land programs, there was a change in natural resource management as well. Previously, the county commissioners had issued almost endless timber permits to companies from off the reservation with little of the money coming back to the Indians. Now, a natural resource management committee established a program of selective cutting and habitat restoration. The committee had planted medicinal plants and reintroduced animals. It also strictly limited hunting. Ten years prior, the majority of the deer and fish on the reservation had been taken by non-Indian sports hunters; today, the statistics were sharply reversed and the harvest was lower. Non-Indians could still hunt on the reservation, but they required a special permit.

Willie Schneider and Moose Hanford sparked the idea to issue the hunting permits based on income. "Sport hunting is a crime against the natural order and against the *Anishinaabeg* code of ethics," Hanford had said. "However, people who really need food have a right to take animals. We can figure out who those people are, in part, by income." Selam Big Bear had made the arguments for culture and residency as well. Big Bear sat on the Anishinaabeg citizenship committee.

Under new tribal enrollment provisions, a commitment to language and culture were now a central part of tribal membership. "It's not that you have to be a fluent Ojibwe speaker," Selam reasoned, "only that you should be sincere about a commitment to remembering your culture and language." Big Bear always used the term "remembering" when referring to language and culture since within the past four generations most people had spoken, but lost, the language. "Hey, it's not my fault, I can't speak Ojibwe," Big Bear would say. "Boarding schools and the Mahnomen principal made sure I couldn't even talk to my grandparents by the time they were through with me."

Willie turned the pickup down a dirt road following D-Day's

insistent pointing finger.

Willie Schneider spoke up now. "So you guys going to do some hunting tonight, *eh?*"

He saw the way D-Day stirred uncomfortably in the seat with the .30–06 under his jacket.

"*Eh heh,*" came the response from the backseat.

Willie quietly slipped his arm around Alanis's shoulders, his movement a part of his conversation.

Mesabe smiled, observing the earnest doings of his young counterpart and empathizing with his challenge. Alanis was a headstrong and cosmopolitan woman who found herself struggling with all of her own expectations, standards, and what she loved. Willie Schneider reminded her of her father, the smell of his sweat, his big hands, and the security of his presence. Except Willie was not a ladies man, but the exact opposite. He was shy and unsure around women. But he was determined. He had set his sight on Alanis and somehow was going to win her heart. The old way, maybe.

"Ever hear an Ojibwe flute?" Mesabe asked Alanis from the back seat of the big truck. Mesabe had read Willie's mind, and he could see Willie shift in his seat.

"No, can't say I have."

"Those Ojibwe love songs on a flute are really something."

"No kidding?" Alanis's voice raised slightly to show her interest and hide her amusement. She shifted slightly, aware of Willie's arm at her back. "Been giving any lessons lately, *Mishom*?"

She smiled into the rearview mirror at the old man who chuckled now. Mesabe elbowed D-Day and whispered something to him in Ojibwe and they all laughed. D-Day's was his loud, raspy laugh. Alanis looked again at the old man and smiled at Willie. She was not sure how she felt about him, but his arm around her shoulder was okay for now. Maybe she would wait for the flute.

"Slow down!" shouted John Brown, and a startled Willie lifted his foot off the gas.

"Turn off them headlights," Mesabe interjected.

The headlights went out, and the world around them turned dark.

"What's going on?" Alanis asked. But Willie suddenly knew where they were and why they were there.

They were driving slowly now onto the outlying land of a large cattle ranch owned by a woman from Oklahoma. The five-thousand-acre spread adjoined tribal land in a couple of places, and had been the center of controversy over the past few years. The Oklahoma woman had never even seen this ranch, named Oxblood. She had inherited it from her grandfather, a big land speculator who had picked up sixty or so allotments decades past. Now she ran the ranch as a corporation from her headquarters a thousand miles away. Over the past two years there had been a number of skirmishes between the ranch operators and the tribe, mostly over environmental problems. A feed lot in the northeast corner drained directly into the Wild Rice River, and sewage and pesticides were ending up downstream. Although the environmental department had issued a series of warnings and tried to condemn the site more than once, the operators would invariably hire an attorney, find a loophole, and restart.

Then there was the problem of the native prairie grasses. The Oxblood Ranch was home to a number of patches of the native prairie grasses the tribe wanted to protect. Although the Indians had tried to purchase conservation easements, the owners were adamant that no Indian had any business on the ranch. A number of the areas had highly prized medicinal plants that tribal members often harvested, now mostly in secret to avoid the No Trespassing signs. People always reported fewer plants to harvest in each subsequent year, but the tribe seemed powerless to stop the destruction. After two years, negotiations had broken down, as had the patience of many tribal members.

Aside from these troubles, everyone knew that D-Day's family had owned four of the allotments that now comprised the Oxblood Ranch.

It was a moonless night with a warm southerly wind. Willie eased the pickup down a section road adjoining the ranch. The old men lost their silliness and commenced thinking about the importance of their mission. About a mile and a half down the road, Willie halted the pickup in response to John Brown's whispered command.

"Where are we?" Alanis whispered, but her question was not answered.

D-Day was the first out, followed by the other three. The old man took tobacco from his pouch and passed some to Willie, who grinned as he accepted it, realizing he was now an accomplice. He was a Vietnam vet, so maybe he was being made an honorary member of the hunting party.

John Brown broke the head off a Marlboro cigarette and passed a second to Mesabe. Each man said a few words and set tobacco out under a large white pine near the truck. Only then did they extract the rifle, wire cutters, and flashlights from the truck. Then Mesabe went back and laboriously lifted himself into the driver's seat.

Prepared, D-Day and John Brown headed off through the woods toward the ranchland. In his usual good spirits, Mesabe began to giggle from the rear guard. He watched the two old men shuffle through the woods toward the fence. Having arrived at his predetermined site, D-Day extracted his wire cutters.

"What are you guys doing?" Alanis whispered, looking with wide eyes from D-Day's wire cutters to the faraway lights of the ranchhouse. "What's going on?"

"I'm collecting back rent," D-Day said out loud, and his two buddies almost fell over themselves laughing.

D-Day neatly cut through the four barbed-wire strands as John Brown pulled them back. Just for good measure, D-Day repeated this exercise every two hundred and fifty feet or so along the fence.

This pasture held the Simmentals. These were special cows that tasted real good. The White Faces were in the feeding lot, but they were less interesting. "After all," D-Day had reasoned back at the elder's home, "you could buy them at the Country Market store along with that funny buffalo meat." The Simmentals also like to roam, and at fifteen hundred dollars apiece, that roaming was a good investment of their time.

After they finished up the east pasture, the two old men trundled over to the workhorses. The owners of the Oxblood bred Percherons, the kind of horse D-Day and Mesabe had used in their days on the logging crews. Those horses knew how to move as well, and with a couple of big gaps in their fences, chances were those horses could be almost in Mahnomen by morning. Watching the two old men from the truck, Mesabe spoke to Willie in a whisper: "The horses aren't for eating. It's just the principle of the thing."

Willie shook his head, thinking to himself, *"Besides, horse stealing was an old Indian trick, and these are old Indians."*

Alanis whispered into Mesabe's ear, "What are you doing now? What if someone sees us?"

Mesabe only giggled again and said, "You watch for lights from the ranchhouse over there." And he pointed a gnarled finger to the west.

Now the hunting could begin. D-Day positioned himself on the side of the fence that was tribal land and waited, cradling the heavy rifle in his unsteady hands. John Brown moved in toward the herd. He set his sights on a cow, fat, but not too old, or too heavy. And she should be tender. Waving his arms in the air, he drove most of the animals toward the fence, keeping a close eye on the heifer. A flash-light illuminated their escape route.

As the animals saw the hole, they accelerated. A surge of fifty cows rushed through the fence. The heifer stayed toward one side and in easy range of D-Day. As the animals set hoof on tribal land, Mesabe hit the headlights of the pickup. The lights stunned the animals and they stood stock still. John Brown motioned to D-Day to take a shot.

The shot almost put the old man on his ass. The cow fell at once, and the other three men cried out in a high-pitched "counting coup" call.

"Howah!" D-Day exclaimed. He was exhilarated. "I shot a buf-falo."

The rest of the frightened herd scattered into the woods except a few of the less intelligent beasts, who stared with vacant eyes at the fallen cow and the old men. D-Day took out his tobacco pouch again as he slowly walked toward the cow. Her face still hot, he put some tobacco in her mouth and kneeled down by her side. He put his hand on the side of her head and spoke softly to her and thanked her for her life: *"Mashkode biizhiki, mashkode biizhiki."*

Alanis looked nervously around to make sure no one at the ranchhouse could see them. The house and the watchdogs were a thousand acres away, so there was little danger. Willie perched himself on the pickup's roof just to make sure: The old men may have been slow, but they were accomplished hunters at this stage in their lives. *Awakaanag.* Accomplished hunters—especially of domesticated ani-mals.

With jerks and starts, Mesabe backed the truck up to tow the cow. In different circumstances, they would have gutted the animal there but the Oxblood Ranch security might have heard the shots. Willie jumped out with a come-along in his hand. He hooked the come-along on the back side of the truck cab and quickly unwound it toward the cow. The old men maneuvered a blanket under the cow, end by end, as the strap of the come-along was fit snugly around both the blanket and the cow. The old men guided the cow, and Willie cranked the come-along. As the cow inched up toward the truck, John Brown and Willie changed places. With a grunt, the younger man shoved the cow into the truck.

Willie buttoned up the back of the truck, and everyone climbed back into the cab. John Brown was shouting *"Howah!"* in imitation of D-Day, and Mesabe was giggling. Even Willie and Alanis were feeling silly now as D-Day laughed and coughed and rubbed a shoulder sore from the kick of the rifle. The truck slowly moved down the section road and out onto Highway 200. Only then did Willie turn on the headlights.

THE LAST DANCE
OF DEPUTY BENNERT

Kevin Bennert had it coming. He had covered his tracks well enough that Hawk Her Many Horses's murderer was never brought to trial in the white man's court. And he had plea bargained himself out of any time on the sexual assault of Indian women. Instead, he opted to get transferred to the next county over.

That left justice up to the Indians.

It began slowly. He had given chase to a carload of Naytahwaush Indians, careening down a road into the deep woods. Lights flashing among the trees along the road, the Indians finally stopped. "Do not move! Stay in the car!" the voice of authority blared over the loudspeaker. Then Deputy Kevin Bennert climbed out of his patrol car and did his best official stroll toward the station wagon full of "skins." All four doors opened abruptly, and Bennert found himself surrounded. The wily entourage escorted him back to the patrol car. There, they extracted his handcuffs and keys, handcuffed him to the driver's door of his own locked police car, keys tossed far into the woods. The happy Indians smiled and waved as they headed the five miles back to town.

So began the low-intensity war between Deputy Kevin Bennert and the people of Naytahwaush. It was, over time, a form of slow, somewhat-public torture that left the deputy rattled and bruised.

More than once the off-duty Bennert found himself in a bad spot with an Indian woman. He had a definite sexual preference for Indian women, but only those he met in bars. In turn, the objects of his desire, it seemed, had forged a silent pact, one that prevailed miraculously in even the most drunken of courtships, and Kevin Bennert would invariably end up with the most unusual of bruises, or tied to a bedpost.

The strangest part was that it happened more than once and he never seemed to learn. It was the blindness of his arrogance that let it continue and got him into the worst trouble. It was Kway Dole, however, who would finish it up three years later. And in the end, he wore his blindfold to his execution.

Kway possessed an internal calmness of soul and a self confidence that allowed her to reason through the most trying of circumstances. This served her well.

Deer hunting in one of her usual and accustomed places, Kway Dole's eagle eye spotted Bennert's patrol car down a backroad. Whether the deputy was scoping out his new lair or scouting for some stolen loot, he was in the wrong place at the wrong time.

Now Hawk had never been Kway's kind of guy. He had been a womanizer by the feeblest of opportunity; his sexual behavior went against the grain of Kway's sense of decency. They had, however, crafted an understanding over the twenty or so years they worked together and lived in the same community. They shared a respect for each other's boundaries and could work side by side on a project, amidst laughs and teasing.

Kway turned over various memories, tastes, and scenarios in her mind. In the small sense, she owed little to Hawk. But in the larger sense, she owed him much. All of their humanity was enlarged by his ways, his character, and his own life. Cold-blooded she was not, but exacting, yes.

So it was that, although Kway was an unlikely avenger in the larger sense, she was Hawk's best bet in the practical sense.

She asked the Creator to forgive her and pulled the trigger, dropping Kevin Bennert in a clean shot through the temple. Then she took a deep breath, loaded her gun into her pickup, and never looked back.

THE RUMMAGE QUEEN

The phone rang and jolted Danielle Wabun away from the morning news. A woman's voice on the other end was overflowing with urgency.

"There's been a *terrible* mistake . . ." the unknown caller began.

Danielle caught her breath. This was not how she liked her mornings to begin.

"Yes?" she replied.

"It's just *dreadful*," the voice continued.

Danielle waited, nervous now.

"It's simply a *tragedy*," the voice moaned.

Danielle could feel her own pulse quickening.

"Yes?" she said again. "What's wrong? What is it? What's happened?"

The woman sighed, took a big bracing breath, and then explained, speaking slowly and deliberately so Danielle would understand the gravity of the situation.

"We had a relief drive last month at our church here in Wayzata to gather clothes and appliances to send to your reservation. . . ." Suddenly she could contain herself no longer: "I accidentally sent you my *good* mink stole." And the woman broke into long-pent-up tears.

Danielle rolled her eyes skyward, but she knew this was a serious matter. The Presbyterians in Wayzata were good allies, and she sure did not want to screw that up. She paused to register the problem and puzzle over a possible solution.

"Which shipment?" Danielle said, assuming her professional manner.

"I'm really not sure," came the response on the other end as the tears cleared up, "only that it would have been in the past three weeks."

Danielle sighed, realizing this would take some major detective work.

"Really, it's *very* important," the woman reiterated, her voice becoming more insistent and demanding. "My husband gave me the fur on our twentieth wedding anniversary, and now there's a charity fundraising ball, and I *have* to wear it."

"OK, OK," Danielle said. "I'll do my best to find it. Give me all the details, and I'll call you back this afternoon." She resigned herself to another day of crisis management at the reservation's recycling program.

As Danielle Wabun patiently took notes over the phone, Alanis Nordstrom pushed her way in the door of the Wabun trailer house parked along the shore of Rat Lake, waving to Danielle's husband and making her way straight to the coffee maker for her morning jolt. Alanis was in town for the week researching a feature story on Danielle's father, Warren Wabun, the aging White Earth patriarch of the American Indian Movement. As she warmed her hands around the steaming cup of coffee, Alanis's eyes scanned the trailer house and caught on the bumper sticker stuck on the wall above Danielle's bedroom door: *She Who Dies With The Most Material Wins.*

True to form, Danielle had a world-class collection of fabric. There were bolts of cloth stuffed into her closet and folded pieces of material overflowing into five or six boxes under her bed and around her room. Twills, velvets, prints, paisleys, polka dots, stripes, African and Guatamalan patterns all danced a rainbow of colors and patterns that caught Alanis's eye everywhere she looked. She remembered that someone had once told her that the love of fabric was the downfall of the Ojibwe women.

"Are you stockpiling for the end of the world?" Alanis teased Danielle as she hung up the phone.

Danielle motioned for Alanis to follow her, replying to Alanis's question over her shoulder. "Hey, you should see my gramma's house if you think I've got a lot. She's got more than a couple of closets and cupboards full plus many half-finished projects."

"So that's why the old lady needed a new house," Alanis surmised.

"Yeah, she finally ran out of room."

Danielle walked around her sewing table to scoop up her two-year-old son, Meegwun, passing him to Alanis along with a coat and boots.

"Here's for practice," she said, adding, "you ought to try it," encouraging Alanis to add to the tribal rolls.

As Alanis wrestled the boy into his outfit, Danielle quickly descended onto the toy collection and returned the precious things to their appropriate places in the room. Finished, she grabbed her briefcase and moved into the living room where her husband, Chris Thunder, and their six-year-old son were busy working on a fishing net and listening to the morning news.

Danielle spoke to all assembled: "We've got an emergency. We need to find a missing mink. Alanis, you can be a journalist tomorrow; my father can wait for his propaganda piece. Today, I am drafting you into service. Alright, let's pull out."

As Alanis looked helplessly to Chris for aid, Danielle marched out of the trailer home. Meegwun ran after his mother, and Alanis followed them, climbing into the cab of the pickup truck as Danielle started the engine and aimed for town.

Alanis watched Danielle in amazement. With her left hand, Danielle held a cup of coffee and clutched the steering wheel. Her right hand manuevered the radio dial to find a station, while at the same time, Meegwun dug under her shirt for some *toodoosh*, a milk-filled breast.

"How the hell do you manage?" Alanis asked in admiration.

"Manage what?"

"Juggling your kids, your work, everything?"

"Do I have a choice?"

"I guess not, but just looking at you here, like there's no problem, anything is surmountable, and nothing seems to phase you."

"Well, in the course of my short life on this reservation, I have come to realize that things can be challenging, but they can be done," Danielle said. "And besides, we've got work to do. We've got rummage to get out, and if we don't get down there to get those trucks to town, there'll be hell to pay."

Danielle, like most other women on the reservation, knew rummage sales as a way of life. Although her father had become relatively successful—first as a radio announcer, then later as an Indian politician—money was always scarce. Few people on White Earth had any, but that did not stop them from shopping. It only required greater sophistication.

Reservation rummage sales were bountiful, but in truth, the best rummage came from the suburbs of Minneapolis and other big cities, where the middle class were prone to clean out their closets and garages each summer weekend. From her youth, Danielle remembered many a visit to the cities with an entire weekend spent scavenging at rummage sales. Her father trivialized these weekend forays as "White Earth Raiding Parties," but Danielle, her mother, and their cronies were undaunted.

Warren himself had benefited from Danielle's resourcefulness. Of all that was left by the white man in Indian Country, the worst, in Warren Wabun's mind, was a receding hairline. By his nature, Warren had always been preoccupied with outward appearances, and over the years as an international spokesperson for the American Indian Movement, the need to look beautiful had only been augmented. While others might have shrugged his baldness off as an inevitable result of intermarriage between Ojbiwe, French, and various other ethnic groups over time, Warren Wabun became preoccupied with the state of his head. Danielle reassured him that there was little need to worry about his hairline. "Wear a baseball hat," she would scold him, "and besides, you're on radio, not TV."

Warren Wabun, however, was not content. He became determined to secure an Indigenous Only hairweave to cover his crown. It took a great deal of diligence, but much to everyone's amazement, one day Danielle returned with her father from a northern Manitoba Cree community where she had located some locks suited for his head. His eyes gleamed anew at the carefully constructed addition to his hair. The hairpiece exactly matched his own hair color and was interwoven into long braids. His daughter was so impressed with his newly confident demeanor that she arranged for a feature story on his new reservation-based radio station with *Minnesota Monthly*, a statewide magazine. Warren Wabun carefully and proudly orchestrated his place in media history by appearing, in his new glory, on the cover.

Today, Danielle had been called upon, once again, to perform nothing short of a miracle.

Danielle was in charge of the reservation's Three R Program, whose motto was "Re-use, Recycle, and Reduce." The program was aimed at reducing reservation garbage and creating alternative industries where appropriate for various products. That was where the rummage came in. As part of the recycling, rummage was carefully distributed to the community and to different organizations and projects that produced a variety of crafts from the old fabric, ranging from rag rugs to quilts and mattresses. With Danielle's firm management, the program not only provided raw "materials" to a number of cottage industries, but also satisfied the rummage demand for the community. For her role, Danielle was known as the Rummage Queen.

Donations, charity drives, and church groups filled semi-trailers with castoff clothing and other rummage that was trucked to the reservation. When the donations were dumped at the distribution center in Pine Point, Danielle took over. Each reservation village utilized a request form to procure baby supplies, car seats, canning jars, ice skates, and other special equipment that Danielle tried to match from the different church groups' shipments. The rest of the rummage was distributed on a monthly basis to the rummage centers in each village as fairly as could be managed. The Elders Congregate Housing Unit and the fabric cooperative, of course, received special shipments, although Danielle heard from a reliable source that a number of the old ladies were raiding other distribution centers just to make sure they didn't miss out on the crème de la crème of the rummage.

Danielle's impeccable sense of order and fairness made the program a success. Not only was the rummage distributed to the communities and cottage industries, it was also economical. The rummage sales subsidized the recycling program and some local village projects. The fabric cooperatives were assessed a minimal fee for raw materials, which also went into the kitty. Then there was the money people made in selling the rag rugs back to the people in the cities, who appeared to like their clothes much better cut up and woven into rugs.

It also seemed that as fortunes and political winds changed, rummage improved. For some undetermined reason, people who were the most concerned with Indians seemed to have a great deal of extra clothing, or perhaps they just expressed their concerns with clothing.

Consequently, as Warren Wabun, Jim Vanoss, Elaine Mandamin, and other spokespeople for the reservation land issues mustered the interest in the masses of the urban areas, the volume of goods sent to White Earth increased geometrically.

"We're not a bunch of crows here," Danielle mocked authoritatively to Alanis. "But I tell you, if we didn't have this distribution network to get the rummage out, we'd be in a hell of a lot of trouble. We'd be overrun with rummage and have a civil war on our hands."

"So then how in the world are you going to find this one coat?" Alanis queried, as Danielle pulled up to the Pine Point distribution center.

"The only way we can," Danielle said, turning off the truck and speaking in the silence after the engine noise died away: "We'll find the boxes from that church group, dump them out, and start digging."

She looked over the steering wheel to the distribution center. Trucks from Rice Lake and Elbow Lake villages were already waiting for their share.

"Problem is, we'll have to move fast," Danielle said, thinking aloud. "Beyond finding this one lost fur, we had better keep things moving and distribute this fine booty of the Earth."

Danielle climbed down from the truck and unlocked the center. She efficiently moved in with notebook in hand and Meegwun in tow. She turned on the coffee pot and a couple of lights, then inspected the Rice Lake and Elbow Lake piles before dispatching them. "OK, they're ready," Danielle yelled to Alanis, who was trying to locate the Wayzata boxes on Danielle's strict instructions. "Tell Rice Lake they can get their stuff."

Alanis waved to Rose Ahnib in the diaper service truck, which was called into rummage duty two Fridays each month, but served babies in three villages the rest of the time.

"So, how's it look?" Rose asked as she ambled over to what appeared to be twenty assorted boxes of clothes and about ten pieces of furniture. Rose, like Danielle, had older children and not much need for the diaper service, but she did have an insatiable appetite for "le rummage."

"Today is the Lutherans from White Bear Lake," Danielle reported. "Some nice stuff, *enit?*"

"Yeah, it's almost spring cleaning time," Rose said as she eyed the boxes like a hunting dog looking for pheasants, "and those *Chimook-omaanag* are settling in with their new Christmas presents and tossing out the old models."

"Hell, I wouldn't look now," Danielle warned. "You open those boxes and Elbow Lake is going to raid you if they see some goodies."

"Alright," Rose said with resignation, "just give me a hand."

Alanis, Rose's son, and the other driver helped Rose load up the panel truck as Danielle looked on approvingly.

"Whew, that was close," Danielle said with relief as Rose climbed back into the diaper truck. "I hate hen fights. These ladies act good, and then after enough of them start digging, all of a sudden, it's war. Rummage is sacred stuff."

The two panel trucks departed, full of their precious cargo, just as Alanis uncovered the boxes from the Wayzata church group. There were some seventy cartons, and Alanis stood shaking her head at the thought of dumping them out on the floor to dig for one fur coat amidst the hundreds of pairs of old pants, T-shirts, dresses, and other clothes. But Danielle got down to business, spilling the boxes onto the floor without ceremony, kneeling down, and tunneling through the piles like a mole.

It was two-year-old Meegwun who finally found it.

"Puppy, puppy," he said, cuddling the short mink.

"A miracle," Danielle said, and Alanis sighed with relief.

Danielle had a battle getting the soft fur away from her son but when she finally did, something caught her eye. She took the mink stole outdoors so she could examine it in the sunlight. Then she handed it to Alanis.

"What do you think?" she asked Alanis, who ran the palm of her hand over the fur.

"Not really my style," Alanis responded.

"No, about the fur," Danielle said again. "What do you think about the fur?"

"Well, it feels coarser than I would have thought and the fur is really long . . ." Alanis said somewhat puzzled, looking from the stole to Danielle.

"Beaver," Danielle said with assurance. "I've skinned many of them, and I know my beaver."

THE INDIAN INAUGURAL BALL

1997

At the Indian Inaugural Ball, the descendants of Chi Makwa and Philomene St. Clair rocked softly to the big band sounds and Indian country western music, and raised the occasional toast of non-alcoholic champagne to the newly elected Great White Father. This one, a man named Bill, had promised to treat the Indians as his family, and, once and for all, improve their conditions. Although the Great White Father was unable to make a personal appearance, he did send one of his younger siblings, the Secretary of the Interior, who blushed, smiled, and shook hands with the finely dressed brown-skinned peoples of the land.

Choctaw, *Anishinaabeg*, Dine, and Lakota women were dressed in their finest ballroom gowns. They swayed to the music with their consorts, who were clothed in fine tuxedoes. Lucy St. Clair and Kway Dole had decided to attend as representatives of White Earth, the former in a navy velvet dress adorned with a simple but exquisitely placed spray of floral beadwork, and Kway sporting, uncomfortably, a tuxedo shirt under an ornately beaded vest. Kway stood on the sidelines, shuffling her feet slightly to the music and wondered at the glamour of it all. Lucy, however, took to the floor on a number of occasions with handsome young men from other nations who whis-

pered softly into her still amazingly crow-black hair and were oblivious to the perils of Ojibwe love medicine.

An abrupt change of pace came when Keith Secola and His Wild
Band of Indians took the stage and sent the ballroom gowns spinning
exhileratedly across the finely polished floors. Dancing continued deep
into the night as the latest set of pasty-skinned BIA bureaucrats pretended to enjoy the surroundings. Indian women from across the
United States preened and gossiped, swaying to the various sounds
and searching for chairs at an occasion at which the high price of
"seats" meant that many could not actually sit. Finally, at the end of
the evening, the women who could not afford seats at the posh event,
sat on the floor in ballroom gowns, danced out from the croonings of
Indian country western singers, bluesmen, and Keith Secola. A good
time was had by all.

Moose Hanford had not attended. Tonight, he looked at the stars,
and in the crispness of a clear winter night of northern Minnesota,
took his snowshoes, and walked across Round Lake while the
Mishinameginebig, the Great Horned Sturgeon, slept soundly deep below the surface.

GIIWEDAHN
COMING HOME
SUMMER 2000

The ancestors were loud and getting louder. Moose Hanford could hear the ancestors even over the music from his tape deck and the roar of the road beneath the wheels as his ex-UPS delivery van hummed down the interstate through southern Illinois. There were forty-five ancestors in the back of the van. Resting. Now on their way home. Sometimes he could hear them sing, other times they were crying out. Now they seemed to just rattle.

The tape of Little Otter singing intertribals accompanied Moose on his journey. When Little Otter's drum stopped between songs, the sounds from the ancestors also ceased for a moment, but the rattling continued. Moose realized this noise was coming from his van. He turned off the casette player and listened closely to the mechanical cacophony.

The van was an old UPS delivery van that had been virtually donated to Moose by the UPS driver who had had the misfortune of having White Earth on his route. The van had been well used by the time Moose had gotten his hands on it, and now it counted two hundred thousand miles more on the odometer before that too broke. Moose sifted through his mind, discarding various squeaks, rattles, and creaks that he had grown accustomed to in his van and focused his mind on a possible source for this new ailment.

He moved the van into the right lane and continued listening intently. He inadvertently drove over a pothole and the rattle became a scraping sound accompanied by the full-bore roar of the engine. Only one thing made that music: an exhaust system gone bad.

Moose quickly scanned the horizon for a place to pull over. *The last thing I need,* he told himself, *is for a cop to stop me, see I'm a skin, and give me a ticket for driving without an exhaust—and start asking me questions.* He sighted a rest stop a few miles ahead. He glanced in his sideview mirror to change lanes and to see if he had left any important parts of his van behind. He drummed his fingers on the door, slowed the van to thirty-five and set his sights on the rest stop, tiptoeing his van the last two miles.

Moose pulled the van into the rest area and killed the engine. He grabbed his pack of cigarettes from the dash, opened the door, and stepped down. He lifted his pony tail off his back and shook the back of his shirt for ventilation. *A bush Indian was not meant to travel the southland during the summer. It must be eighty-five degrees with no wind. Too warm for an Ojibwe.* He stopped for a moment and scanned the scene. The rest stop was vacant.

Moose lit a cigarette and walked toward the back of the van. With some effort, he bent over and examined the muffler, reaching his hand toward it. "Shit! It's hot," he inadvertently yelled. Sure enough, the hanging clips had broken and most of the exhaust system was dangling precariously from one remaining anchor. He realized duct tape would not fix this one.

There was a lot of responsibility in this journey and it weighed heavily on Moose. People around White Earth joked that Moose must have been Mole Clan on account of his uncanny knack at finding things in the ground. The only problem was that there wasn't a Mole Clan on White Earth, and so his Marten Clan tendencies would have to account. Moose had discovered the grave diggings in the first place. Then, with Elaine and Danielle Wabun's help, they had come up with an amazing inventory of the people and belongings missing from the reservation through the years. Where they were now was anybody's guess, but they bet the Smithsonian Institution, Peabody Museum at Harvard, Minnesota Historical Society, and the University of Minnesota were the first places to look. The list of missing persons and their belongings ran to fifty type-written pages comprising approximately two hundred and fifty ancestors.

With some digging of her own, Elaine traced the work of a Smithsonian researcher, one Dr. Ales Hrdlicka, who had made several "scholarly" forays to White Earth in the 1910s. He had dug up the remains of forty-five White Earth ancestors, labeled them, packed them away in wooden crates, and shipped them one thousand miles away to Washington so they could be measured, cataloged, and studied. And there they remained.

The White Earth Government, with the agreement of the *Midewiwin* Society, had drafted several polite letters to the Smithsonian. The *aanikoobijigan*, the ancestors, were to come home, the religious leaders wrote, as were all of the traditional objects of the *Anishinaabeg*, particularly those from White Earth. Finally, after years of wrangling, they succeeded in winning an agreement from the Smithsonian that the remains of some of the ancestors could be repatriated. Moose's journey was the first mission to bring back the ancestors, and it was not surprising that there were some technical difficulties.

The Smithsonian's was known to be the largest collection with more than thirty-two thousand remains in one location, not to mention a million or so "artifacts" that were held in various boxes, drawers, and warehouses at the museum. The Smithsonian's White Earth collection was a result of the physical and social anthropologists they had enthusiastically dispatched over the years.

The Peabody at Harvard had a similar number of "specimens," and over the past few years had also begun to return remains and objects to Indian tribes nationally, and to a lesser extent, internationally. The Maoris and Tasmanians had been picked over particularly badly, and they had waged an aggressive campaign for the return of their objects that had been underway for almost twenty-five years.

Smaller public collections at state historical societies and universities were also under pressure, and both the Minnesota Historical Society and the University of Minnesota had joined with the various reservations to form local historical societies and museums so they had somewhere to return artifacts.

The curator at the Smithsonian had been courteous, even helpful. The Smithsonian, it seemed had become a repository for all bastions of colonial and military expansion. In an era when collecting the heads of Indian men was a common practice of the military and anthropologists, the Smithsonian, over the years, had received the booty of ornithologists, generals, and anthropologists—men who literally lifted the human remains off burial scaffolds to send east for scientific journals and presentations.

From Denver, Alanis Nordstrom, with her penchant for research, had volunteered to painstakingly review the anthropologists and Indian agents' records for White Earth and, after a few trips to Washington with more of her ubiquitous frequent flyer coupons, had matched to the best of her ability people, documents, and sacred items. Under a new law, funerary objects, human remains, and objects of cultural patrimony were required to be made available to their people.

Moose and George Agawaateshkan took the trip to Washington. The Great White Father's closets were full. The Smithsonian's Office of Repatriation had twenty full-time staff members, all busy trying to sort out whose femur belonged with whose skull and where they might have come from. It was a complex task in the face of tens of thousands of cases.

Moose and George followed the lanky Smithsonian anthropologist through the maze of rooms in the immense building, the doors clanging shut in one airtight and fireproof section after another. The man with a clipboard led them on and on, through the rooms, while the air seemed increasingly more precious and less available. Thousands of green boxes lined shelves built from floor to ceiling and contained bones, birds squished behind glass, reptiles, insects, and dinosaur parts. Moose and George walked through rooms where ancestors languished in small boxes the size and length of a femur, the largest bone in a human skeleton.

At first it was a hum, somewhere in the back of Moose's mind. Slowly, death chants, lullabies, love songs, and war songs became a composite of music, chants in his mind and ears, as their voices crescendoed. An immense graveyard of the unwilling dead, out of order. He broke into a cold sweat, beads dribbled down his face and back, as he followed the anthropologist and George Agawaateshkan through the vault.

George was singleminded and hummed a song to himself, and in that way he kept the music of the others at bay. Moose's eyes scanned the names written on the boxes: Inuit, Kiowa, Pawnee, Oklahoma, New Mexico, Florida, Florida, Florida. George, however, stared straight ahead, until the anthropologist stopped. The boxes read "Minnesota, White Earth Ojibwe." The Smithsonian man looked at his clipboard and flipped through the inventory list, running his fingers over the numbers in the aisle. George and Moose watched quietly.

"These are all of them," the anthropologist finally announced. "You can look them over if you want, and we'll bring them out for you tomorrow."

George nodded. *"Miigwech,"* he whispered, "thank you."

"I'll leave you now," the anthropologist said, looking at his watch. "Should I come back in an hour?"

"OK. Good."

It was in this vast warehouse of the collected remains of people from around the world that George Agawaateshkan, with shaking voice and trembling hands, made an initial inventory of the White Earth ancestors and those contents of their graves the Smithsonian would return to them. Moose gently moved the bones as George carefully placed medicine bags, clan markers, moccasins, and other articles of clothing in with the old people. Then George wrote it down as best as he could in his notebook, listing from what village or site the bones had originated, names if possible, and any other notes.

The men worked a full two days with the forty-five ancestors, and when they were done, they placed each femur-sized green box into a larger box for shipping. Finished, they went to a local Piscataway native man's sweat lodge, cried tears that were lost amid their sweat, and prayed to get the smell of death off their bodies before they headed home. Moose was designated to drive the ancestors home.

George flew back to attend to lengthy preparations at home. He was to arrange for a reburial ceremony as well as to determine what articles might go into the White Earth museum.

The museum was located in the old St. Benedict's Mission in the community college complex. The museum housed memorabilia from White Earth history, some ceremonial objects, copies of birchbark scrolls, and other aspects of the cultural traditions of the White Earth *Anishinaabeg*. Most of the religious objects, however, had been removed from the exhibits and were either in use or in "safekeeping" with various families. The pipes had previously been displayed in the museum in the border town of Detroit Lakes. Now all the pipes that belonged on White Earth were back in the correct place, and as best as people were able, were presently in use in the different ceremonies in the villages.

The same was true of the *Midewiwin* water drums and the big drums, both of which were in use in the villages and not on display or stored away in a backroom in the museum. Most of these drums had been stored for fifty or so odd years since the day they were taken by the priests or Indian agents. In later times, museum curators might have preserved the drums for observation, but not for use. The drums were now repaired by each of the families in charge of the twelve drums returned to White Earth.

The White Earth museum now played a different role: The displays and collections chronicled popular culture. For instance, the museum displayed the old fur press that the Northwest Company had used in trading with the Indians almost a century ago. The press had compressed furs so the trader could cheat Indians. Also on display were the black hats and some gambling sticks from an old moccasin game at White Earth.

The museum had a beaded outfit worn by Bugonaygeeshig when he traveled with a delegation of White Earth chiefs to Washington to negotiate for better treatment. Bugonaygeeshig's outfit was on display alongside Selam Big Bear's ribbon shirt and blue jeans, which he had worn to Washington to testify against the taking of the land in the White Earth Settlement Act in the 1980s, almost one hundred years later. The truth was, it was easier to get the ornately beaded outfit of the old headman than it was to get those jeans and the shirt. Moose had persuaded Selam's wife, Georgette, to make Selam a new, even fancier ribbon shirt, and the museum budgeted for a new pair of Levis to replace the old ones.

There was also a display of shoes, illustrating traditional shoes and social shoes from different generations. When Georgette had suggested this to the White Earth Historical Society, people had laughed and said she had a "foot fetish." But after they saw the collection, everyone admitted that it was pretty damn interesting, all the kinds of shoes

Indians had worn in one hundred and fifty years or so. Those were the kinds of things the Indians wanted in their own museum, and they were not necessarily the kind of things the white people liked to look at. These things made the people of White Earth feel a part of their history, not as though their *aanikoobijiganag* were "objects" to look at and "things" to take apart.

So George Agawaateshkan had flown home, leaving Moose with the responsibility of bringing the ancestors home. Moose had meticulously prepared his old UPS van for this trip. The van was fitted with shelves that were ideal to carry the ancestors. He had wrapped the wooden boxes in wool blankets and then strapped them onto the shelves so they were safe and secure. He slept in the cab when he stopped; he wasn't going to leave the ancestors on their own now. On one hand, he had to make sure that nothing else happened to them. On the other hand, it was out of respect for them. Someday, when he himself walked down the pathway of the souls and met with the ancestors again, he wanted to at least be able to say that he tried to make their long journey home comfortable.

Moose took another puff on his cigarette and then focused his mind on repairing the van. His tool set was onboard, as his van was prone to odd noises, parts unceremoniously left behind on the road, and breakdowns. But what he needed now was a long piece of strong wire to rig up an exhaust system repair. He checked behind the seat of the van. Nothing. He put his cigarette out and slowly started walking around the van, looking at the ground, his eyes scanning his surroundings for any bit of wire or, ideally, a clothes hanger. Again nothing; the rest area was unusually clean. He started walking toward the restrooms, figuring the garbage can might yield some useful bits in the least. As he crossed the parking lot, Moose looked up at the sound of an approaching vehicle.

As if by some mysterious radar that attracts hippies to Indians, an aging Volkswagen van pulled into the rest stop. Moose watched the van drive slowly by. It was painted brilliant purple from front bumper to tailpipe with rainbow mandalas on the side windows, American flags as curtains, *Free Leonard Peltier* and *Garcia Lives* stickers on the rear bumper alongside the Colorado license plate. Rock 'n' roll drifted out the open windows like a trail of marijuana smoke. Moose observed the entrance of the Deadhead out of the corner of his eye as he began to dig through a garbage can. The van stopped, and Moose continued to scavenge, now acutely aware of being observed. He shrugged and picked up a stick to aid his search through the garbage. No hanger. He turned his back on the van and went to check the men's room. Nothing. With one eye on the van, he gingerly opened the door to the women's room and checked inside. No luck.

Moose exited the women's room and began walking slowly back toward his van just as a big hairy guy with a paunch covered by a tie-dyed T-shirt stepped out of the van. His reddish hair stuck out in all directions, absent of any wind. The man stretched his arms and wiggled his hips slightly to loosen up, most of his body continuing to move in several directions simultaneously even when he was standing still. His arms still outstretched, he looked to be poised for flight. Moose cringed and stopped in his tracks, still weighing the limits of his options.

With his radar lock on, the Deadhead moved toward Moose with a familiarity only Deadheads have for complete strangers. "How's it going, bro?" the Deadhead hailed him.

Moose winced and calculated quickly in his mind just how badly he needed that coat hanger. Besides, this guy did not look like someone who had hung up his clothes in quite a spell.

"Well," Moose said, "my tailpipe is falling off but besides that, I'm OK."

"Hmmm. . . . Where you from?" The Deadhead was obviously less concerned about the present than the overall story.

"White Earth," Moose said. "Minnesota."

"Long way from home, eh?"

"Yup."

A pause.

"That'd be Ojibwe, right?"

"Yup." Moose was feeling cheap with his information.

Another pause as the Deadhead looked over Moose's ailing van from afar. Moose popped the question:

"You wouldn't happen to have any wire, like, say a coat hanger, would you?" He was both hopeful and skeptical.

"Let me take a look," the man offered. "By the way, my name's Mike," he said, offering a soul-brother's handshake to Moose.

"Moose," Moose said.

Mike dug into his van with a vigor that belied his paunchy build. He seemed hopeful that he could help an Indian. Tie-dyed clothes were thrown in all directions and boxes of cassettes were dumped out. Finally, Mike blurted out from the depths of his van, "Hey, I've got it!" With a hard pull, a length of speaker wire came free in his hands. Mike appeared out the door, pregnant with the pleasure that he was valuable to his Indian brother.

"But your tunes . . ." Moose began.

"Worry not, bro. I've got six speakers set up in my van. I can live with only five."

Moose smiled and thanked him, turning now to the task of fixing his exhaust system. He walked back to his van with Mike following hopefully behind, wishing for a small morsel of Moose's affections. Moose laid down on the pavement and worked himself under his van to survey the damage. The scent of patchouli oil told him Mike had joined him under the vehicle.

"What you got in the van, buddy?" Mike said as they worked side by side to lift the exhaust pipes back into place. "If you don't mind my asking, that is."

Moose had anticipated this question and now weighed his answers. Potatoes or bones were his two choices. He sensed Mike's earnestness and gave in.

"Bones," Moose said, grunting as he wrapped the speaker wire around a muffler.

Mike's face lit up, privy to new information.

"How's that?" he asked.

"The bones of our ancestors," Moose explained.

"Wow!" the Deadhead responded. "Where did you get them?"

"We're going home from Washington. They were at a museum out there, and we want them back." Moose generously offered the information to his ally.

Just then, another car pulled into the rest area and parked close to Moose's van—too close. A door opened and shut. Moose and Mike could hear the sound of footsteps on the pavement coming closer. They looked out from under the van to see two black, shiny boots.

"Uh oh," Mike said.

Moose held his breath.

The boots bent as their owner leaned down. Moose and Mike looked upside-down into the face of a highway patrolman. They could see themselves reflected in his mirror sunglasses, two grime-covered men on their backs with uncomfortable looks on their faces.

"What's going on here, boys?" said the patrolman in that expressionless drawl officers of the law have perfected.

Moose looked over at Mike, and Mike looked back at Moose. "I'll explain," Mike whispered to Moose, and then repeated it louder to the patrolman as he lumbered out from underneath the van.

Moose could hear them talking but could not understand anything they said from his listening post. Presently he heard the trunk of the patrol car open and then shut. *The cop's arrested him and thrown him in the trunk,* Moose worried to himself, concerned for a moment, wondering if he should intervene for his new ally.

Suddenly there was the high-pitched sound of squeaky wheels, and the next thing Moose knew, the patrolman was next to him under the van, with Mike sliding in on the other side. The officer had removed his hat and sunglasses and in his gloved hands he now carried pliers and a wirecutter. He was laying on a mechanic's dolly that he must have retrieved from the trunk.

"I've been reading up on this whole issue of repatriation," the patrolman said. "Let me see if I can lend a hand here."

As Mike held the exhaust pipe aloft, the officer ran the speaker wire around it and over part of the chassis frame. Moose felt like a fifth wheel.

"Got any duct tape?" the patrolman asked.

"Yeah, sure," Moose said, somewhat confused at how he had been so quickly marginalized. He dragged himself out from under the van.

As he retrieved the duct tape from his toolbox, a fake-wood-sided station wagon with Pennsylvania license plates pulled into the rest area and parked on the other side of the van. All five doors swung open at once and a man, woman, four children, and a golden retriever came spilling out. The man stretched, the woman yawned, and the children and dogs raced for the restrooms.

"Howdy," the man said in his best frontier accent when he saw Moose. He looked around at Moose's van, the highway patrol car, and the brilliant purple VW van. "What's all the excitement about?"

"Well, my van's exhaust broke, and we're fixing it . . ." Moose began, only to be interrupted by the patrolman who was suddenly standing beside him, wiping his sweating forehead with the back of one his gloves.

"He's carrying an important load," the officer authoritatively told the family. "He's bringing back remains of his ancestors to be reburied."

The man and woman looked surprised, then the woman asked Moose, "They're probably from the Smithsonian, I'll bet?" The man looked questioningly at his wife as she explained, "I heard all about this on public radio."

Moose looked at them both quizzically, "Yeah, they are."

"Is there anything we can do to help?" the man offered.

"No, sir," the officer said. "We're just finishing it up. Exhaust system's as good as some wire and duct tape can make it."

They all stood for a moment not knowing what to say next. Then the woman chimed in: "Well, have you all eaten?" She pulled a wicker picnic basket from the back of the station wagon and began handing out sandwiches primly wrapped in waxed paper. "That one's tunafish," she told Moose as she thrust the sandwich into his hands. He wanted to tell her he was not hungry, but he suddenly realized he had not eaten all morning.

Before Moose knew what had happened, he was sitting at a picnic bench with a red-checked tablecloth eating sandwiches with Mike the Deadhead, the patrolman, and the Walker family from Harrisburg, Pennsylvania, who were on their way to see the Grand Canyon. The officer and Mrs. Walker were discussing repatriation while Mike ate tunafish sandwiches with glee. The Walker children had just returned from under the van where they were inspecting the repairs. Exhaust grime now accompanied the Kool-Aid mustaches on their faces.

"Well," Moose finally said. "I need to get going."

"Yes, you better," said the patrolman, nodding.

"*Miigwech* to you all," Moose said.

The whole picnic table responded with a chorus of *miigwech,* and Mike told Moose to look him up if he was ever in Colorado.

The big Indian extended his hand and walked toward his van. He jumped into the driver's seat and started it up. Everything sounded good. He looked into his sideview mirror to see the people at the picnic table waving to him, and he stuck his hand out the window in return. He wheeled the van out onto the turnpike and north toward Champaign to take the ancestors home through Wisconsin. *"That should be some smooth traveling,"* he said to himself. *"Besides, that's Ojibwe country so the old people will like that."*

Once he was out on the road and up to speed, it seemed to Moose as though he heard a lot of noise from the back of the van again. Noise, and even some singing. This time he realized that the new rattles were the old people, not the van. Once again, the ancestors were loud and getting louder.

That was why he decided to move his tape player into the back of the van. Moose had a good boombox cassette player and an excellent collection of music. On this trip he had tossed aside most of his country western and rock music and opted for his more traditional collection. This seemed to work out just fine with the old people.

He played grass dance songs part of the way back, and then started in with some special tapes he had made of "traveling songs" from Big Drum ceremonies. That's what he put in now, a nice tape of traveling songs from Leech Lake. *"That should keep those old people happy,"* he thought as he turned up the tape player in the back of the van. Then he shifted into high gear and headed home.

NAAS'AAB MAA JIITWE WIN
THE REBURIAL
Fall 2000

The graves were shallow, etched into the clay soil with which White Earth held its children. Amazingly enough, the skeletons returned by the museum were intact, making it possible to place them individually. A number of the *aanikoobijiganag* had been identified by George Agawaateshkan, and clan markers and medicine pouches had been prepared by the related families. Georgette Big Bear, Kway Dole, and several other women wrapped the ancestors in Pendleton blankets and star quilts. Now the ancestors were ready for their long journey ahead. Alanis returned to White Earth for the ceremony and helped Elaine prepare the feast.

Mesabe, George Agawaateshkan, and Selam Big Bear began the ceremony, praying in Ojibwe to the four directions, to the Earth, and to the Creator. They prayed that this ceremony would put things in order and that the Spirits would once again take the *Anishinaabeg* home. Then George, representing the *Midewiwin* Society, explained what he had done:

"We are born here, and we have a certain time to be here. There are many things that we harvest and benefit from when we are on our Mother the Earth. We are blessed with life, and strive to live a good life: That is our responsibility on this Earth. When our time comes, we give back to the Earth and to the Creator. Our spiritual being goes to the Creator, and our physical being goes to

our Mother. That is our returning to our Mother, and that is how we reciprocate for the gifts of life that have been given to us during our time on Earth. We give our lives then."

As he paused, heads nodded in concurrence. This ceremony was not about sorrow, it was about correcting the order of things.

"We must petition the Earth Spirit and the Creator Spirit on behalf of these aanikoobijiganag. *The disturbance of the natural cycle was not of their doing, but was from the outside. We petition for restoring the natural cycle, and we do that through prayer, ceremony, and song."*

Then George began to sing for the *Midewiwin* people.

As they finished with the prayers, several men continued the ceremony and songs. The ceremony was known as the Wiping Away the Tears Ceremony. Elaine, and Claire and Lucy St. Clair joined in to *zhaabowe* in the appropriate places.

They held the ceremony on a bluff in the Buckboard Hills, overlooking the Mississippi River headwaters. The burial site had come to Mesabe in a dream. The graves themselves were more isolated from the elements, but they still overlooked the Mississippi. *"The old people were here at the beginning, they should be here at the beginning of this river as well. That way they can watch over it,"* the old man explained.

It had taken months for all the songs, protocol, and ceremony to be learned. Many of the oldest songs and ceremonies had been forgotten at White Earth, vanquished by the missionaries years ago, so now what had once been "common knowledge" had to be recalled from other reservations, books, and memories of the oldest people. Each song had an order, and each clan had certain songs and ceremonies needed to help the ancestors on their way. To return so many was a large responsibility.

For the men, George Agawaateshkan had guided them in their work, painstakingly teaching songs for each part of the ceremony and each clan. The women asked an elder from Red Lake to instruct them as they were to "dress" the bodies, a responsibility reserved for women who would bear no more children.

For Moose Hanford and Willie Schneider, the reburial put to rest those who had followed them since Vietnam. Willie knew all too well that most of those he had killed in the war never had a proper burial and many were never even found. And while the sweats and ceremonies he had done since had addressed their spirits and his own spirit in some way, the *Waas'asb Maa Jiiiiwewin* ceremony talked to those spirits again, and they were finally put to rest.

For Selam Big Bear and Moose, the ceremony was about re-ordering the world. Their direct ancestors were some of those returned, the same families that, four generations back, had begun the drum ceremonies in White Earth village, families that had been torn from the earth by Doctor Hrdlicka and his assistants at the Smithsonian forty years later and had not been home since. Selam's grandmother had screamed out when she saw the anthropologists dig into the earth by their house, only to be taken away and, as punishment, shipped like a cow to the mental institution for Indians in South Dakota. For the Big Bear family, that violation of the sacred seared their souls for generations and caused a grief that could not be resolved by any Christian prayer. Only now could his family heal; only now could his nation heal.

For Moose's part, he had made a special effort to find the remains of his ancestors, Ishkwegaabawiikwe and Situpiwin. They too had been stolen away, but not to the Smithsonian. They had been taken as recently as the 1980s to the University of Minnesota, blessings of Warren Danielson. Now, they rested in boxes in some storage room, Ishkwegaabawiikwe still with her skinning knife, Situpiwin with her long braids of hair lovingly kept by Ishkwegaabawiikwe and laid at her side.

Alanis whispered prayers throughout the feast preparation. Her distant relations as well were contained in the boxes of ancestors, but to her the ceremony was about becoming whole again. A family history is a mirror of a people's history. Disassembled and violated, the longing to be whole never wanes until whole again. She had found that her own path home was only a single strand in a web of generations who still wandered, looking for their clan markers.

Several men carefully placed the *aanikoobijiganag* into their graves. In each grave a medicine bag containing some essential traveling components was placed on the body. Either George or Selam added tobacco to the bodies as they were covered with soil. That done, Willie Schneider and Moose Hanford completed the *jiibegamig*, the small wooden gravehouses, and placed them over the bodies of those *aanikoobijiganag* who had been in the *Midewiwin* Society. Willie, George Ahnib, and some young men from Rice Lake Village had carried the wood up the hillside for the graves. Now they carefully finished the houses and placed them over the bodies in each of the individual graves. On those whom they had been able to find their lineage, George carefully placed a clan marker to the side of the gravehouse. On those whom no one knew, they were buried simply in blankets without clan markers, but with tobacco and prayers for their long journey.

The Indians in attendance were dressed in their ceremonial best, and the white people were dressed for church, which was fine with the Indians. Reverend Swenson's wife, Jane, and a number of other women had prepared hot dishes and Jell-O salads for the feasting, which were added to the traditional foods of deer, moose, wild rice, berries, and hominy corn.

They assembled in a large circle surrounding the old people and those conducting the ceremony. There were a fair number of non-Indians there, some from Reverend Swenson's congregation.

The singing and feasting lasted for four days. A number of families had set up camp near the burial site to continue their visiting and to care for the ceremony. Most non-Indians just came for the day, although the Swensons stayed and camped through the four days. On the last day the drum finished with traveling songs to send the *Chi-Anishinaabeg* on their way.

Charlotte Oshkinnah, now eighty years old, stayed up late each night to talk about the old days and point out to her grandchildren and to the rest of those there, the dancing spirits in the northern lights. The lights seemed their brightest ever. She couldn't take her eyes off them.

THE THIRD MIRACLE
2000

There are few people who are witness to a miracle in their short time on this Earth. Yet Claire St. Clair was one of these special people who was privy to not one but three such acts of God in her lifetime.

Claire witnessed the Deer Woman's return in the spring of 1991, an event that caused a major spiritual transformation in her life. She had been one of the most devout Catholics in the recent history of the reservation, but the sighting caused her metamorphosis into, in the words of her friend Selam Big Bear, "the most pagan woman on the reservation." She had become a member of the Big Drum Society and active in the *jiisakiiwigamig*, the shaking tent.

In the course of being born for a third time—since that is essentially what it was—Claire became only the twenty-fifth Minnesotan in history to win the state lottery in an amount of more than ten million dollars, the second miracle. As the lottery primarily financed environmental projects, the lottery committee was extremely interested when it discovered that the winner was an elderly Indian woman from the White Earth Reservation. Miss Dodd of the public relations department saw an excellent promotion opportunity for Minnesota, Indians and the environment being so closely associated. Miss Dodd even had visions of placing a picture of Claire on the new posters for the lottery, replacing the loon in the bulk of promotion.

Claire, however, had no premonition about the role of image in marketability, and over the advice of her second cousin, Alanis, invested her lottery earnings in a permanent. The result, according to both the hairdresser and Claire, was magnificent. With her new 'do, Claire was quite something. The intent of the beehive she now had piled on top of her head had been to look like Dolly Parton. On her rather large and dark frame, the result was a little different. Claire looked much more like one of The Supremes, thirty generous years older. The effect was accentuated by Claire's brand spanking new floral jumpsuit and very high heels.

After the furor over the fourteen million dollars died down, Claire and Elaine developed a trust fund and an investment plan to use the interest on the lottery winnings for land acquisition, leaving the principle intact. In addition, a federal appropriation came as a part of a national interest in financing land re-acquisition on reservations and the return of federal land to Indians. By the year 2000, the law had financed the re-acquisition of more than ten million acres of Indian land across the nation.

White Earth had benefited heartily from the program and had been able to purchase fifty thousand acres of land. This, combined with other acquisitions and negotiations work they had done, comprised almost one hundred fifty thousand acres of land. In total, the tribe now owned over half of the reservation. That, in itself, had changed the balance of power on the reservation.

While some things changed, some things remained the same. Although the return of Indian control of the land signaled a new balance of power on the reservation, there were a few holdouts from the old Settler Occupation. Many non-Indians had been eager enough to sell their land back to the Indians and move to sunnier, more affluent areas where they felt at ease. Others elected to stay and work it out. These individuals appeared to realize that things would be different. Over time, in fact, many of these individuals had not only survived the transition, they flourished in the new economy and culture.

Then there was the third type, obstinate individuals and enclaves who felt this was their "promised land." They had come to settle on the reservation like woodticks on a warm dog. The land was cheap, and the Indians appeared to be docile. They began a vigilant occupation. They lived in isolation and refused, for the most part, to relate in any way to the Indian people in whose midst they had come to settle.

Instead, they fortified themselves behind signs of Private Property and No Trespassing.

And, by the mid-1990s, almost every different religious, sport, and other denomination of "do gooder" in the country had, it seemed, set up a summer camp on the reservation. Several charismatic church groups seemed the most entrenched of this persuasion; almost like barnacles, they resisted any storm or wave. To them, the reservation was their own private refuge, and the Indians were just a part of the scenery. Even Claire, who had been one of the few up to their standards, could not enter into a dialogue with them. They were as a rock, unshaken.

It was in the early spring of 2000 that Claire witnessed the third miracle. She was driving toward Round Lake from north of White Earth Lake when the twister came in. It was not that Claire was reckless, it was just that since her turn to traditionalism she preferred to avoid most parts of American society, including the newspapers, TV, and town but excluding the lottery and, of course, Indian bingo. These she continued to play religiously to demonstrate her continued commitment to what she called "the two paths of the *Anishinaabeg*"—Christianity and traditional spirituality.

On account of these principled decisions, she had not heard the radio weather report or tornado warnings. Fortunately, her route was well sheltered by trees and hills, but as she passed the Maple Grove Town Hall, she felt her car surge to the left and realized that this was no ordinary storm. She stopped her car and ran inside.

"Aaniin, aanikoobijiganag, aaniin Ningaabii'anong," she began her prayer to the powers of the Ancestor and the West. She made prayers to the Thunder Beings and to the Great Wind.

Claire then grabbed her scapular, which she still kept under her blouse in reverence to Father Ginney. She prayed carefully and fervently to all the Saints who might be blowing in that Dakota windstorm. As she completed fifteen minutes of *Anishinaabeg* prayer and ten minutes of Catholic prayer, she sat and rested on a chair in the old town hall. Peering out the window toward the west and down the road, she was satisfied that she had done all she could.

While so-called civilization had come from the East to the *Anishinaabe*, this wind came from the West. *Wabun,* the East, signified the beginning, and *Ningaabii'anong*, the power of the West, signified the end of the day and the changes brought by this. *Wabun* would be the making and *Ningaabii'anong* would be the unmaking. Others with less perspective might have resented the latter and favored the former; but the *Anishinaabeg* understood that both the making and the unmaking were essential parts of life and necessary to keep the balance. After all, what was dawn without dusk and what was life without constant change?

That was precisely why Claire prayed and gave thanks for the force and only took care to ask that the people were not harmed.

The twister put down somewhere southeast of St. Benedict's Mission and began slowly moving east. As the force shook the town hall she clutched her medicine pouch in her left hand, her scapular in the right, whispering alternately to each. She, however, had no fear.

Claire was the only person who witnessed the strike. It was as if the *Oditibitidoodi*, the Wind that Tumbles, came in a precise path to the Christian Retreat Camp. Almost like a small child eating dinner, the twister selectively laid waste to the Chapel, the camp director's house, the large meeting hall, the bunkhouses, and the classrooms. All that was left was an outhouse.

Just before the twister moved south, Claire understood exactly the "unmaking." The wind moved into Christian Retreat Acres, the retired subdivision for, Claire assumed, old campers. Here, only one house was taken, the most brash and ostentatious log mansion in the enclave. The other twenty remained shaken but unscathed.

Then as quickly as it had come, *Oditibitidoodi* lifted, and only the strong winds of *Ningaabii'anong* remained, as always, making a change when no other force could. Fifteen minutes later, as the wind subsided, Claire took to her car and drove toward the camp. It was clear that a calling of God might have brought them to the reservation, but only an act of God could make them leave. This work was final.

ISHKWEGAABAWIIKWE
LAST STANDING WOMAN
2001

At fifty-seven and still a fearless beauty, Lucy St. Clair was now a grandmother many times over. Her six sons had all seeded fruit, and many village children had characteristic St. Clair features. She felt great reassurance in her progeny and delighted in each new delivery. Yet, above all, she remained entranced with love and babies.

Lucy had given birth to six sons and one daughter out of love, only three out of any marriage. Her sons had all been born without incident at the St. Mary's Hospital in the reservation border town of Detroit Lakes.

Her daughter, however, was a different story. Born in a South Dakota Indian Health Service hospital, the birth was a nightmare in which her daughter would languish her entire life.

It was the winter of 1970. Since the baby's father was working in Nebraska at the time, Lucy had driven herself to the hospital just after her water broke. Alone but unafraid, she began a delivery characteristic of a woman who had already borne three children, a short precise labor that was to last for only two and a half hours. The Indian Health Service fortuitously located her medical records a few minutes before the birth, but had been unable to find a doctor to attend the delivery. The obstetrician was in Rapid City at a meeting. Two nurses alternated in watching Lucy, taking care of other patients, and awaiting the return of the doctor.

Although she argued she was more comfortable walking around, the nurses insisted in strapping her to the delivery table while her labor progressed. They gave the Indian woman no credit for knowing her own reflexes and conditions. When Lucy said the baby was coming, they did not believe her, and constricted as she was, she was in no position to help the infant. She screamed as the baby came out, but the nurse had her back turned and only caught the baby after she had fallen to the floor.

The child, Sarah, was to live, but would be forever plagued with a paralysis of her left side and splitting headaches from the fall. Sarah was her only daughter, and from that time forward, Lucy never forgave the government for their miscarriage of Indian health. She carried with her a vehement hatred, to be reflected at every possible chance.

Not surprisingly, when the opportunity emerged for a new midwife program on White Earth, Lucy was the first in line. Weary of the Indian Health Service and the largely indifferent treatment by white doctors in border towns, in 1996 the White Earth people built the *Anishinaabeg* Health Center on White Earth Lake.

A midwife program served many needs, as did the traditional mental health and ceremonies programs, wherein practices like the sweat lodge, doctoring, and the *Midewiwin* were integrated into one program. Here, victims of abuse, mental illness, and other forms of *giiwanaadizi* or craziness were treated, as were those who suffered from chronic medical problems ranging from cancer to asthma. Western Medicine and *Anishinaabeg* Medicine were merged.

The sign over the big, double doors read *"GigisAkaajigewigamig."* The translation was "A place where they are pregnant," and happily, many were. These were Lucy St. Clair's grounds during the day.

At night, however, there were other medicines.

No one had appointed Lucy the Cupid of White Earth, but none would deny her the position. Not only was she good at what she did, she was still fearless. At the Renewal Ceremony held the summer following the *Oditibitidoodi* or tornado, Lucy had been given a new name, Ishkwegaabawiikwe, or Last Standing Woman. The name, as it was intended, fortified her stamina and determination and, some would say, gave her a license to practice love medicine.

There had been an exchange of goods. Willie Schneider, head bowed in a humble plea, had passed cloth and tobacco to Lucy. After considering the request, she was ready. Lucy carefully closed all the curtains of her house and pulled the blinds. Content that no one could see her, she sat down at the table and contemplated the order of things. Lighting first sage, then cedar, Lucy deliberated as she walked around her kitchen. Satisfied, she took out a small hand drum and began to sing. In her words and song, she invoked spirits and helpers, and in other songs, the love of the Ojibwe for generations.

As the medicine grew in strength, Lucy focused on a small mound of brown powder she had carefully placed on the table. Singing and calling, she drew upon all her strength to merge the power with the medicine, increasing the potency of the original substance manifold. Finally, she picked up a small bone and sent that medicine to its intended object, far from the reservation. Far from home. As the medicine took to the elements, Lucy continued singing until all the medicine left her house. In the end, she was exhausted but elated.

It started slowly. The love medicine worked its magic on Alanis. Some nights a dream, others, awakening from a night of tossing in her bed in Denver, she had Willie's name on her breath or his face imprinted in her mind. Willie had got under Alanis's skin, and he intended to stay there.

Alanis, for her part, looked at the world through slightly puzzled eyes. For a woman who prided herself on being in control, this new set of emotions and a growing adoration for the reservation boy jostled her senses. Coming back to White Earth "only to visit," as Alanis told people, she found herself drawn to Willie's quiet allure, and Willie swooped in while he had an advantage, asking her to lunch, the movies, and even once, to accompany him in checking his leech traps. The medicine set in. Willie persisted, and Alanis was in love.

The quandary of love medicine is tenure. A heart captured under a cloud of chant and medicine, procured with the help of powers

unseen, is a difficult one to keep. There the medicine must be renewed or in the most favorable of circumstances, the medicine only
removes obstacles to affection and love. Then a clever suitor can, with
a careful and ardent courtship, woo his or her subject and secure the
desired love.

Willie Schneider, although not practiced in the wooing of women,
had taken some lessons. There was the initial exchange of goods with
Lucy St. Clair. That secured Lucy's assistance. A later exchange got
him some tutoring in pre-bedside manners. Moose Hanford, Willie's
most long-term friend, offered a few more suggestions as well. "You
could drop a deer on her doorstep," he suggested, thought the better
of it, and adjusted his advice. "or maybe just a hind quarter."

So it was in a somewhat clumsy but earnest manner that Willie
Schneider courted Alanis Nordstrom. He did so successfully. And, as
was frequently the custom in White Earth courtship, Alanis happily
became pregnant with Willie Schneider's child.

At her house in Denver, Alanis tossed and turned until she finally
turned home. *Giiwe*. She drove her Saab past the prairies, past the
border, and into the woods. She was coming home to White Earth.
Not just for Willie, although he was quite the persuasive and persistent fellow, but for herself as well. Weary of wandering, the smell of
pines and the glitter of deep lakes made her breathe easy and feel at
peace. *Giiwe*. Home.

Lucy St. Clair smiled as she named the child. She had done well, and
felt in some way a resolution to her part of the sequence. That was
why she passed on the name. Ishkwegaabawiikwe, Last Standing
Woman, was her own name, a good one at that, and now it, like her,
could have a new life.

There were other gifts she passed on to her *wen'enh*, the person
whom one names. She also passed on her skinning knife and its sheath,
quilled in yellow and blue. She said it went with the name, and it too
was a good one.

It was a year later when Alanis sat next to Elaine at the powwow.
She held her daughter close to her chest and turned her so she could
watch the people dancing to the drum.

Epilogue

DIBAAJIMOKWE
THE STORYTELLER

It was the child who had the gift of the story and the word. The child began to tell stories before she emerged from her mother. In her pregnancy, the mother remembered stories she had heard as a child and others she could not remember having heard. The stories called to her in lessons and memories.

At first she resisted them, continuing her daily work and her life as she had carefully planned it. Each month as the child grew, the stories came forth with more force. And soon, they formed a web that surrounded them both and linked them from past to future. While before there seemed to be no time, now there seemed to be nothing but time, as each story joined their lives to a whole.

Before she came into the world, the child remembered their arrival in the Land of White Clay. She remembered the good years in the wealthy land, and that was her foundation for courage and strength. She also remembered the descent into the abyss of land stealing, the plagues of sickness (the monster that destroyed people but not memories), and the poverty and starvation of generations lost. She remembered the endless stream of refugees as she watched her people walk from the refuge of White Clay and lakes to the cities, hoping for food and a way of life. Then she remembered the return and the long struggle for change.

Her coming was signaled by the departure of the oldest person in the village, Mesabe. He was at once both the story and the teller. His memory contained six generations of history and knowledge. He re-told how the people had survived in the first three generations and could instruct in the essence of survival for the next three and those to follow.

His passage appeared to open the door for her entrance into life. It was also his life that brought forth the work of hers. When he passed over, he had outlived four of his five children, his wife, and at least seven of his grandchildren. He was a hundred years old, and his changing of worlds marked the ending of one time and the beginning of an-other.

JOURNAL OF
ISHKWEGAABAWIIKWE

Emiwak mewinzha gii-aawan gaa ako-ishwaasobiboonagak giiwan gii-saagijiwidood aw George Ahnib iniw aabajichiganan gaa-izhi-abajitoowaad imaa anaamakamig endazhi-biiwaabikokeng iko gaa-tazhi-anokiiwaad ingiw biiwaabikokewininiwag. Miki sa gwayak wayaabang gii-pi-izhi-niigiyaan niin.

Mii dash igo miinawaa iwapii gaa-ako-nizizho-anamie-giizhig gii-pi-izhi-niigiyaan, minnawaa dash bezhig giiwen inini, akiwenzil, Mesabe gii-izhinikaazo, aw dash igo gayewiin gii-nibo.

Gii-pi-nitaawigiyaanmoozhag apane ko ingii-ni-zoongide'e. Mii dash igo iw zoongide'ewin geget igo gii-pi-izhi-giiginiigiyaan. Ow dash idog zoonigide'ewin ingii-miinigoo gii-ondinigeyaan imaa inga omakwaman odoodemiwaag, ingiw dash igo indinawemaaganibaniig imaa ko giiwen gaa-tazhi-ayindaawaad jiigi-gizhi-ziibiing mewinzha.

Mii sa iw indizhinikaazowin Ishkwegaabawiikwe ezhininikaanigoziyaan, iw dash gaa-pi-izhinikaazhid aw niiyawan-en Lucy St. Clair ezhinikaazod.

Ow dash ingii-pi-ozhibii'ige aanagonaa wnji-nandamikwendamaan iw gaa-pi-izhiigikinoo'amaagooyaan niin sa go. Gii-agaashiinyiyaan anooj igo aw ingo ingii-tadibaajimotaagoo igo gaye ingiw indinawemaaganag. Geget sa debwewin omaa atemagad.

Giishpin wiin igo wiikwajitoowaad egindar jig wewani ji-gikenindizowaad, anooj igo ingii-atoon omaa ozhibii'iganing ji-gikendamoozhiwewimagwaa ingiw gwayak ezhi-gikendamaan gayeniin iw sa gaa-pizhi-gikinoo'amaagooyaan. Mii sa iw Zhawenimigoowin gii-izhi-bagami'ayaamagak imaa wayeshkad, bekish dash igo niigaan kayaa da-ayaamagad iw zhawenimigoowin gaaginig apane go gaaginig. Mii iw keyaa ge-izhiwebakiban.

Mii gawiin igo indaa-debwetanziimin iw sa ezhi-nibide-ayaamagak, mii sa imbimaadiziwininaanin, danaasag ingoji go keyaa eni-inikaag ahishaa, mii sa gaawin ingoji. Dawaaj dash igo ji-debwetamingiban iniw imbimaadizim-wininaanin ji-izhi-inikaag imaa biindig wayaawiwiyaminagak, mii sa anishinaabe-bimaadiziwining, ji-wiikwajitooyuaang iw sa anooj anaasing wii-tagoshkaagozigaang.

Aanish mii sa iw wenji-ganawendamaang iniw anishinaabewinikaazowinan igo gaye ikodowinan. Mii imaa go gaye ge-onji-nisidotamaang imbimaadiziwininaanin ji-gwayakoseyaang imaa anishinaabe-miikanaang. Mii go gayeniiawind iw wenji-naanaagaadawenindizoyaang geoo ji-wanendanziwaang aw anishinaabe iw gaa-izhi-bagidinind ji-iahi-gaagiigidod mewinzha sa go. Awegwen ge-mamoogwen gefoo ji-aabajitood ga-izhi-gaagiigidod mewinzha sa go. Awegwen ge-mamoogwen gegoo ji-aabajitood ga-izhi-mino-bimaadizid, mii iw neyaab aanind minik igo ge-wi-bagidinang imaa sa go. Giishpin igo gashkitooyaang gegoo, mii akawe booch igo gidaa-miigwechiwendaamin iw sa gi-miinigooyaang.

Aaniish mii sa iw keyaa ezhiwebiziwaagobanen ingiw ishkweyaang keyaa indaanikobijiganinaanig, mii iw gaa-izhi-gikendamoogobanenag, mii iw gaa-ni-dowaagobanen ingiw anishinaabed mewinzha. Mii sa go iw minik.

I was born exactly eight years to the day after George Ahnib took out the logging equipment. I was born two weeks after the old man, Mesabe, walked down the pathway of the souls to the next world.

As a child, I was bold. It is a trait I believe I inherited from my mother's clan, the *Makwa Doodem*, the Bear Clan of the Mississippi. My dad, however, was a Loon, and he gave me my formal clan. Suited him funny, the Loon. He was a man who stumbled with words and was cheap with them when he did use them. But on occasion, he would fulfill his own destiny, and his voice would echo loud, long, and far.

The Bears are different. In times past, they were warriors, the *ogichidaa,* those who defended the people. Sometimes we still are. We are what we are intended to be when we have those three things that guide our direction—*our name, our clan, and our religion.*

I wrote this because I am called to write. I have done the best I could and have tried to tell some of our story from my mother's words and from the words of my relatives. There is a great deal I have omitted, but in the least, I tried to be honest with the memories and the principles.

There are many stories here. And, there is much to learn for the future. For all the pain and heartache we have felt, there has been and will be, an equal amount of joy. That is how everything works. There is always a struggle to maintain the balance.

I do not believe that time is linear. Instead, I have come to believe that time is in cycles, and that the future is a part of our past and the past is a part of our future. Always, however, we are in new cycles. The cycles omit some pieces and collect other pieces of our stories and our lives.

That is why we keep the names, and that is why we keep the words. To understand our relationship to the whole and our role on the path of life. We also understand our responsibility. We only take what we need, and we leave the rest. We always give thanks for what we are given. What carries us through is the relationship we have to the Creation and the courage we are able to gather from the experience of our *aanikoobijigan*, our ancestors, and our *oshkaabewisag*, our helpers.

Signed,
Ishkwegaabawiikwe
2018

GLOSSARY OF
ANISHINAABE TERMS

Glossary note
The Ojibwe language used in this novel is the dialect of White Earth Reservation, utilizing the double-vowel system. Several small exceptions exist in the text, including some common names, historical names, and the excerpts from the St. Columba Episcopal Church Ojibwe hymnals.

aababishkaw: inside out, as in to skin a rabbit.

aanikoobijigan: ancestor.

AAbita Niibino Giizis: Mid-Summer Moon, July.

Agwajiing: literally "outside," the *Anishinaabe* name for the Minnesota state sanitarium at Walker, Minnesota.

Anishinaabe: literally "the people," but also used for a person, an Indian, Ojibwe. *Anishinaabeg* is the plural form.

Anishinaabeg Akiing: the people's land.

Anishinaabekwe: *Anishinaabe* woman.

asabikenhshii: literally the "Spider," the *Anishinaabe* name for cancer.

asemaa: tobacco.

awakaanag: domesticated animals.

bawa'iganaak oog: wild rice harvesting stick.

biboon: winter.

biidaaban: dawn.

boozhoo: hello, greetings.

Bwaan Akiing: land of the Dakota.

Bwaanag: Dakota people.

Bwaanikwe: Dakota woman.

Chimookomaanag: white people, Americans.

Chippewa: a corrupted term for Ojibwe.

dakoniwewinini: literally "the Men Who Hold Someone," referring to tribal police.

dewe'igan: drum.

dibaajimokwe: a storytelling woman.

dikinaagan: cradle board.

doodem: clan or totem.

Gaawaawaabiganikaag:White Earth, named after the white clay found in the area.

Gashkadino Giizis: Freezing Moon, November.

giga-waabamin miinawaa: see you again.

Gichimookomaanag: literally the "Big Knives," referring to white people.

giimooj: secrecy.

giiwedahn: home.

giiwanaadizi: crazy, insane.

Gichi Manidoo Giizis: the Great Spirit Moon, January.

ininaatig: maple sugar trees.

jiibay: ghost.

jiibayag niimi'idiwag: northern lights.

jiibegamig: gravehouse.

jiisakiiwigamig: a small triangular hide lodge known as the shaking tent.

jiisakiiwinini: the man who could see into the future through the shaking tent.

Maajaa'ind: sending off ceremony.

makakoons: birchbark basket.

makwa: bear.

manidoo: spirit

Manidoo Giizisoons: the Little Spirit Moon, December.

manoomin: wild rice.

Manoominike Giizis: Ricing Moon, September.

mazinaakizigan: photographic camera.

Makadewikonayewinini: literally "the Men Who Dress in Black," *Anishinaabe* name for the early missionaries.

Midewiwin: Grand Medicine Society.

miigwech: thank you.

mindawe: to be dissatisfied with what is given

Mishinameginebig: the Great Horned Sturgeon.

mishtadim: horse, called the "big dog" by the *Anishinaabeg*.

mooka'ang: dawn, sunrise.

ma'iingan: wolf.

Namebini Giizis: Sucker Moon, February.

niimiidiwin: powwow.

Ningaabii'anong: the land of the west.

nookomis: grandmother.

nooji'ikwewe: the act of actively seeking women.

Ode'imini Giizis: Strawberry Moon, June.

Oditibitidoodi: literally "the Wind that Tumbles," a tornado.

ogimaa: chief, leader.

ogichidaa: warrior, those who defend the people. *Ogichidaaweg* is the plural form.

ogichidaakwe: female chief, leader.

Ojibwe: corrupted term for *Anishinaabe*. Also spelled Ojibwa or Ojibway.

Onaabani Giizis: Crust on the Snow Moon, March.

Oshki Anishinaabeg: the new people.

miiniingwaan: eye boogers.

waawiyaasenagweyaab: literally "a round light rainbow," or sundog.

Waabigwanii Giizis: Flower Moon, May.

waabooz: rabbit.

Waaban aki: the land of the east.

waawaashkeshi: deer.

wemitigoozhi: Frenchman.

Wiindigoo: a cannibal or monster. *Wiindigooweeg* is the plural form. The term is sometimes used to refer to the white people.

wiiyaas: meat.

zagimeg: mosquitoes.

zhaabowe: a woman's style of singing characterized by a high-pitched call.

ziigwan: spring.